Chicken Parents Chicken Schools:

Reclaiming Your Influence and Authority

by
By Roland L. and Sherry C. Wong

PublishAmerica
Baltimore

First printing

ISBN: 1-4137-4616-0
PUBLISHED BY PUBLISHAMERICA, LLLP
www.publishamerica.com
Baltimore

Printed in the United States of America

Acknowledgments

Chicken Parents Chicken Schools: Reclaiming Your Influence and Authority, represents the cumulative experiences we have had as parents and educators. Those experiences were shaped by many individuals who deserve our thanks. We would particularly like to acknowledge our parents, Hans and Ethel Wong and Jo and Jerry Catron for their support in making us the people we are today. We would like to thank our sons, Tyler and Travis Wong, for being the central cast in our own living laboratory; in which we tested our methods for raising confident, compassionate, responsible, well balanced adults. The experiment worked; you are everything we could want and more. Thanks to the many excellent teachers who shaped our own educational experience as well as to those exceptional educators with whom we've both had the pleasure to work over the years. We would also like to thank "the Buffalos" for decades of friendship and support as we all learned to parent together.

Thanks to Linda Finch and Diane Wong for their careful review and feedback on the manuscript and to Ted Roumelis for his encouragement.

This book is dedicated to the countless committed teachers and parents who struggle daily against a system that makes their jobs infinitely harder than necessary.

Table of Contents

Preface

Yet another parenting book; another treatise on how to improve the state of education. Why is this book different from the thousands of others that fill bookstore shelves? It's different because it tells the truth; because it challenges you, the reader, to tap into your own history and your own common sense, rather than relying on the self-styled experts who have managed to convince us that parenting and teaching are mysterious, complicated jobs that require the enlightenment of their years of scholarly study.

I am a teacher and a parent. I have a college education but no advanced degrees. My "expertise" comes from over thirty years of working with young people, as a parent, teacher, and coach. In those roles I have worked with over 7,000 young people. The ideas and techniques I share with you in this book are things that I have seen work over and over again in my interactions with my sons, students, and players. They have been tested and refined in countless situations and have consistently produced positive results. Rather than ascribing to a particular school of educational or parenting thought, my philosophy is built on personal experience and continuous reflection. I have tried and discarded many ideas and techniques. What gets retained and integrated into my approach to parenting and teaching is *what works*. I regularly hear from former students who thank me for making a powerful difference in their lives, for being "different" from so many of their other teachers.

I don't hold myself out as an "expert." Rather, I offer you a perspective and a philosophy that has worked well for me. The ideas in this book represent a fusion of my personality, my experience, and my situation.

As co-author, Sherry brings another perspective and area of expertise to this book. As a curriculum developer, writer, and trainer, she has spent the last twenty years helping parents, schools and communities apply the prevention science/youth development research to their work with children and teens. She is the author of *Communities That Care Prevention Strategies: A Research Guide to*

What Works (1996, 2000) and *Communities That Care Community Planning Kit* (1996). She also managed the development of numerous research-based curriculums, including *Parents Who Care™*, *Preparing for School Success™*, *Preparing for the Drug Free Years™*, and *SOAR™ (Skills, Opportunities, And Recognition)*. She has worked with hundreds of communities across the country as a *Communities That Care®* consultant and is a frequent presenter at conferences.

Finally, Sherry and I have spent the last twenty-three years parenting our own two sons, who are now happy, well-adjusted young adults.

As a parent or a teacher, we encourage you to use the ideas in this book as a catalyst for creating an approach that is effective for you. Don't be afraid to use your common sense and your own experiences, both good and bad. Most importantly, know what results you want and have the courage to do what it takes to get those results. Don't let anyone call you "chicken."

Chicken Parents Chicken Schools: Reclaiming Your Influence and Authority is based on a simple approach that we call **Big Five/Five Steps**. This commonsense framework helps you identify a vision for your child and a road map for reaching that vision.

The first step in this framework is identifying your **Big Five,** which helps you clarify your vision of the kind of adult you want your child to become. Your **Big Five** represent the most important fundamental qualities and characteristics that you want your child or student to have as an adult. They represent the priority areas on which you should focus your time, energy and attention. Taking the time to really think through these parenting or teaching priorities will pay off immeasurably. The clear focus provided by the Big Five gives you direction in every day situations with children. Whenever you have a decision to make, the benchmark becomes, "How will this contribute to my Big Five?"

The second step is to **Identify the Lesson.** Everything you do teaches a lesson, whether you intend for it to or not; it's up to you to decide what your child will learn. So, one important way to reach the vision you have for your child as an adult is to constantly ask yourself, "What will my child learn from this?" and, "Will that lesson contribute to the kind of adult I want her to become?" These two simple questions help take the guesswork out of day-to-day decisions about parenting or teaching. For example, when you are tempted to give in to your child's whining, tantrums, or arguing, ask yourself, "What would my child learn if I gave in?"

The third step is to **Take Charge.** Taking charge means that you embrace your role as the responsible adult in a child's life. It means that you face and conquer the fears that prevent you from fulfilling that role. You realize that your job is to set and enforce guidelines that will help your child or student gradually learn to manage her own behavior.

The fourth step is to **Balance the Approach.** This means that, as the responsible adult in a child's life, you are always striving to balance the opposing forces that threaten to divert your child from the vision you have for him as an adult. Balancing the approach means that you allow children to experience pain as well as pleasure, happiness as well as sadness, failure as well as success. It means that, as an adult, you model a balanced and stable life yourself. Balance provides the even keel that keeps young people on track as they navigate the stormy waters of growing up.

The final step is to **See if it's Working.** You may have heard Albert Einstein's definition of insanity, "The definition of insanity is continuing to do the same thing but expecting a different result." Yet many parents and teachers continue to use the same child management techniques even when those strategies aren't producing the desired results. The best technique for your child or student is the one that works. It's not rocket science; it's not complicated; it doesn't require a PhD in child development. If it's not working, try something else. If that doesn't work, keep trying until you find something that works. It's important to remember, however, that when I say "what works" I mean that it works in both the short-run and for the long-term. Too often parents sacrifice the long-term outcomes they desire for their child (the Big Five) for the short-term goal of making life easier right now. Again, logic and commonsense are your greatest allies. Discipline is really a problem-solving exercise. Approached in a logical and rational manner, most discipline problems can be resolved.

You'll learn how to use the **Big Five/Five Steps** approach throughout this book.

Caveats and cautions: First, I have attempted to reflect the experience of parenting and teaching both boys and girls through the alternating use of feminine and masculine pronouns. However, my parenting experience has been exclusively with boys, so you will find my stories and examples often reflect not only that gender bias, but also the specific talents and interests of my own two sons. Therefore, you may notice a preponderance of sports examples and anecdotes. If these situations don't reflect the types of experiences you have with your children, please substitute the appropriate activities, but don't lose sight of the concepts they are meant to convey.

Second, although the examples you will read about in this book are true, all names have been changed to ensure the privacy of those individuals.

Lastly, although I will exhort you to accept your responsibility as the adult in your family or classroom and I am committed to adults holding a firm line to ensure young people learn the lessons they need to learn, I want to make it perfectly clear that I do not sanction physical or emotional abuse of children. Please do not use this book to justify behavior that in any way steps over those boundaries.

I encourage you to reflect long and hard on the challenges I present in this book. Parenting and teaching are tough, stressful jobs. I'm convinced that neither parents nor teachers are adequately prepared for the realities of shaping the lives of the children in their care. Your job as a parent or teacher is far too important to blindly swallow the advice of the so-called "experts." It is only through constant observation, reflection, and refinement that you can develop a powerful, effective approach to the important work you do. This book will stimulate your thinking; it will challenge the status quo. I hope it will force you to think long and hard about what you believe to be true. I hope that by the end of this book you will have decided that children deserve better than chicken parents and chicken schools.

CHAPTER 1: THE PROBLEM

Parents

She rummages through her drawer and finds her new leotard-peach and turquoise stripes on a black background. After pulling on tights, she wriggles into the leotard, bends at the waist and gathers her long hair into a ponytail, which she secures with a black velvet hair band. As she passes the full-length mirror she pauses, twirling to appreciate the effect of her ensemble. In the living room, she selects her favorite exercise video, pops it into the VCR, and Tuesday's exercise routine begins. She moves through the warm-up stretches, feeling the stresses of her typical 16-year-old high school day melt away. As her heart beats faster and the sweat begins to dampen her leotard, she feels the familiar surge of power that accompanies these workouts. She's in control, she's taking responsibility for her own health, and she's on her way to looking *really* good in that bikini!

The back door slams and 13-year-old Derek swaggers in, stopping to throw his backpack on the hall table before heading toward the kitchen for his after school snack. He hears music coming from the living room and stops as he realizes it's Carrie's exercise video. Not one to pass up an opportunity to make his sister's life miserable, he forgoes the leftover pizza and heads into the makeshift aerobics studio. He flops down on the couch with a mischievous smirk on his face, contemplating the perfect opening line, but having used up his daily ration of creativity in Mrs. Fletcher's Language Arts class, he blurts out, "I think that was a 6.5 on the Richter scale."

Carrie whips around and snaps, "Shut up, dickhead!"

"You shut up, lard-butt!" Derek yells.

Over the music, Carrie screams, "Get out of here you little f......er!"

In her bedroom talking on the phone, Angie cringes as she hears the familiar sounds of her children at war. She quickly tells her friend that someone is at her door and she'll call her back after dinner. Leaving the sanctuary of her bedroom, Angie wonders why her two children just can't get along.

As she walks down the stairs toward the living room, the name-calling has escalated. Screaming over the music and the barrage of obscenities, Angie tells Carrie that she has warned her not to use that kind of language.

Carrie snarls, "What are you yelling at me for? I was in here first and that little faggot came in and started bugging me."

Derek immediately counters with, "It's not my fault if you have a fat ass!"

"Shut up, you puke!"

Derek tries to plead his case that he has just as much right to watch TV as Carrie does. Carrie defends her use of the TV, explaining that she only uses it for 30 lousy minutes. Disgusted, Angie threatens to trash the TV so no one can use it. The teenagers ignore the warning, having learned that such consequences never materialize in their household.

Angie pleads, "Why do you have to do this all the time? Do you have to ruin every evening for me?" When Derek hurls one more insult at Carrie, Angie decides that she is going to solve this problem once and for all; this Saturday she is going to buy Carrie a TV and VCR for her bedroom so she can do her aerobics in private.

Problem solved? If you think so, you're a CHICKEN parent. If I were you, I'd read on.

Schools

It's never good news when an emergency faculty meeting is called in the morning and this gathering is not to be the exception. Teachers arrive in virtual silence, anticipating the worst possible news—attempted suicide, car accident or maybe even the death of a student. Experience has taught these junior high teachers that imagining the worst possible scenario can help cushion the sting of the inevitable bad news.

The principal breaks the uncomfortable silence with a firm tone, quickly moving through the greeting and standard announcements. Her comments are direct and void of emotion. She informs the staff that a convicted sexual predator has been enrolled in the school and will begin attending classes immediately. Early in her statements she makes it clear that acceptance of this student is not negotiable. As more administrative information is given, teachers begin to scan the room, wondering who will be "fortunate" enough to have this student in class. The principal insinuates that this student will be on the disciplinary fast track, meaning that she will try to move him out of the school as quickly as possible, but teachers are cautioned to give him every fairness granted to other students on campus. When questions are raised about the legality of this student being allowed to attend school and interact with other students, the principal responds that, since the student has paid his debt to society, he has the right to return to school. She forcefully adds that revealing his past to students or parents could bring legal action against the staff member and the school. After a few additional questions about the responsibilities of the teachers who will have him in class, the student's schedule is read and the meeting comes to a close, with the Principal asking those teachers who will have the boy in class to remain for further instructions.

When William arrives on campus the following day, he draws the usual attention given a new student. A good-looking kid, his appearance and manner give no hint of his time in juvenile prison. His energetic and friendly personality allow him to easily fit in with his ninth grade classmates.

During his first full week on campus, William is caught pulling down the pants of a 7th grade girl during gym class. He is suspended for one day. The girl's parents, upset but assuming the incident is a typical junior high prank, are not informed of the perpetrator's background. A few days later William is observed pressing his body against a number of other girls, many of whom complained to teachers about his behavior. After bringing their concerns to the attention of the administrators, teachers are told to seat the boy away from any girls and to watch him very closely.

Days later, a teacher witnesses William pinning a seventh grade girl against a brick wall and kissing her on the mouth. When the frustrated and angry teacher brings this incident to the attention of the Principal, her response is to ask, "Was the kiss a big kiss or a small kiss?" Questioning of the girl confirms that the kiss was unwanted. The Principal and Counselor call William in, reiterate the rules, and have him sign a "No Touching Contract," forbidding him to touch girls in any way at any time during the school day.

The very next day William is seen behind a locker kissing another seventh grader.

Problem solved? Do you get what CHICKEN is now?

Parents and Schools

Jenny flunked over 80% of her classes in both 7th and 8th grades and now has a perfect "F" status halfway through her ninth grade school year. Following standard procedure for failing students, the school counselor has initiated this conference with all of Jenny's teachers, her parents, and Jenny. The assembled group sits quietly, waiting for one teacher who is a few minutes late. The teachers avoid direct eye contact with Jenny's parents until the counselor has made formal introductions. Jenny's mother sits poised and confident in her well-fitted and expensive suit. Her father, appearing irritated by this early morning meeting, slumps in his chair, his body language clearly communicating his desire to be anywhere but in this room.

The counselor begins the conference with a candid review of Jenny's academic situation, his careful words and tone sculpted through decades of experience. As each teacher describes Jenny's performance in his or her class, the phrase "is failing" begins to lose its power and a clear pattern of non-performance becomes evident.

Jenny's mother responds by sharing her daily schedule. A surgeon, she is a busy woman and the demands on her time are great. She is often at the hospital at 5:30 in the morning and seldom leaves before 8:00 at night. She expresses some concern that she is not home as much as she would like to be, but then quickly assuages her guilt by revealing her husband's even more demanding schedule. Breaking his silence, Jenny's father confirms that his growing business devours most of his waking hours. Jenny's mother comments that teenagers these days are so much more independent than kids were in her day. Jenny herself is always on the go and is rarely home until after her parents have finished work, often after they have gone to bed.

Jenny's mother explains that Jenny has always been a good student and that she believes that the problem is a lack of communication between the school and parents. In other words, it's *not Jenny's fault*. Therefore, she has come prepared with a solution. She hands each teacher and the counselor a stamped, self-addressed envelope, instructing them to write a note the next time Jenny is failing a class or in trouble at school. Of course, she presents no suggestions for how she will follow through on these communications. Throughout this discussion, her husband remains silent, still slumped in his chair and appearing frustrated at the demands of this meeting on his time.

Jenny's teachers are appalled and incensed by the mother's ridiculous "solution" but they remain silent. The mother interprets their lack of response as support for her plan. The meeting adjourns with the teachers left stewing in anger, frustration and unspoken words. They learned early in their careers that candidly expressing their feelings and thoughts usually created conflict, rarely changed the outcome, and risked jeopardizing their jobs and their reputations. In the safety of the empty hallway, they release their pent-up emotions by crumpling Jenny's mother's envelopes in their hands and hurling them into the garbage can. They head for their first period classes, licking the wounds of misplaced blame and feeling the shame and cowardice of not having spoken their minds.

A few months later Jenny is selling her body on the streets.

Jenny knows what CHICKEN is.

What's Chicken?

In order to define CHICKEN, we must first clarify the unique responsibility that comes with being a parent or an educator. As a parent, your primary responsibility is to prepare your child to function independently in the adult world. This requires that you first have a vision of the kind of adult you want your child to become. With that long-term outcome in mind, your task is to structure your child's environment so that decisions are made based on the answer to the question, "What will my child learn from this?" and, "Will what he learns lead to the kind of adult I want him to become?"

Educators also see their role as contributing to the development of the whole child; preparing children with the academic, social, and emotional skills they need to function in school and later on in the larger world. Like parents, teachers must prioritize their time and efforts with children. If students have not yet learned the basic social skills needed to operate in the classroom, then long division may need to be delayed for a few days while they learn how to take turns, listen to others, follow directions, etc.

So what is being CHICKEN? Think back to your grade school playground; the thick mustard yellow lines, the high-pitched screams of girls being teased and chased, the never-ending games of hopscotch, tether ball, tag, or basketball. You probably also remember moments of major significance, burned into your mind as if they happened yesterday; the challenges and confrontations that characterize playgrounds everywhere; challenges of academic egos, contests of athletic prowess, the dares of mischievous pranksters. All initiated by someone calling someone else CHICKEN, the ultimate challenge. But what did it mean? Why did it hold so much power? And why could that word get us riled up enough to do things we would otherwise not even consider doing?

Being called CHICKEN cuts deeply to our inner psyche because it usually contains at least a kernel of truth. It slices through all the protective layers we have built around ourselves and exposes our fears, weaknesses, and vulnerability. It puts us in touch with that part of us that we would rather ignore and push to the side. It sheds light on the shadows of our insecurities. And, of course, the worst part of being called CHICKEN is that someone else is astute enough to uncover the frailties we have worked so hard to mask.

Today's parents have abdicated their responsibility to be the adults in their children's lives; preferring the far easier and apparently more palatable role of buddy or best friend. The lack of assertiveness by today's parents is appalling. Ill-behaved children run roughshod over parents who avoid confrontation like the plague. The standards to which we hold our children are rapidly decomposing. The ever-decreasing time devoted to family is irresponsible. Self-absorbed lifestyles and decadent attitudes increasingly shape children's perceptions of adulthood. "Experts" promoting the panacea of self-esteem compromise the healthy development and maturation of the independent child. Sacrificing for the good of the whole is almost extinct. In a nutshell, today's parents are *afraid*. All parents? Of course not. However, over the last thirty years as an educator and as a parent, I have observed a very disturbing trend in the way people view their job as parents.

I am calling today's parents CHICKEN. Many of you will squirm because this definition contains some degree of truth. I hope to spur you to action; to challenge your assumptions about parenting; to take a clear-eyed look at what your parenting is producing.

Let's go back and take a look at story number one. (These stories are true although, as they say on television, "the names have been changed to protect the innocent.")

Angie is a mother who is frustrated and overwhelmed by the conflicts that pummel her each and every day. She longs for relief from her torture, craving answers to her problems. But, like so many other parents, she doesn't see the forest for the trees. She just wants her children to stop driving her crazy! Whatever the price, she's willing to pay for an immediate end to her misery. This time it will cost Angie a new TV and VCR. What will it cost tomorrow? Unfortunately, Angie is not solving the problem, for herself or for her children; she is simply providing a short-term detour. Buying her way out of the sibling conflict won't teach her children how to resolve their differences in productive ways. On the contrary, she is upping the ante, teaching them how to use their arguments to get what they want.

Is Angie stupid? Is she a selfish, unloving parent? No. Like so many parents, Angie's behavior is motivated by fear. Choosing the more effective and long-term solutions would be too scary. She worries about inflaming an already horrible problem. She's afraid that if she comes down too hard on the kids they might run away. She's afraid her kids will hate her. She doesn't know if she can be consistent enough to see a long-term solution through. She doesn't want to have to spend the time it would take or the energy it would suck from her already depleted reservoir. She just wants the fighting to stop! She is CHICKEN.

In the second story, William is the only person who is not afraid, because experience has taught him that adults seldom back up their rules with consequences. Because they are held responsible for whatever takes place in their classrooms, including one student's harassment of another, teachers are afraid of being sued over

William's behavior. They are afraid to have him out of their sight and spend most of their class time tracking where he is and what he is doing, even if it means neglecting the needs of other students. The principal is afraid that if this situation is not handled well it will damage her reputation and prevent her from getting a promotion to a district administrative position. She is also afraid of any adverse publicity that could result if parents or the press found out about the situation. The young girls that William victimizes are afraid for obvious reasons. The teachers and administrators charged with protecting and nurturing all the children in the school are CHICKEN.

The greatest tragedy is found in the final story. Both her parents and the school failed Jenny and she paid the price. Although this incident happened many years ago when I was a young and inexperienced teacher, to this day I am ashamed to admit that I was one of the teachers involved and wish I could have that moment back. Jenny's parents' refusal to face up to the reality of their daughter's needs, their eagerness to employ a quick fix that served their needs without regard for the ultimate consequences for Jenny, combined with the culture of fear and powerlessness that prevented her teachers from advocating on her behalf, are inexcusable. One thing you can count on is that when parents and schools get together as dueling CHICKENS, there will always be a child who pays.

Vision for Your Child

Do you know what kind of adult you want your child to become? Visualize your child when she is twenty-five years old, sitting across the table from you at Thanksgiving dinner. What do you hope to see? What kind of qualities and characteristics does this person have? I refer to these as the **Big Five**– the most basic standards and positive characteristics you want your child to have as an adult. For example, I want my sons to: 1) be responsible, 2) lead a healthy, balanced life, 3) have respect for people, creatures, and the earth, 4) find passion in work and play, and 5) know what they believe in and stand up for those beliefs. Your **Big Five** may be similar; they may be completely different. What is important is that you have spent the time necessary to clarify these priorities. These become the guiding principles for your decision-making as a parent.

Narrowing the spectrum of parental priorities will immediately do three things for you. First, you can focus your time and attention on a limited number of important parenting issues. This relieves you of the bombardment of daily decisions about which issues are significant and which are unlikely to have a lasting impact on your child's development. Secondly, identifying your parenting priorities reduces the feeling of being overwhelmed, overloaded, and helpless, and makes you a calmer, more rational, more confident decision-maker and role model for your child. Thirdly, a limited number of parenting priorities helps you be more consistent, both individually as well as between each of the child's parents.

This is not a book for parents who wish to be stroked and told everything will be okay if they just love their child enough and spend lots of time building his or her self-esteem. It's not for parents who believe that parenting can be fit in to the available spaces in their personal calendar. It's not for parents who believe that an hour of "quality time" is an adequate substitute for the daily experiences that build the strong bonds that protect children from the inevitable vicissitudes on the pathway to adulthood. It's not for those who believe that good parenting means eliminating frustration, pain, disappointment, and failure from their children's lives. It's not for parents who believe that, "If Mom and Dad are happy and getting their needs met, then the kids will be happy, too."

If you are one of those parents, but you are willing to challenge your comfortable assumptions in order to be the parent your child needs, then keep reading. If you are already behaving like the mature grown-up in your family; if you have taken responsibility for preparing your child for adulthood by allowing him to experience both the frustrating, painful, difficult parts of life as well as the happy, pleasant aspects, then this book will reinforce the wisdom and courage of your choice. If you believe that you have all the answers; that your positive, "Mc-parenting" approach to child rearing will actually produce a responsible, mature adult who is prepared for the full range of life's experiences, then I hope you still have the receipt for this book. You are not ready to hear the truth. Take the book back to the store and continue living in your fantasy world. Or, perhaps, you should put it on a shelf, just in case. When your child is fourteen and out of control, you just might be ready to face reality.

If you decide to keep reading, be prepared. This book will tell the truth. It is likely to be unsettling. It may be unpleasant. It may shake you up. It will contradict what the "experts" have been telling you. In fact, it is likely to get a rise out of a few degree-laden scholars. If you have the guts, read on. If not, well I guess you are just CHICKEN.

CHAPTER 2: DYSFUNCTIONAL SYSTEM

Like parents, today's schools suffer from a "chicken" culture. Schools are big business. The nation's public schools spend $300 billion annually to educate 46 million students in 91,000 school districts. The nation's largest school districts employ tens of thousands of people, including 115,000 in New York City Schools and 61,000 in Los Angeles Unified Schools[1]. In smaller communities, the school district is often one of the community's largest employers. Over the last several decades, school districts have begun to think of themselves as the large businesses they are, rather than as the mom and pop non-profits they may have been in the past, and school administrators are increasingly encouraged to consider themselves the CEO's of their schools. However, there are some fundamental differences between public schools and private corporations.

In companies in the private sector, the goal is clear and explicit. Profit is the bottom line. This is not to say that business leaders don't have to constantly balance the needs of employees, shareholders, and customers; but, at the end of the day, companies don't stay in business if they don't make money. Decisions about new work processes, new employee policies, or new organizational structures are all viewed through the lens of their impact on the bottom line. With more mothers of young children in the work place, companies have experimented with flexible schedules, on-site childcare, and telecommuting. Although each of these innovations may benefit working parents, they will only be adopted if a positive impact on the bottom line can be demonstrated. If flexible work schedules help the company attract and retain skilled workers at minimal cost, then their adoption can be justified. In contrast, despite the fact that on-site childcare proved a valuable recruitment and retention tool, most companies that experimented with it have since abandoned it as too expensive.

This clear and well-accepted focus on a financial bottom line greatly simplifies the job of running a large, complex corporation. Whether they like it or not, everyone accepts the fact that profit is the driving force behind every decision, great or small. If a decision pleases employees and production increases, then it's good for the company. If the company's attention to the environment brings more customers, then it's good for the company. If changing advertising strategies reaches a greater audience, then it's good for the company. Whatever the decision, the final arbiter is impact on profits. The desired end result is clear. One very simple question can be asked to determine the wisdom of any decision: How does this impact our bottom line?

Bottom Lines

School systems, however, operate very differently. The bottom line in schools is murky at best, invisible at worst. Rather than being a clear and well-accepted focus, the bottom line in schools seems more like the price of a hotel room—completely different depending on who you are, whom you ask, and when you ask. This lack of focus leaves schools floundering in a sea of uncertainty and misdirection.

There seem to be three major bottom lines guiding decision-making in today's school systems: 1) the financial bottom line, 2) the legal bottom line, and 3) the educational bottom line, in roughly that order of importance. Over the last several decades the "business" of schools has been undermined from all directions.

Financial

The financial bottom line in schools and school districts is a factor of the number of students enrolled. Each student brings with him or her thousands of dollars of state funding. Although certain groups of students, such as disabled students, English-as-a- Second Language students, and high-risk students also bring federal dollars with them, the additional funding is rarely enough to meet their special needs. This funding structure sets up a system that encourages schools to compete for students and the dollars they represent. The most "desirable" students, however, are those that are the least expensive to educate, which, of course, excludes students with special needs. Administrators struggling to maintain their profitability go to any and all lengths to compete for new students, particularly those in the more "desirable" categories. Schools scramble to position themselves as the premier school, touting the number of Advanced Placement courses offered, the special programs available, the SAT scores their students get. Determined to be viewed as cutting edge, principals and teachers flock to conferences to learn the latest educational fad. Supporters of this free market system of public education believe that competition for students will improve the quality of schools overall, forcing them to become more "consumer-oriented." This approach may be valid for businesses, where it is clear who the customer is and the corporation has little stake in what the customer chooses as long as it produces a profit. In public schools, however, the "customer" is less easily defined. Is the customer the parent? The child? The employers who will eventually employ the student? The general public who is footing the bill?

In fact, schools will, indeed, change as a result of pressure from their customers. The important question is, will they change in ways that better fulfill the mission that we as a society have for public education? Or will they change in ways that are designed to please their constituents, to keep people happy, to avoid conflict? In the case of public education, does the customer always know what is best?

This pandering to the customer influences a myriad of decisions at all levels of the system. Several years ago, my superintendent sent a memo to all district employees informing us that her goal for our district was to be the "Nordstrom" of school districts. She was referring to the Nordstrom Company's legendary philosophy that "the customer is always right." Nordstrom employees are renowned for going out of their way to make their customers happy. The implicit message to us was that we, too, were to go out of our way to make sure that our customers were happy. Interesting that this district leader believed it was more important for our customers to be happy than it was for our students to be educated, productive citizens.

In another school district in my area, I have watched the Superintendent and School Board enact policy and reverse that policy so fast it makes your head spin; simply because they are constantly trying to please *all* of their customers *all* of the time. We all know that you can't please everybody and attempting to do so usually means that nobody is ever happy. The current dysfunctional system, in which the financial bottom line is focused on attracting and retaining students at any cost, perpetuates this insanity.

At the individual building level, principals are also driven by this need to keep the customer happy. If a group of parents wants more Advanced Placement classes, then the principal better find a way to get them what they want, or they may take their student, and the associated dollars, to another school that will. If some parents and students want a strong arts program, then the smart principal will make sure that program is fully funded, even at the expense of other kinds of programs.

In the classroom, the "customer is always right" philosophy is particularly pernicious. For example, after receiving her semester grade, one of my students came up to my desk to question the "C" grade she had earned. I showed her the points that had produced the grade and she cried, "But I don't WANT a 'C'!" As an unhappy customer, she felt that somehow her *feelings* about the grade she received should have the power to change the grade she had actually *earned*. Teachers who feel it is their responsibility to keep students happy are easily distracted from their more primary responsibility of ensuring that students are educated.

Here's how the system works with this dysfunctional financial bottom line. Teachers have to keep their customers (students and their parents) happy in order to get recognition from, and avoid punishment by, their boss, the Principal. Principals have to keep those same customers happy in order to get recognition from, and avoid punishment by, their bosses, the District Administrators. District Administrators have to keep the customer happy in order to get recognition from, and avoid punishment by their bosses, the School Board. The School Board must keep their customers happy because, in most School Districts, their customers are the ones who elect them. It's easy to see how this financial bottom line can distort decision-making and produce unintended consequences that negatively impact students.

Legal

The second bottom line that drives school decision-making is the legal bottom line. The past several decades have seen an explosion of legal challenges to schools. Each year new laws are added to the ever-growing list and educators must learn the intricacies of each one: IEPs (Individual Education Plans for Special Education students), 504 laws (designed to meet the needs of students with medical or emotional conditions that hinder learning) and Washington State's BECCA Bill (for truancy), just to name a few. The Students' Rights movement of the seventies opened a Pandora's box by making students' rights paramount, even when ensuring the legal right of an individual student jeopardizes the rights of the group.

This absurd imbalance between the needs of the individual and the needs of the group has had profound consequences in all areas of education. I experienced a good example of this type of situation during my sixth season of coaching junior high cross-country. It was the second day of practice when a new student showed up , with paper work in order, and dressed to run. It was obvious from her appearance that she suffered from several severe disabilities. She wore exceptionally thick glasses, walked with a distinct limp and was very difficult to understand when she spoke. However, as she had both her doctor's and her parent's permission to participate, I began practice. After general announcements, we proceeded with our routine stretches. I watched her very closely, trying to assess her abilities and possible limitations. Still uncomfortable with the situation, I went to the office to try to find out more about her condition, but no one there could tell me anything. So, I returned to the team and we took off on our customary early season two-mile route, running along the shoulders of the suburban streets that surround our school. It quickly became clear to me that this student was incapable of negotiating the roads and most definitely couldn't keep up with the rest of the twenty plus runners. So I escorted her back to the campus and told her to sit on a bench until the team returned. The next day I investigated her condition further. In talking with the school nurse and her special education teachers, I was shocked to find out the degree of this student's physical disabilities. She was legally blind. A shunt in her brain was required for proper blood circulation and she suffered from various muscular abnormalities. I immediately informed the principal of the situation and made it clear that I could not possibly be responsible for this girl while also supervising the other twenty students, as she needed constant supervision to guarantee her own safety. The parents were strong advocates for their daughter and wanted her to have the same opportunities as her peers. They knew the law well and had a history of flexing their power in such situations. In most of these situations, the dysfunctional system has taught administrators and teachers that it is better just to give in to the demands of potentially litigious parents. However, I was adamant in my refusal, which resulted in a convening of all the involved parties to discuss the situation. As expected, district officials informed me that I had to allow this student to participate in cross-country. When it became clear that the needs and rights of this one student were going to be allowed to override the needs of the other team members, I had no choice but to inform the principal that, if she was allowed to run, I would resign as coach. The entire program was jeopardized for one individual.

In the classroom, laws and policies protecting the individual rights of students are equally out of whack. The passage of the Americans with Disabilities Act provided students with a new excuse for inappropriate, irresponsible, and out of control behavior. Designed to meet the needs of students with legitimate medical or psychological conditions that interfere with their ability to function in the classroom, the "504" process has generated a rush of parents seeking to have every conceivable condition designated as a "disability." Once students are identified as "504," the school system must make "every reasonable accommodation" for their disability. There are many legitimate conditions for which this designation is a necessary and valuable tool. For example, I had one student who had such severe migraines that she often was unable to come to class. Her 504 designation allowed her to work with her teachers to ensure that she could keep up with her class work and not be penalized for her condition. However, the language in the law is so vague that its misuse was inevitable. Just a few of the examples of 504 "conditions" I have encountered in my own classroom: school phobia, difficulty concentrating, and inability to control anger. The required accommodations might include more time to complete homework or tests, no consequences for absences or tardies, being allowed to move about the room during class, freedom to leave the room when angry, etc. The use of this new loophole to rescue kids from responsibility for their own behavior is so pervasive that, in one of my math classes recently I overheard the following conversation. One student was complaining to another student about what a pain in the neck it was to have to do homework every night. This student often came to class unprepared. His helpful neighbor quickly volunteered, "Hey, why don't you just get on a 504? That way you can have as long as you want to turn in your homework and you get extra time and help to take tests. It's great."

Although the 504 laws provide much-needed support for students with legitimate needs, widespread misuse further undermines teachers' ability to hold high expectations for all students. In effect, it legitimizes and excuses laziness, procrastination, lack of self-control and a host of other behaviors that students are fully capable of learning to manage. Once again, students pay the price. The student whose inappropriate behavior is allowed to continue never learns the skills he or she will require to function effectively in the real world. That student's classmates suffer because they are forced to put up with behavior from one student that is often disruptive to the overall classroom learning environment.

Armed with the knowledge that the legal system will always err on the side of protecting the needs of the individual student, parents and students are filing lawsuits in alarming numbers. Reluctant to incur the time and expense required to fight yet another lawsuit, school districts often choose to give in to even the most absurd and counterproductive demands. Once again, this distorted legal bottom line contributes to faulty decision-making that reinforces the dysfunction of the system.

Educational

So what about the third bottom line—education? I think we would find fairly universal agreement that this *should* be the real bottom line in schools, not the financial and legal bottom lines that currently overpower the system. So, if we all agree that this *should* be the bottom line, why has the current dysfunctional system been allowed to continue? We may find some answers by looking at our own history. How did schools in the past manage to keep their focus on the educational bottom line and not become distracted and pulled off course by the legal and financial bottom lines that plague today's educators? I would submit that, in days past, the bottom lines for parents and educators were more similar than they are today. Each entity had basically the same end in mind for young people. With that common focus, parents supported schools and schools supported parents. A truly symbiotic relationship existed. Parents trusted the judgment of teachers and administrators on educational matters and schools trusted parents to parent their children. Each partner had a legitimate, agreed-upon role to play in producing healthy, productive citizens.

Unfortunately, this mutually beneficial relationship has been seriously weakened over the last several decades, to the point where neither party is really sure what the other wants. Parents, schools and society as a whole all had a part in the demise of this valuable partnership. As detailed earlier, the Student Rights movement ushered in an era of families and schools as adversaries, not as collaborators focused on a common goal. As the self-esteem movement captured the attention of a new generation of parents, they increasingly challenged established educational and discipline policies in schools. Rather than teachers and parents standing together as a team of adults with the long-term best interests of students in mind, the dynamic shifted to one of parents and students banding together *against* teachers. Often this new partnership is solely focused on ensuring that the student's immediate needs (or wants) are met and her rights are protected, with little regard to the long-term consequences for the student's development. This realignment of parent/student/teacher alliances is well illustrated by a situation I recall from my years teaching in the junior high. A colleague of mine, one of the most effective teachers I know, was walking through the student lunchroom one day when a seventh grader dipped his French fry into ketchup and proceeded to launch it at the back of my colleague's neck. The teacher, a veteran who knew the value of constantly scanning your environment when amongst students, had seen the offender smirking at him and whispering with his friends. He walked back to where the student sat with his buddies, his demeanor clearly challenging the teacher to call him on the assault. The teacher calmly bent over the student, quietly said, "You're lucky I'm not twenty years younger or I'd kick your ass," then walked away, knowing that this approach would leave the teenager suitably humiliated in front of his friends. Indeed, as he walked away he heard the boy's friends snickering. The next morning when the teacher arrived at school, he was called in to the Principal's office. He was told that the student had gone home and told his parents what had happened and the parents were planning to sue the teacher and the school, because he had "threatened" the student and the student was now afraid to come back to school.

When the teacher recounted this story in the faculty lounge later that day, my first thought was how different this scenario would have been when I was a student. First of all, I couldn't imagine ever going home and telling my parents that I had dipped a French fry in ketchup and thrown it at a teacher, because the punishment for doing so would have been far more severe than anything the school could ever have imposed. But, assuming I had done so, there was no question in my mind that my father's reaction to being told about the teacher's response to me would not have been to call his attorney. The more likely reaction would have been, "I don't care if I'm not twenty years younger. I'm still going to kick your ass."

When I voiced my reaction to the other teachers sitting in the room, they resoundingly agreed. Although I certainly am not condoning teachers threatening students, the reaction I would have gotten from my father communicated to me that my parents and the school were united in making sure that I learned how to be a responsible, civilized human being. In contrast, the student in this example learned that he could not only avoid punishment for his totally unacceptable behavior, he could actually *get the teacher in trouble*! All he had to do was take advantage of the adversarial relationship between parents and the school and claim that his "self-esteem had been damaged." The parents quickly jumped on the lawsuit bandwagon, ready to protect the rights of their child, regardless of the thoroughly damaging lesson he would learn.

So, if we all agree that the appropriate bottom line for schools should be an educational bottom line, then how can we cure this sick patient and undo the damage done by the current dysfunctional system?

Changing the Bottom Line

First we need to have discussions between all interested parties that confirm our agreement that the bottom line for schools should be an educational one, not the current financial or legal bottom lines. Once we have agreement on this fundamental common goal, then we need to further articulate what we all mean by an "educated" young person. In other words, if we agree that the main purpose of schools should be to produce "educated" students, then we need to come to some consensus on what an educated student looks like. This process harkens back to the Big Five concept that we suggested for parents in Chapter One. Schools, too, need to define their Big Five-those fundamental attributes or characteristics that are the most important components of an educated student. To be an effective tool, the process of defining the school's Big Five should include all of the potential consumers of the public education system—parents, students, the business community, and the community at large—as well as teachers, administrators and other school staff. Just as in a family, the process of identifying the school's Big Five is as important as the final outcome. Once the Big Five are identified, then everyone associated with the school can use them as a benchmark for making all kinds of decisions. For example, if one of the school's Big Five is "respectful behavior," it shouldn't be hard for school staff to decide whether or not swearing should be tolerated. If students and parents have been involved in the discussions about the Big Five, when a student is disciplined for swearing in the hallway, school staff can simply point to the Big Five and explain that swearing is not an example of respectful behavior, therefore it is not permitted.

If we agree that making kids responsible for their actions is one of the school's Big Five, then the parent who tries to rescue a misbehaving child from the consequences of her actions can be firmly reminded of this important goal. We all know how destructive it can be when children divide and conquer by playing one parent off of the other. This is equally true with parents and schools. When parents and schools present a united front to students, everyone wins.

Teachers and administrators win because the bottom line is clear and concise and it can be used as the foundation for decisions. This frees educators to concentrate on teaching, not policing. Parents win because they know exactly what is expected from their kids. Finally, children win because they know precisely what the boundaries are so they don't need to expend their energy constantly testing the limits. Their energy can be directed toward learning.

Once schools have defined their Big Five, then the question becomes, what is the best way to produce the qualities we've defined as the Big Five? Once again, the dysfunctional system often does exactly the opposite of what we know works to reach these important goals.

If we want students who are responsible, compassionate, good critical thinkers, effective problem-solvers, and motivated learners, what things should schools be focusing on to develop these qualities in students?

Good Teachers

Research has shown that the one thing that is most consistently associated with student success is the presence of a high quality teacher[2]. So, if having a high quality teacher is the most reliable predictor of student success, one would assume that society's attention and resources would be focused on this single important ingredient. Unfortunately, the focus seems to be everywhere *but* on this essential component. We have raised standards, implemented high-stakes tests, introduced new curriculums, adopted block schedules, restructured schools—everything *but* investing in the teachers whose impact is so critical to student success. In fact, the dysfunction of the system itself is one of the primary obstacles to getting and keeping good teachers.

Of course, there are the obvious obstacles of absurdly low pay compared with other similar professions and the lack of opportunity for advancement over the course of a career. When you talk with new teachers, or those considering teaching as a career, it is evident that teaching is not a profession destined to attract the nation's best and brightest. In my early years of teaching in 1981 and 1982, our two-year contract allowed for an 11½ % raise the first year, followed by a 10½

% raise the next year. Such raises are unheard of today. In the past ten years of teaching in one of the best districts in Washington State, any raise I received was quickly devoured by inflation. In fact, in those ten years I have lost over 8% of my buying power. Teachers rarely receive the cost-of-living increases or similar inflation fighting advantages that other professionals receive. In fact, when extra money becomes available from the State, that additional compensation is almost always tied to additional work on the part of teachers. I guess this way the State can prove to the public that they are getting something for their money. It is also common practice to pay teachers hourly for these extra work hours. We are the only occupation I know of that will work overtime for less than normal hourly pay. That's right! Teachers in my state are actually paid less than our normal hourly wage for extra time spent in workshops or mandatory training. I get a pay *decrease* for working overtime. I have never heard of a district paying *more* than per diem for overtime, as is the case for the rest of the working world. Can you imagine going to work tomorrow and having your boss tell you that you must work an extra two hours that day and that you will be compensated at a rate of 66% of your normal hourly wage? That's absurd! You wouldn't stand for it. It's unfair and ludicrous. You'd have a few choice words for that boss and make it clear that he/she is never to approach you again with such a ridiculous idea. And for you bosses out there, can you imagine the reactions of your employees after you have submitted such an offer. Forget it! You wouldn't even contemplate such a foolish idea. But this is normal practice for schools across the country. Coaching stipends, supervising school activities, teaching Traffic Education, etc. are all under the same asinine compensation guidelines.

To add insult to injury, not only are teachers expected to work overtime for less money, we are also expected to work a considerable number of additional hours for free! Virtually all of the teachers I know take additional work home with them. Some subject areas require more outside work than others. Subjects that involve a good deal of writing produce reams of essays and reports to read and correct. Spelling, grammar, punctuation, and content, all have to be corrected. A teacher assigns a two page essay in her three junior English classes, due Friday. She averages thirty students per class. That weekend she will be correcting ninety essays, reading 180 pages of student work. Students and parents demand prompt feedback, so they expect their papers to be returned early the following week, so the dutiful teacher uses her own time during the weekend to finish grading the papers. This scenario is repeated in all departments, in every school, in every state, throughout the country. Think of the astronomical number of unpaid hours accumulating throughout the nation in just one week. Now multiply that by thirty-five more weeks. That's a lot of teacher time that is unpaid, unappreciated, unnoticed, and increasingly expected by the public.

Teachers are routinely expected to donate their time for the good of the school. Imagine that you are an accountant and your boss summons you to her office and tells you that the following policy changes will be effective immediately. You are required to attend meetings before or after work for business purposes, you are to do your own tax law research at home, you are to prepare and organize for tomorrow's tax returns at home, you will be asked to do the work of any employee who doesn't show up that day, you are required to help train new accountants who are having trouble adjusting, you will be responsible for the maintenance of your office, you are required to respond to every client the day they call, you might be asked to supervise an office gathering or entertain at the office party, or volunteer your time for any event that is associated with the firm. Oh and by the way, you will still be expected to do your usual full day's work and you won't be receiving any extra pay for your extra duties. Who's jumping up to join that club? All these things and more are everyday life for teachers. We are required to attend regular faculty meetings, either before or after our contracted day. In order to stay current in our subject matter, we are expected to read professional journals and other publications. However, there is no time allowed during our school day for this preparation, so we have to do our reading at home on our own time. Preparation for the next day is often done at home the night before, as our daily "planning" period is often used to meet with students, parents or other staff. We are often required to sacrifice our planning period to cover classes for other teachers who have to be out of the building. Because there is often no formal system for supporting and mentoring new teachers, that task usually falls to more veteran teachers. Budget cuts have reduced janitorial service and teachers are increasingly asked to contribute to the maintenance of their classrooms. The availability of voicemail and email has given rise to a belief on the part of parents that a teacher should respond to them immediately, or at the very least, by the end of the day in which the message was left. And, of course, what "good" teacher can turn down the endless requests to chaperone dances, supervise clubs, tutor struggling students, run the clock at the basketball games, etc., etc., etc.

Okay, so we expect teachers to work extra hours for less pay, to work additional extra hours for *no* pay, what else could we possibly expect from them? You guessed it. We expect them to actually use their own money to help make ends meet in the classroom. I have never encountered a teacher who has not spent his own money for something that was needed for his class. For several years I car pooled with a colleague whose wife was an elementary teacher. One day as we were discussing the financial woes of the teaching profession, he commented that his wife spent over a hundred dollars a month on things she needed to run her class effectively. We decided to ask around our campus to find out what the average teacher in our building spent out of his or her own pocket for classroom supplies. All of the teachers we surveyed reported having spent some amount of their own money that month and many actually had surpassed the one hundred dollar level for that month. A recent national report found that teachers spend an average of $400 a year of their own money[3].

Although most people's response when I tell them I'm a teacher is something like, "Wow, that must be really hard." or "Gosh, I can't imagine doing that for the kind of money you guys make," many people also believe deep down that teachers have it pretty easy. After all, they get *all* that vacation time! Let me correct a few misconceptions. Teachers are contracted for 7.5 hours per day. We are only paid for 183 days out of a year. (The number of days will vary from district to district but will usually be within a few days.) Those of you who believe teachers are paid for the summer months are correct in your assumption but incorrect in your analysis. In fact, teachers are only paid for the 183 days they work. They are not paid for the two and a half months that school is not in session. However, many districts allocate teachers' pay over twelve months anyway. The district takes the total pay for the 183 days and divides it by 12. This ensures that teachers have a paycheck coming in each month. I guess districts don't think teachers are mature enough to be paid their money after they have earned it. During those summer months that the district is holding onto the money I have already earned, they are also keeping the interest that accrues. Could that possibly be the real reason for this payroll scheme?

A friend of mine received his college degree at the age of 43. His company paid for his tuition and any expenses associated with his degree. I guess his company figures that the better educated the employee, the more valuable he will be to the company. I'm sure that the education system would agree, but they certainly don't put their money where their mouth is. In most states, teachers are required to complete a fifth year of college to retain their teaching certificate. Some states require teachers to get a Master's degree as part of their continuing education. The entire expense of this required education falls directly on the shoulders of the individual teacher. The cost of $15,000 for that additional education can be a prohibitive burden for a new teacher earning $26,000 a year.

When college students are choosing their majors we give them ample reason not to choose education. How can we expect the best and the brightest to go into teaching when the financial rewards are so out of line with compensation in other professions? How can we attract well-balanced men and women to be role models for our children when they know they are doomed to financial mediocrity at best? How can we draw the best people into teaching when their salary often does not allow them to qualify to purchase a house in the city in which they teach? How much longer can we continue to hope there are still exceptional people out there who will sacrifice their personal financial future for the good of society?

However, compensation is not the only thing keeping young people from going into the profession and chasing good teachers out. We need to look deeper to fully understand the reasons for the fact that our country is currently experiencing a dire teacher shortage, which is predicted to reach crisis proportions in the very near future.

Let's look at the composition of a typical public middle school or high school classroom. At the beginning of the semester, teachers receive a list of students who have identified issues about which the teachers need to be aware. A typical classroom might contain three "mainstreamed" Special Education students, with a variety of physical, emotional, or learning disabilities; a couple of students who have alcohol or drug problems; one or two who have been physically or sexually abused; one whose parent is seriously ill or dying; many who have various physical ailments (kids who need to be in front because of vision problems; kids who have trouble controlling their bladders; kids who need to eat during class; kids who need hearing equipment; kids who have allergies; kids who can only do very specific actions-walk but not jump, jump but not run, run but not over a mile, run but not lift, lift but not run; blood conditions; asthma conditions, skin conditions, you name it, I've seen it); a bunch who are angry at parents, the school, or just authority of any kind; a sizeable number who are sexually active; boys who are violent and girls who are victims of that behavior; pockets of students who are dealing with divorce and parental conflict; many who work part-time jobs to the maximum of hours the State allows; several who show symptoms of excessive pressure to achieve; many experiencing serious conflict with parents or siblings; most suffering from sleep deprivation. This is in addition to the normal trials and tribulations of adolescence—acne, puberty, dating, cliques, bad hair days. It's important to remember that the classroom I just described is typical of my own experience in an upper middle class, suburban school district. Needy students do not just exist in inner city, poor school districts. With all of these special needs, the classroom teacher is supposed to stay informed, understand the full range of implications for the classroom, adjust programs and lessons to fit specific needs, treat all students fairly, tolerate behavior that is often outside of the boundaries of acceptable classroom behavior, and oh yeah, teach.

Good Administrators

Dealing with this complexity in the classroom requires the support and reinforcement of strong leadership. An effective principal facilitates and supports success in the classroom. Unfortunately, because of the design of the system for selecting and preparing administrators, effective principals are all too rare.

Unlike the system for advancement in most professions, becoming a school administrator is not based on demonstration of exceptional competence and skillful performance. If I wish to become an administrator, all I need to do is make that decision; neither my skills as a teacher nor my ability to lead other teachers is considered. I am not promoted by a superior who has observed my performance and deemed me worthy of advancement. I am chosen from no select group. I have demonstrated no special expertise, talent, skill, or competency. I just decide to leave the classroom and seek an administrative position. Yes, I have to successfully complete an accredited administrative program. I have to attend the appropriate classes and satisfy the designated requirements. But I have not known one single individual who has applied for admission to the Administrative Certification program and been denied. After completing these requirements, I would be eligible for a Principal or Assistant Principal position.

During my career in teaching I have worked with many administrators— a few exceptional, others totally incompetent, most simply functioning. To understand why there are so few exceptional administrators, it's helpful to ask why a teacher would choose to leave the classroom to seek an administrative position. My observation, confirmed by most of my colleagues, is that there are three common reasons. The first category includes those individuals who truly believe they can do more for education as a leader of a school. Their heart is in the right place, their focus is on the right things, and their motives are genuine. They are able to translate the leadership, management, organizational, and instructional skills that made them successful in the classroom to the task of running an entire school. When this type of individual does have the requisite competencies for running a school, they can make the difference between a school that is truly educating kids and a school that just struggles to survive from day to day. An effective and enthusiastic Principal has the power to motivate her staff and make them feel as if they are valuable and appreciated. I have worked for such a Principal and can attest to the fact that it makes a world of difference in my attitude as well as my teaching. If teachers' energies are going to be devoured by the myriad of challenges in today's classrooms, the support and leadership of a good principal can be a godsend.

Unfortunately, this type of administrator is not the norm. Often new administrators, with the best intentions, land an administrative position only to find that it is not what they expected and, even worse, they don't have what it takes to be successful. However, they have invested two years of graduate school and a small fortune out of their own pocket to reach this occupational level. So, rather than admitting defeat, they continue to wage an uphill battle. As they fail to win the confidence of the staff, they rely on reinforcement from other administrators. This administrative group develops its own identity and the division between teachers and administration builds. Administrators also are responsible for evaluating classroom teachers, which further polarizes the two groups. There also appears to be an unwritten code within the administrative group that they will stick together. No matter how obvious a mistake or how painful a problem created, they will back each other as a united force. They have the power, so teachers fear them and what they can do.

The second reason teachers seek administrative positions is because they are unsuccessful as a teacher. Again, these individuals have spent five years of college and tens of thousands of dollars preparing for their chosen profession, but when they actually get into the classroom, they find that it simply isn't a good fit. When these types of people become administrators, the system is immediately compromised, because, as leaders of their schools, they are responsible for providing evaluation and instructional guidance to teachers. But how can people who left the classroom because of their incompetence as teachers provide valuable feedback and support to teachers? In my years of teaching I can honestly say that there has been only one administrator whom I felt could actually give me constructive suggestions for improving my teaching. The others demonstrated on a regular basis that they lacked the knowledge needed to run an effective classroom.

The most conflict I ever had with an administrator was with a principal who had approximately one and a half years of classroom experience. It was clear from the very beginning that she did not like teaching or being with kids. Her manner with students was often described as cold or unfeeling. She avoided contact with people, delegating duties to her staff as much as possible in order to remove herself from uncomfortable dealings with students, parents, or teachers. She often found refuge in her office with the door closed and window shades drawn. She clearly lacked basic people skills, a serious problem for someone in a position that requires interaction with 65 educational staff, 900 students, and over a thousand parents. Over the course of a decade as principal of this school she polarized the faculty and created an atmosphere of tension and hostility. Scores of teachers transferred from the school, including myself. Students who had once experienced a fun-loving, supportive campus atmosphere, now attended school under a cloud of tension. Parents questioned her abilities, teachers filed grievances, district administrators conducted investigations, and the teacher's union got involved. But even as the complaints piled up, the grievance files grew thicker, and good teachers fled to other schools, she remained firmly ensconced in her position. She was put on probation, ordered to attend people management classes, sent to therapy, reprimanded multiple times, and yet she was still allowed to continue to run a school. At one point, a mediator and the district's attorney had to be called in to resolve the conflict. A team of district administrators was called in to conduct interviews with the entire staff. The conflict was so great that the school developed a negative reputation throughout the district. Despite the chaos, the disruption, the negative impact on staff and students, this individual was protected. She remained in her position, all powers intact, receiving all the financial rewards and benefits that accompanied this job, until her retirement.

The final reason for becoming an administrator is to seek power. This type of administrator will eventually fail, drowning in a sea of conflict and rebellion. For these individuals, the pursuit of power stems from their inability to feel powerful in other parts of their lives. They left the classroom because they couldn't handle the kids well, but hope maybe they can handle the adults. So the only remaining avenue for asserting their power is the school. This type of motivation is the exact opposite of what is required to successfully lead a school.

One overarching reason why teachers go the administrative route is simply that it is the only pathway to get more money. The educational system is set up so that the only way for a teacher to advance financially is to get on the administrative track.

Early in my teaching career, a colleague and I regularly squeezed in a short workout during our thirty-minute lunch break. We usually had time to run a few miles before returning to campus. Our principal was not only aware of this activity he actually appreciated our efforts because we would often catch smokers off campus, saving him the trouble of policing those areas. My colleague and I were both well-respected teachers who had always received glowing evaluations. We continued to practice this routine for the bulk of the school year, missing a few days due to weather or scheduling conflicts. To our surprise, we found out later in the year that the vice principal had been charting our activities, marking the time we left and when we returned. He had compiled files on both of us, filled with the charts he had been keeping throughout the year. When he confronted us with this "issue," we called our Union representative, who confirmed that our contract clearly stated that teachers had a "duty free 30-minute lunch." Exercising during this time was permitted and the issue was dropped. So why did this administrator feel the need to go to all of this trouble to chart our activities? He didn't like us "getting away" with something. He wanted to control us. He chose to waste his time charting our activities instead of using his time to help the teachers he was supposed to be supporting or students who begged for guidance. He needed to quench his thirst for power.

The ultimate outcome of this faulty administrator selection process is a glaringly dysfunctional system. We have no screening system in place to identify unqualified administrators. We have no system to identify those who would do well as school leaders. As administrators move through the process and find employment, we put them in charge of evaluating skills they often never had and certainly have no idea how to teach. We set up a polarizing division between administrators and their staffs. We give power to people who have proven they cannot handle it and refuse to remove anyone from their duties even after they have shown repeated incompetence. Rather than providing support and leadership to the teachers in their buildings, administrators all too often become the straw that breaks the camel's back, the ever-present wall into which teachers must bang their heads on a daily basis. The problems of today's classrooms can suck the life out of a teacher. Teacher burnout is a real and serious problem. The challenge of serving the needs of today's students can break even the strongest and most committed individuals, sending them searching for other jobs. The demands are great, the time commitment absurd, and the rewards few. But good teachers rarely leave the profession because of the teaching or the students. They leave because of all the unnecessary obstacles that keep them from teaching and interacting successfully with students. Poor administrators drive good teachers out of the profession, and they are leaving in droves. Thirty percent of teachers leave the profession within their first three years[4]. If having a high quality teacher is the most important thing we can do to ensure student success, then we must fix the system that allows incompetent administrators to chase good teachers away.

Learn From Teachers

Let's take another look at the question we posed earlier. If we want students who are responsible, compassionate, good critical thinkers, effective problem-solvers, and motivated learners, what things should schools be focusing on to develop these qualities in students?

Who better to answer this question than the professionals who have spent their lives educating children? But is this the way decisions are made in the educational system? Absolutely not. In fact, quite the contrary is true. I am always amazed to see the next sweeping educational trend devour the system like a ten-foot wave crashing to the shore. Usually, classroom teachers are the last to know about these changes. They are assured that the new approach is supported by mounds of research, has been tested in schools for years with incredible success, and will produce the results that all of the other strategies have failed to deliver. It generally takes only a few minutes of exposure to this new silver bullet before teachers begin formulating questions about the practicality of actually implementing this new approach in their classrooms. They point out the potential pitfalls and obstacles and ask for clarification on the myriad of logistical issues that must be resolved. Amazingly, these questions are often met with the stock answer, "Well, we're still looking into that, but we're confident that problem will be solved." Of course, the problems usually aren't resolved and, after a few years of experimenting with the new approach, it joins the scrap heap of other discarded programs. I have never been asked the following questions by those who have the power to institute positive change, "What changes would you make to improve education? What can we do to help you in the classroom? How can we help make you a better teacher?"

The Total Quality Management approach pioneered by the

Japanese and adopted by hundreds of American companies in the eighties and nineties brought a fresh new approach to improving organizations. Rather than relying on experts and top management to improve systems and processes, those who were closest to the work were asked for their ideas. This approach created a flood of ingenious ideas that could only have come from those who encounter the problems on a daily basis. In addition to generating fresh new solutions, engaging workers in solving problems also increases their commitment to implementing the changes. Who better to ask than those who are most affected by the change?

The current dysfunctional educational system flies in the face of this logical and effective improvement process. We listen to the experts, most of whom have either never stood in front of a classroom and taught successfully, or whose teaching experience is so far in the past that it cannot possibly provide an accurate barometer of today's school climate. Policy decisions made by State legislators who have no knowledge of the realities of today's classrooms have the power to powerfully impact schools and teachers.

We listen to the self-serving dialogue of the business community, we cater to the whims of the parents, and we give value to the whining rhetoric of the pampered student; but what we refuse to do is to ask for input from the very people who have the most knowledge of the situation, the most experience to draw on, and the greatest investment in positive change-teachers. We should not be surprised when this year's educational fad runs its predictable course. In the end, we will scratch our heads, puzzled at another failed program. But not to worry; you can rest assured that another silver bullet is waiting in the wings to take its place.

What if, instead of our current ineffective strategy, we asked veteran teachers what they believe are the most important ingredients involved in producing a well-prepared student? As both a teacher and a parent of public school students, I have met countless teachers over the years whose judgment I would trust far above any "experts."

One such teacher was Mrs. Salazar, my son's first grade teacher. Having talked with other parents, I was quite pleased that my son would be in Mrs. Salazar's class. Her reputation was outstanding and she was known to create miracles with her students. As the year progressed, Mrs. Salazar exceeded every expectation I had for her.

She was well-organized, had high standards for both academics and behavior, expected the best from all students, and the kids loved her. It also became quite clear to me that she was her own person. Despite the ever-changing dictates of district administrators, Mrs. Salazar just continued to do her own thing. It was this experience that made me begin to seriously question what we recognize in the educational world as accepted truths. Over the course of her long career, Mrs. Salazar had proven that she knew what worked. Field-tested with thousands of students, her methods were sound and reaped consistently positive results. In horse racing, Mrs. Salazar would be a sure thing.

What a great, untapped resource. Wouldn't you think the experts would be dying to pick Mrs. Salazar's brain, along with all the other "Mrs. Salazars" across the country? Imagine the head start enthusiastic college interns would have with the time-tested wisdom of this sage veteran. On campuses across the country there are teachers with the same skills and teaching abilities that Mrs. Salazar demonstrated. Yet the culture of education and the dysfunctional teacher training system is such that this invaluable resource is rarely tapped. So, Mrs. Salazar, and hundreds of teachers like her, quietly move into retirement with a quick thank you and an obligatory retirement party. We let a wealth of experience and wisdom slip away.

Veteran teachers are fully aware of the complexities of today's educational system. We understand how badly parents want their kids to excel. We understand the magnitude of the pressure on students to achieve. We see the political games played within the school district. We experience on a daily basis the financial limitations of the system. We see first hand the successes and the failures of programs. We realize the pressure placed on schools by the community. We experience the anger and frustration of the public demanding measurable improvements in schools. We recognize the lack of confidence in the school system. We sense the blame pointing our way.

Teachers spend their working lives in a living laboratory, constantly testing new ways of working with each student, seeing what works, discarding what doesn't, gradually building our own unique teaching style that works for us as teachers and for our respective students. We struggle daily with students to move them toward understanding, despite the seemingly overwhelming baggage many students bring with them into the classroom. We see the light go on when those moments arrive. We guide a class to group enlightenment and help them discover answers to life's tougher questions. We are there for the tears of sorrow and the tears of joy. We support students with our attention and our presence. We know students because we are with students for eight hours a day 180 days a year. We know what we are doing. We know how to fix many of the problems. We can help focus everyone's attention on those things that will bring about the most constructive change. We have all this knowledge and wisdom, but no one is asking and no one is listening.

The education system in America today is a dysfunctional, unresponsive, ineffective mess. We allow financial and legal considerations to drive decisions, rather than sticking to an educational bottom line that requires decisions to be made based on their contribution to students' educational well-being. When the one thing we are sure of is that the teacher is the most important factor in student success, we have a system that routinely fails to ensure that good teachers are drawn to, and kept in, our classrooms. We tinker around the edges of the problems in our schools, jumping from innovation to innovation, but never committing the time or the resources to focus on those few things that could actually make a significant difference. Until we admit that the system is profoundly flawed, and commit to dramatic, systemic changes, our schools will continue to flounder.

CHAPTER 3: THE EXPERTS WERE WRONG

Like other decades, the seventies gave birth to its own oddities—platform shoes, disco, polyester pants, and bad haircuts. Most of these fads were harmless and short-lived. From the vantage point of a new century, we reminisce with a knowing chuckle as some of them are resurrected by a new generation of teens who view the seventies as ancient history. However, if we look beyond the surface of fashion and music trends at the underlying social, cultural and economic conditions of that time in our history, we see the beginnings of the profound shift in parenting philosophy and parenting practices that plagues us today.

By the sheer force of our numbers, the Baby Boomers reaching adulthood in the seventies impacted everything we touched. Having left our indelible mark on childhood and adolescence in America, we were poised to transform the perception of adulthood and parenting. Raised in peaceful, affluent post-war America, we were the most privileged generation of Americans ever; with more money, more education and more leisure time than any generation in history. Yet the world that shaped our development was one of assassinations, Vietnam, racial conflict, the sexual revolution, student riots and Watergate. These images, which came into our living rooms on a daily basis through the wonder of television, fostered a climate of distrust, hopelessness and pessimism and gave rise to a Peter Pan generation that entered adulthood determined to avoid the responsibilities that came with that role. We wanted things easy; we wanted to be "fulfilled;" we wanted to have fun. Above all, we wanted to be free to be different from the generation before us, to be free from the rules, the constraints and the conventions that had imprisoned them.

The women's movement, fueled by the birth control pill and the resulting sexual revolution, radically changed the landscape of family life and parenting by giving women unprecedented freedom to plan their families and their careers. Within the span of a generation, the percentage of married women in the workforce went from 40% in 1970 to 70% in 1996[5]. As they moved into the workforce, new mothers often lost the informal networks of extended family and friends that had supported previous generations of mothers and prepared them for motherhood. An increasingly mobile society also meant that new mothers were less likely to have Grandma available to help show them the ropes of parenting.

The dramatic social changes of the sixties and seventies produced in the Boomers an unparalleled level of disdain for the wisdom and practices of our elders—the "generation gap" was coined to describe this chasm between Boomers and our parents.

As more and more families accrued the benefits of a second income, we increasingly found ourselves in a situation where we had more money than we had time, knowledge, or support. All these changes contributed to Boomer parents' search for help—we needed it fast and we wanted it our way.

This "Sputnik Generation," raised with the conviction that, if you want to get ahead in life, you have to get a good education, believed that knowledge was the key to success in all areas of life. But, unwilling to turn to the traditional sources of expertise on parenting (our own parents and other wise and experienced elders), we sought out experts elsewhere.

The experts came in droves—PhDs, therapists, child development gurus—ready to tell us what we wanted to hear, prepared to dispense the secrets of personal success and perfect parenting (and of course, make a few bucks along the way). Pandering to the unique qualities of this new generation of Boomer parents, they promoted a philosophy of parenting as:

- Easy—You can have a baby without disrupting your lifestyle.
- Painless—Parenting needn't entail the sacrifice, agonizing decisions, or unpleasant confrontations of your parents' generation.
- Fun—Parenting can give you a chance to experience your childhood again as your child's best friend, and, even, perhaps, to right the many wrongs done to you by your own parents, by giving your child everything you really wanted as a child.
- Perfect—By following the guidance of this bevy of experts, you too can have a perfect child.

Positive Approach

This new philosophy of parenting was characterized by its positive approach. As with most things adopted by the Boomers, this positive parenting approach was also the polar opposite of the hopelessly dated and ill-informed approach favored by our own parents.

Gaining momentum through the seventies, the sound of the positive thinking movement grew deafening and infiltrated every area of our lives. Positive affirmations, such as "I feel good, today's going to be a great day!" and "I'm smart, I'm capable and I can do it!" promised to lift our spirits and make us feel good about ourselves. The happy face sticker and "Have a nice day!" became ubiquitous.

As parents, we heeded the child development experts' advice to use these positive techniques because it helped build our children's self-esteem. We were urged to provide non-stop praise, recognize and reward children just for being themselves, frame everything in positive terms, eliminate the word "no" from our vocabulary, and diligently protect our children's fragile psyches from the pain of frustration, rejection, failure, unpleasantness, or disappointment.

We saturated our kids with praise; confident that this was the pathway to making them feel valuable and capable. We reinforced their efforts with candy, toys, and money. Convinced of the damaging effects of competition, we took pains to ensure that "everyone is a winner," regardless of effort or ability. Houses and classrooms were decorated with the most recent creations of youthful artists, every effort a masterpiece. We cultivated children's self-worth and fertilized their self-esteem with heartfelt sunshine tokens.

I remember a technique called "positive commenting" that I encountered at my son's cooperative preschool. Teachers and parent helpers were encouraged to continuously make positive comments on what children were doing. "Johnny, you are playing nicely with the blocks." "Jessica, you are doing a nice job on that picture you are painting. I like the colors you are using." The idea was that adults could help encourage children's language and self-esteem by recognizing their activities. However, as with so many of the positive parenting techniques, a good idea taken to the extreme and used indiscriminately often backfires and fails to produce the results you had hoped for. One day as I watched my son and another child playing with blocks, with this ongoing adult chatter providing the soundtrack to their play, I realized how annoyed my son was that these adults just wouldn't shut up and let him play! He knew that it was a "technique." He knew that their comments would be the same regardless of what he was doing, so he quickly wrote them off as insincere and worthless. As a result, he made a point of avoiding certain activity centers and, once the narration started, he would stop whatever he was doing and move to another area.

For parents, the perceived benefits of this positive approach were immediate and rewarding. The dreaded "terrible twos" didn't have to be terrible if you never told your toddler "no." Dual income or divorced parents, feeling guilty about the limited time they had to spend with their children, didn't need to waste their precious "quality time" being disciplinarians. We didn't have to be the bad guy; we didn't have to be the mean, authoritative adult. We had found the perfect Baby Boomer parenting fit. We became our children's best friends. We learned their language and related at their level. It was fun, it was easy, and somehow it seemed to fit the Baby Boomers' Peter Pan mentality. We got to be the adults without ever really growing up!

We had the money to buy the rewards, to pay for the best classes and equipment. Determined that our children have all of the advantages, we started them in lessons at the earliest age possible to give them the head start we never got. As more and more families began to experience the financial rewards of two working parents, it wasn't long before mom and dad, a well-oiled money-making team, could provide their children with all of the advantages their own parents could not provide.   Men and women both swallowed this new parenting philosophy because it fit our needs and desires; it allowed us to continue the "me first," instant gratification lifestyle to which we had become accustomed. If doubts crept into our minds, if we wondered if it was just too good to be true, we had only to pick up the next book, written by the latest expert. They kept writing the books and we kept reading them. What a great symbiotic relationship—the experts told us what we needed to hear and we provided a living and fame for them in return.

Women's Movement

As women solidified their well-deserved position in the work force, they had to cope with the new realities of parenting while working full-time outside the home. Convinced by the burgeoning women's movement that they could, and *should*, have it all, mothers looked to the experts to tell them that their children wouldn't suffer. Researchers (often Baby Boomers in dual-income families themselves) rose to the challenge, dutifully pacifying parents with evidence that it's not the *quantity* of time spent with children that counts, but the *quality* of the time spent. What a relief! Parents could put in a full day's work, pick up their child from daycare, prepare dinner, do the household chores, and rest assured that the time spent bathing their child and reading a bedtime story was an hour of quality time so intense that it magically made up for an entire day spent away from a loving parent.

The unspoken message in this philosophy was that there must have been something dreadfully wrong with the way our parents raised us. Their child rearing tactics were primitive, passé, and, ultimately, damaging. Our drug problems, divorces and battles with our inner child must be the result of the psychologically destructive methods used by our parents. The clear message, "Don't do what your parents did!" fit our generation's Peter Pan personality perfectly. We certainly didn't want to be connected to our parent's generation; we were young and hip. Life was to be experienced; live for the moment; stay young and never grow up. We were ripe and ready for a new way of parenting. We wanted to hear that we could be our children's best buddies, because, if we could be their friends, we wouldn't need to be their parents. Parenting wasn't going to be the big authority trip of past generations. We were going to revolutionize the entire parenting process. *We* were going to do it right.

This positive parenting process has become so ingrained in our society that to question its credibility or effectiveness risks being labeled a negative person. As so often happens in American society, our all or nothing, more is better approach reigns. If one aspirin helps a headache, then five will surely be better. If one drink a day can reduce heart disease, then finishing the six-pack will keep me heart attack free. If children's self-esteem is so important to healthy development, then we must go to any and all lengths to protect and build that self-esteem.

This distorted reality means that children should never hear the word "no." They should never hear criticism. All of their efforts should be recognized as equally special and precious. If reinforcement and rewards result in a cooperative response, then bring on the M & M's ™. If negotiating with our child lessens those nasty verbal spats and power struggles, it's certainly worth it to ensure that our limited time with our children isn't ruined by unpleasantness. If we want children to feel that they are important and valuable, then we certainly should allow them to interrupt adult discussions and make their immediate needs known at all times. If experiencing loss makes children feel bad, then we must go to any length to soothe every emotional pain. If attempting a challenging task results in feelings of incompetence or anxiety, then we must never set high standards. If success is uplifting then we must never allow our children to experience failure. If you agree with these statements, then don't be surprised when your child grows up to be unmotivated, spoiled, egotistical, irresponsible, rude, and generally unprepared for adult life!

In keeping with the Baby Boomers' desire to repudiate adulthood for as long as possible, we seem to choose to view parenting from the perspective of our own childish selves, rather than as the parents we have become. It's as though we are reliving our own childhoods, except that this time we get to have everything our way.

Positive Approach in Schools

Just as Baby Boomer parents were revising the script on child rearing, schools were forced to rewrite rules and policies to reflect this positive new twist. Teachers were told that, rather than telling a child no or providing consequences for unacceptable behavior, we should ignore negative behavior, wait for the desired behavior to appear, and then reward that behavior with prizes and candy. Behavior that teachers may previously have found inappropriate was now characterized as "the child expressing his creativity." If a child was mean and hurtful to other students, we were supposed to excuse the behavior because she had a bad home life. Uncivilized behavior– talking when the teacher or another student is speaking, interrupting the teacher, using profanity–was deemed less important than the student's right to free expression. As the excuses for students' out-of-control behavior piled up–poor home life, attention deficit disorder, learning disabilities–and with dwindling support from parents and administrators for behavior standards, many teachers simply gave up the battle and adopted an "anything goes" attitude.

Deceived

So where did the experts go wrong? We were misled in two ways. First, we were convinced that there was an easy, "right" way to parent; a silver bullet that would eliminate conflict, banish discomfort, and produce the "special" children we felt we deserved. We thought that if we just followed the prescriptions of the child development gurus, we could produce the perfect child and do so without any disruptions to our adult lives and without any conflict or pain. We believed that if we read the right books, purchased the best learning toys, responded with the right body language, established the optimal open dialogue, and repeated enough positive parenting slogans, we would enjoy the happily-ever-after, conflicts-resolved-in-thirty-minutes family life portrayed in our favorite sitcoms.

Why did a generation of intelligent, well-educated, well-intentioned parents fall for this poppycock? Because we were afraid. We were chicken. Who were we to challenge the experts? What did we really know about parenting, other than the dated, uninformed techniques that our own unenlightened parents had used on us? What if we trusted our instincts and did the wrong thing? Surely we weren't grown-up enough to make our own decisions about how best to raise our child? We didn't want *that* kind of responsibility.

We disregarded the commonsense practices of generations of parents, thankful to abdicate our parental authority to the experts. After all, if there were so many PhD's who had gone through years of schooling to become experts in this area, surely *we* couldn't be qualified. Unfortunately, this over-reliance on the experts led us to refute the lessons we had learned about parenting from our own families. Rather than building on our own experiences, learning from both the good *and* bad things our own parents did, we chose to ignore the value of our own childhood experiences. Instead of supplementing those valuable childhood experiences with new ideas from the experts or from other experienced, successful parents, regardless of their official expertise, we chose not to do the hard work of pulling together the best ideas from all these sources and creating a parenting process that works for us and our children.

We lost sight of the fact that no one else loves our children like we do; no one else knows our children's unique personalities, temperaments, talents, and eccentricities as well as we do; no one else has the stake in our children's future that we have. No one else, regardless of advanced degrees, stature, intelligence, or expertise, is better qualified than we are to make the daily decisions about our children's lives.

Unfortunately, making all of those daily decisions is a lot harder than parenting by the book, particularly when "the book" provided a built-in excuse for taking the easy, positive route. So, it wasn't all that difficult to convince Boomer parents of the superiority of this method, because it meant less time and effort on our part. We didn't have to spend the time required to do the dirty work of parenting. We didn't have to subject ourselves to the consequences of our children's unhappiness, anger or rebellion when they came face to face with the consequences of their behavior. We didn't have to deny our children, punish our children or say "no." We didn't have to be the bad guy. We could be the cool parent. Rather than keeping the long-term needs of our children as the driving force behind our parenting decisions, we could choose the easy, short-term solutions that made all of us *feel* better. Perhaps Nancy Reagan had the right slogan after all; she just was talking to the wrong people. She should have been urging Baby Boomer parents to "Just say No" to the experts leading us astray. Shame on us for taking the easy way out.

The second way we were misled by the positive parenting experts was that we lost sight of the power of life's inevitable negative experiences to teach valuable, necessary lessons. Having been convinced by the experts that the slightest setback, disappointment or frustration could scar our children's fragile psyches forever, we went out of our way to censor ourselves and shield our children from the big, bad world.

We were too chicken to take advantage of moments that were a bit too hot to handle; moments that are the crucible for molding the values and characteristics of the adult we want our child to become. Can you recall an incident from your childhood that was one of those defining moments? One of those moments that possesses the power to teach you a lesson for life? If you are like most adults, those moments are not moments of great joy and triumph. They are moments of pain and discomfort; events so potent that we recall details and feelings with crystal clarity.

When I was nine years old I had the most horrible and upsetting experience of my life. My brother, a friend, and I were planning an afternoon bicycle trip. Although my mother disapproved of our straying so far from our familiar turf, we took great joy in venturing beyond the boundaries. The summer day made for a pleasant ride and my excitement grew as we pedaled towards our destination. My friend knew of a pristine viewpoint overlooking Seattle's Elliot Bay. It was only a short distance from our local play field and offered the promise of an unmatched view. When we arrived at the undeveloped lot, my friend led the way through the jungle-like vegetation. We followed him to a small clearing, where we were rewarded by a spectacular view of Elliott Bay and downtown Seattle. The buildings seemed so close it felt like I could reach out and touch the skyline. As we savored the view, we quizzed each other on which buildings we could name. Once we had exhausted that game, we turned to another competition: targeting trees with rocks and batting stones with sticks. Before long our play was interrupted by visitors, two young men who we assumed were also looking for solitude at this spot. We soon realized, however, that their intentions were far more sinister. Verbal threats quickly progressed to physical intimidation. After tying us up and placing us against a dirt bank, they took turns throwing rocks at us and whipping us with sticks. When they tired of that game, they kicked and beat us. This torture lasted a few hours, culminating with our attackers rolling us down the hill through sticker bushes. Fortunately, my friend's hands had come untied and he freed my brother and me from our bonds.

Bruised and bleeding, I ran home as fast as I could. Hours late for dinner, I arrived home to find a police officer already in my living room. My mother dashed to me, devouring me in her arms, squeezing me tightly. Although I felt secure in her arms, I knew that my father held the trump card in judging this situation. I glanced over at him standing across the room, speaking to the police officer. As he made eye contact with me I could see the relief evident on his face. I was fine.

My mother had us take a bath, eat dinner and, with the episode of the day still fresh in our minds, she insisted that we go to bed early. As I lie in bed, staring at my bedroom ceiling, I wondered what my father was going to say to me. Would he gush with love, relieved that his son was home safe? Or would he punish us for straying outside our approved play area? He did neither. Moments later he came up the stairs and sat on the bed next to me, silently looking me over as if to satisfy himself that I was, indeed, safe and sound. "Why didn't you fight back?" he asked, in a tone that suggested that he was really quite perplexed. It was clear to me, however, that he didn't expect an answer, and he got up and went back downstairs.

At the dinner table a few weeks later, my father casually informed my brother and me that he had signed us up for judo lessons at the local YMCA. That was the beginning of the most influential activity of my life. I took judo lessons for about two years, participating in tournaments and developing the many skills that judo has to offer. In my late twenties I returned to the sport, earning a black belt and learning invaluable lessons. I learned more about life participating in judo than from any other experience I have had. How remarkable that the most torturous, frightening event in my young life was the catalyst for the most powerful, life-changing experience I would have in my fifty years.

When I look back at that experience, I wonder how today's experts would assess my parents' handling of the situation. I'm certain they would chastise them for not encouraging me to talk about my feelings, possibly even bringing in a counselor to help me cope. My mother's matter-of-fact attention to our physical needs (bath, food and rest) would be viewed as neglecting to validate the tremendous emotional trauma we had experienced. My father's "Why didn't you fight back?" comment would surely elicit gasps of horror. Imagine the impact on my self-esteem!

On the contrary, I believe my parents' response was brilliant. Rather than fueling my fear and insecurity by focusing on how I *felt* about the experience, my father's comment conveyed to me the very real possibility that I could take charge of situations, that I didn't need to be the victim of a bad experience. Their matter of fact response told me that, yes, bad things do happen, but the way to handle bad things is to take action to prevent them from happening again.

My father took the opportunity to teach my brother and me a powerful lesson about life through a horrible experience. How lucky we were that he used it to our advantage instead of allowing it to erode our confidence and label us as powerless victims. He chose to turn a potentially scarring experience into one that built our confidence and expanded our belief in our own potential.

Can you recall an episode from your past that was painful, frightening, upsetting, but that taught you a valuable lesson about life?

Regardless of whether or not you agree or disagree with the methods your parents used, explore the connection between how your parents parented you and the kind of adult you are today. Are you responsible? Honest? Hard-working? Compassionate? Curious? Independent? What did your parents do to develop those characteristics? Now think about whether or not the methods used by your parents are consistent with what today's experts are promoting as good parenting.

I believe that one of the major differences between the parenting style of Baby Boomers and their parents is in the outcome on which their parenting is focused. The older generation of parents focused on the impact of their parenting decisions for the long term. They responded to situations with the goal of teaching their offspring lessons that would shape their personalities and establish values for the future. Today's parents, on the other hand, with their fragmented, over-scheduled lifestyles, don't even have time to *think* about their long-term goals for their children, much less to undertake the difficult task of ensuring that those goals are met.

Our parents intuitively and subconsciously identified their Big Five. In their world, where larger families precluded parents from hanging on their child's every utterance, where children were not seen as equal to adults and families were not meant to be democracies, they saw their responsibility as producing successful adults, not "special" children. Yes, they paid the price for this long-range approach–the discomfort and unpleasantness that often results when a child doesn't get what he wants; the guilt and self-doubt when a child says "I hate you;" the tantrums, silent treatment or outright hostility that children employ to get their way; the time and effort required to follow through with consequences. However, they accepted the fact that parenting isn't supposed to be easy; it's not always fun and games; it can be difficult and frustrating, which is why it requires an adult to perform the job.

When I was disciplined as a child, I recall being very upset. As I lie in bed visualizing the torture my parents would experience as a result of the silent treatment or withholding of my affections that I would impose, I thought I had the power. But as I watched my parents function perfectly fine despite my schemes, it became crystal clear to me that they were in charge and I was not. My reach was limited. As the adults, they had a specific job to do; they had more knowledge and experience than I; they were responsible for me; and they made the rules.

Another parenting philosophy that has fallen out of favor in recent years is the use of fear to help manage children's behavior. I was afraid of my father. Today's experts would undoubtedly dismiss this as damaging and inappropriate. However, my experience as a child, a parent, and a teacher, has taught me that fear can be a very valuable and positive tool. Think for a moment about why you didn't do certain things as a child. How often was the reason fear of being caught? Think about how often fear governs your behavior as an adult. Why do you stay within the speed limit? It's not to save gas or be law abiding. You're afraid of getting a ticket! My wife conducted an informal survey of her Baby Boomer female friends and asked them why they delayed sexual involvement. The majority of these women responded, "Because my Dad would have killed me." Fear is a valuable tool. Used sparingly and appropriately, it can impress upon children the significance of a variety of important lessons. And, more importantly, it can inspire appropriate and safe behavior.

You're the Expert

How have generations of parents survived without the advice of the experts to whom the Baby Boomers so willingly bow? As my mother once told my wife when she encountered the stack of parenting books on our coffee table, "People have been raising children for centuries, it's not rocket science. Do you *really* need to read a book to learn how to play with your baby?"

So, if I've convinced you that the experts aren't a good source of parenting information, then where else should you turn? One of the best resources for parenting is your own experience. You experienced parenting as a child. You've observed other families and how they handle parenting issues. Time spent reflecting on this already accumulated knowledge and experience is a natural and valuable starting point.

When was the last time you purposely scheduled time to think; just you and your thoughts, one-on-one? Comedian George Carlin says that if he could make one suggestion for rearing kids today it would be to schedule a one hour "nothing" time each day. Sound advice from a man known for making people see the humor in the contradictions and absurdities of human behavior. I recommend that you schedule one hour every day (or at least on as regular a basis as you can) to just think or look out the window. One hour to ponder the events of the day or just sit with no demands or activities to attend. Most of the world's religions and cultures promote some type of meditative or reflective practice and, especially for parents, this routine can be a powerful and sanity-saving tool. You can use that reflection time to review where you have been, what has happened in your life, where you are today, what is important to you now, and where you are going. The bottom line is that children need parents who are emotionally stable and secure and it's difficult to maintain that balance in a chaotic world without regular reflection on these important questions.

Reflecting produces many positive benefits, some for you and some for your children. Reviewing the events, both good and bad, that have shaped your life, will help you look at those events from the perspective of a mature adult who is trying to shape the life of a child. When you were a child you saw things from that youthful point of view. As an adult you are better able to understand the reasoning and motivations of those involved. Spend time thinking about your own childhood; strip off the childhood filters that prevent you from exploring the underlying truths of those experiences. Our own childhood is the starting point for the way we parent. Some people are happy with the way they were parented and will strive to replicate that experience for their own children. Others desperately want to avoid making the mistakes their own parents made. Some parents actively learn about parenting, from books or by talking with or observing other parents. Others parent by trial and error. We know that under stress most people will fall back on the parenting behaviors they learned in childhood. If those behaviors are things you want to continue with your children, great. If not, then you need to consciously delve into your own childhood and identify which parenting behaviors were valuable and effective and which you want to avoid. Then you need to really think through how you are going to build new parenting habits so that, when you find yourself in a stressful situation with your child, the new behaviors won't be hijacked by your primitive brain's more instinctive, learned responses.

Take yourself through a journey into your childhood, with the goal being to heal past wrongs, view your childhood through objective adult eyes, learn from the events that shaped your life, adjust your approach accordingly, and change behaviors and practices for the betterment of all. This journey will likely elicit a variety of feelings. Don't be afraid. You are in control and you make the decisions.

A few things to think about as you depart on your quest. It can be fun and uplifting to reminisce about the good times and happy moments, but you will often learn more from the tough times. So don't be afraid to contemplate the bad things that have happened in your life. Don't avoid the painful or difficult experiences you had as a child. Also, in addition to focusing on specific, isolated incidents, be sure you look at the big picture of how the events contributed to your overall development. Both perspectives are important and necessary.

Here are a few suggestions for topics to consider during your reflection time. First, think about the qualities that you like in yourself—generosity, sense of humor, responsibility, determination, risk-taker—whatever qualities you value most in yourself. Then go back in time and try to trace the pathway that led to the development of each of those characteristics.

For example, I recall a situation that taught me the meaning and value of caring about other people. I was in second grade. I had a neighbor friend named Jeffrey with whom I hung around on a regular basis. Those were the days when kids could roam freely in their neighborhoods with little adult intervention or supervision. I didn't know much about Jeffrey's family and, being a typical egocentric seven-year-old, I didn't particularly care. I just knew Jeffrey was fun to hang out with. One day we were playing near my house right about dinnertime. I told Jeffrey that I had to go home for dinner and innocently asked if he would like to come. Jeffrey and I walked the short distance home and I asked my Mom if Jeffrey could stay for dinner. She gave me that look that said she wasn't particularly thrilled with this request five minutes before dinnertime, but she said of course Jeffrey could stay. We sat down to dinner, undoubtedly one of our usual family fares, spaghetti or meat blanket, something designed to fill up four growing kids. As we began to eat, it was clear that Jeffrey was shoveling food so fast that, as my Mom said, "It looks like you're eating as if there's no tomorrow." When he came up for air, he looked a little embarrassed and, with the honesty of a seven-year-old child, informed all of us that this wasn't his day to eat. I looked at my Mom to help clarify this odd pronouncement, but quickly realized that this was a topic that was to be left alone. After we finished dinner that night my mother called Jeffrey into the kitchen. I watched them have a short conversation, which ended with Jeffrey walking back into the living room smiling broadly. He ate dinner with us every other day for some time after that.

My childish brain couldn't comprehend a scenario in which someone who lived in my neighborhood and went to my school would have days that they ate and days that they didn't. Although my family was certainly not well off, we always had plenty of food available. I had a hard time imagining myself eating every other day. In fact, my brothers and I had trouble even making it from dinnertime to breakfast the next morning and would often be back in the kitchen within hours bugging my Mom for a snack. This episode opened my innocent seven-year-old eyes to a world I had no idea existed. I realized that other kids I knew were going hungry. Kids I played with lived in situations that differed greatly from mine. I learned that I was lucky not to be one of them. And I learned that there were people like my mother who were willing and happy to help those in need. What a great lesson.

I also remember vividly the day I learned about determination. My older brother, who was bigger and stronger than I, took every opportunity to demonstrate his superiority. From my younger and weaker vantage point, his purpose in life often seemed to be dominating and overpowering me. One day, when I was ten and my brother twelve, he challenged me to a wall-sitting contest. Since I had no choice but to participate (I knew from experience that he would *make* me do it), I decided that this could be my chance to show him how tough I was and to plant a tiny seed of doubt in his head about messing with me. We took our positions on the wall. Minutes passed and I was determined not to give up. After fifteen minutes my brother started to show signs of wavering and I knew at that point that I could actually win this time. After five more long and painful minutes, my brother grudgingly conceded the contest, stood up and turned on the TV. But, even though I had won, something inside me said not to stop. I just knew that this was an opportunity to send a message to my brother. I sat on that wall for a total of forty-five minutes and only got off because I was called to dinner. My legs screamed in pain. I could barely maneuver the stairs down to the dining room, my muscles cramping in rebellion from the abuse. But, despite the pain, I had never felt so good. My brother treated me a little differently after that and I knew I had gained a degree of independence from his power. I remember realizing that I had broken through a boundary that had been self-imposed; I had let my brother convince me that, because he was older and bigger, he could always win. That day I learned that my own efforts could determine my success or my failure. I learned that I had control over the outcomes in my life and if I could muster up the determination to outlast the next guy, I could be victorious.

I learned about the power of determination through pain and anguish. I had to experience that pain in order to learn to believe in myself and to go beyond my limits. It was the suffering that taught me how to endure. Yes, I realize that sitting on the wall longer than my brother may not be an earth-shattering accomplishment, but it had a profound influence on my life. I believe that long ago triumph of determination over a bigger, stronger opponent laid the groundwork for me to run three marathons and earn a black belt in judo. I believe it taught me the value of tapping into my inner strengths to overcome difficult odds. I believe this one silly sibling challenge had a profound and lasting impact on the adult I grew up to be. Don't discount the power of negative life experiences. It is my personal and professional experience that the hurtful, painful, difficult, and challenging episodes in life are the most valuable in shaping one's personality. They provide the true challenges that build character and bring out one's strengths and abilities. What if my parents had been like so many of today's parents and rushed to save me from this difficult experience? What if my mother had rushed in and chastised us to "play nicely together" or told my brother to "Be nice to your little brother, that's not fair to challenge him when he's smaller than you." What if my Dad had come upstairs and insisted that I stop my vigil after my brother had given up, because I might hurt myself? Any of these intrusions may have kept me from learning a powerful lesson about myself and about my place in the world. Don't be afraid to let your child experience something painful or have your child suffer a little bit. That pain or suffering from which you rescue them may just be the one incident that teaches them the most valuable lesson they will ever learn.

Expert Teachers

If you are a teacher, this reflection process is equally valuable. You just need to direct your reflections to those aspects of your own school experience that you feel were important in making you the person you are today. Think about those teachers who really made a difference in your life. Were they the teachers who let you get away with anything? Was their influence the result of telling you that everything you did was wonderful and special, regardless of how much time and effort you put into it? Did those extraordinary teachers impact your life by focusing more on your self-esteem than on building the attitudes, skills, and competencies that would make you a successful adult? I doubt it. So what specific things did they do that produced such a significant impact? Discover those things and use them in your own classroom. Although the experts may try to convince you otherwise, teaching and learning haven't fundamentally changed much in the last century. Sure, what we teach may have changed, but kids are still kids and they need adults in their lives who are willing to do the tough work of helping them grow up to be responsible, independent, self-sufficient adults. The very things that your favorite teachers did for you can and will still work with your students. Don't let the bandwagon-hoppers tell you otherwise.

The important advantage that each of us has as a parent or a teacher is that we were all children and adolescents once. We all had parents or other caregivers; we all experienced scores of teachers over our years of schooling. That experience is a goldmine if you are willing to take the time and energy to sift through it and uncover the valuable nuggets. Explore the lessons of both the good experiences and the bad experiences. Remember the importance of balance in young people's lives.

CHAPTER 4: THE SELF-ESTEEM FALLACY

The one area in which the experts have had the most persistent and damaging impact on effective parenting and healthy child development is in their consistent trumpeting of positive self-esteem as the holy grail of child rearing. Despite volumes of research debunking self-esteem as the panacea for all of society's problems, the self-esteem fallacy endures. In *Greater Expectations: Overcoming the Culture of Indulgence in America's Homes and Schools*, William Damon, professor at Brown University and director of its Center for Human Development discusses the research that has attempted to establish links between self-esteem and positive child development. "An examination of these studies reveals that this is one of the many areas where popular mythology is wholly out of touch with the scientific findings."[6] Research in the past twenty years attempting to link children's self-esteem with intelligence, achievement, social/ emotional maturity have not even demonstrated a *correlation* between self-esteem and these developmental outcomes, much less any evidence that positive self-esteem *causes* healthy development[7]. So how did this pervasive myth get started and why do we hold so tightly to it? Like so many of the parenting practices that have been promoted by experts over the last twenty years, the self-esteem fallacy has its roots in solid knowledge about child development, but that knowledge has been distorted and misapplied in ways that often produce exactly the opposite effects intended by well-meaning parents and teachers. Psychologist Abraham Maslow's theory of the Hierarchy of Human Needs[8] puts the research on self-esteem into its proper context in human development.

While so many of the experts' theories have led us to ignore our own instincts about child development and parenting, Maslow's hierarchy has withstood both academic scrutiny, as well as the test of real life and human experience. In my experience with, and observation of students, no other concept rings as true or explains human behavior as accurately as Maslow's simplistic human needs pyramid.

Maslow's theory explains the motivation behind human behaviors. The hierarchical nature of the pyramid illustrates how certain needs must be met before other needs can be addressed. In the first level of the pyramid are the physiological needs that must be met to keep us alive. Humans will do whatever is necessary to meet these essential physiological needs for food, water, oxygen, and a suitable body temperature. If not satisfied, these basic needs impede progress up the levels of the pyramid. Therefore, when a child is hungry, his energy will be focused on getting that need met and not on security, love and belonging, or esteem.

Once these basic needs are met, attention and energy can be focused on the next level–safety and security needs. Feeling safe and secure is necessary for us to function normally. Like the physiological needs, if the need for safety and security is not met, we will find it difficult to concentrate on building caring relationships and developing the competence that leads to positive esteem. Just as hunger makes it difficult for a child to function optimally in school, a child who feels unsafe in her family, school, or neighborhood will expend her energy trying to get that need met, often at the expense of positive relationships with teachers or peers and development of the skills needed for academic success.

Fortunately, the majority of American youth live in situations where resources are available to fulfill these first two basic levels of needs. Of course, there are far too many children who go hungry, too many students who attend schools in less than safe neighborhoods, and children from all socioeconomic backgrounds who live in families where instability and/or violence are a harsh reality. But that's another book.

Once our physical and safety needs are met, we can turn our attention to emotional needs. A committed, attached relationship with an adult who cares about the child's future is essential to healthy development. This bonding has been found to be a major component of successful passage into responsible adulthood. Parents must understand the titanic significance of this need to their child's development. The time necessary to fully establish this bond is much more than a couple of hours per day. Eight hours of work and a significant percentage of the typical parent's other waking time completing domestic chores does not leave sufficient time for building this strong bond. Consistent and abundant time is the simple formula needed to build this strong parent/child bond. Children who experience this positive, loving relationship with a parent can then reach out to form caring relationships with other adults and with peers, laying the groundwork for the development of a strong sense of personal esteem, the next step in Maslow's hierarchy.

Dependent on the previous physical needs being met and on the foundation of a bonded relationship with a parent or other primary caregiver, the need for esteem encompasses both self-esteem and the esteem one gets from others. This esteem is grounded in a person's feelings of competence and sense of being valuable in the world. Children and adults alike are keenly aware of their accomplishments, measuring themselves against others as well as against their own previous capabilities. Few of those achievements are glorified with trophies and public accolades. Rather, they are moments of brief contentment, barely acknowledged. For adults, successfully completing a day's work, getting dinner on the table, running all the domestic errands, or making it to our child's game are all accomplishments in their own right, often greater achievements than they may seem to us at the time. For children, each stage in their development provides valuable opportunities to master new challenges and develop feelings of competence. If you want to see self-esteem in its purest form, observe the face of a toddler taking his first steps; a child leaving the supportive hand of her parent behind as she pedals a bike for the first time; a teenager experiencing the independence of a newly-acquired driver's license. In other words, self-esteem is a *result* of authentic feelings of competence, not the *cause* of those feelings.

Once these lower level needs have been met, individuals can move into what Maslow calls the *growth needs*. These include 1) cognitive needs: the need to know, understand, and explore; 2) aesthetic needs: the need for symmetry, order and beauty; 3) self-actualization needs: the need to find self-fulfillment and realize one's potential; and 4) self-transcendence needs: the need to connect to something beyond the ego. At the highest levels of Maslow's hierarchy, you have reached your potential and achieved balance in your being. Happy, content, satisfied, you live in a state that only a small percentage of humans will achieve.

As articulated so eloquently in Maslow's theory, an individual's feelings of self-worth are fundamental to a well-balanced psyche. This feeling of esteem is so important that it merits a specific level on Maslow's hierarchy. As such, it is critical that we focus on the development of a strong esteem with our children. I am a staunch advocate of strategies that effectively contribute to the satisfaction of this important need level. However, so much inaccurate and counterproductive information has been spread about self-esteem in the last several decades, that this entire chapter is devoted to debunking these damaging myths. It will also help readers apply the research on self-esteem and healthy child development in a way that produces the intended goal—healthy, happy, independent, productive adults.

Let's start by taking a closer look at exactly what is meant by self-esteem or self-worth. As defined by Maslow, self-esteem is a result of feelings of *competence* and being *valuable* in the world. In other words, children, like adults, feel good about themselves when they believe someone would notice and care if they weren't around. They feel good about themselves when they master challenges, when they develop new skills–social skills, physical skills, emotional skills, or cognitive skills–when they contribute in a valuable way to their family, their school, or their community. In other words, children *feel* valuable and competent when they are given opportunities to *be* valuable and competent. But that takes work! It takes effort on the child's part and effort on the adult's part. And, as is the norm in contemporary American culture, we prefer the easier pathway to self-esteem. We prefer to believe that, if we just *tell* children enough how wonderful and special they are, they will *believe* they are wonderful and special and they will *behave* in wonderful and special ways.

In fact, the most pervasive and potentially destructive of the myths about self-esteem is that it is something that a parent or teacher can *give* a child. In countless child rearing books and articles, the experts exhort parents and teachers to "build" children's self-esteem. However, promoting a child's positive self-esteem is more like planting a garden than it is like building a house. When you build a house, you start with a blueprint, use the correct building materials, put them together as outlined in the blueprint, and, voila, you get the house as designed. Any two builders, given the same blueprint and the same materials would produce pretty much the same house. Developing a child's positive self-esteem is a more complex and organic process, in which the child's unique personality interacts with the environment he or she experiences. As the "gardener," the parent's job is to provide the conditions necessary for the child's positive esteem to grow and develop.

So what are these conditions? The experts would have us believe that the secret to building positive self-esteem is to tell a child often how wonderful and special he is and he will believe it and feel good about himself. They would encourage us to always be positive and to eliminate experiences that make the child feel bad. They would warn us against pushing children too hard and urge us to praise children regularly, giving children plenty of recognition for effort as well as accomplishment. "Every child is a winner" has become the mantra in classrooms, homes, and sports. In practice, this advice has mutated into a philosophy that places primary importance on children *feeling good about themselves*, which has been further distorted into children *feeling good*.

Consequences

The first unfortunate consequence of this misguided focus is that parents and teachers have taken this to mean that their job is to protect children from all unpleasantness; that the pathway to successful adulthood is paved only with happy, pleasant experiences and positive feelings. Taken to its logical extreme, this philosophy suggests that children should never experience pain, discomfort, frustration, anger, or disappointment, or any other negative emotions. Their every need should be met; their every want fulfilled; they are the center of their universe. In fact, "building" a child's self-esteem in this way most often produces exactly the opposite of what adults had intended. Coming to terms with the fact that one is not the center of the universe is an important developmental task that helps prepare children to take on the responsibilities of adulthood. The positive parenting philosophy traps children in an overly protective, self-centered bubble that prevents them from learning the lessons required to move into the other-centered world of responsible adulthood.

The second consequence is that by taking on the responsibility for building children's self-esteem, we ignore the critical importance of the child in this equation. The child becomes a passive receiver of accolades and recognition.

Let's look more closely at how the positive parenting approach to self-esteem backfires. First, let's examine how continuous, unspecific praise and recognition undermines the goal of positive self-esteem.

The most important characteristics of praise are that it is genuine and that it is perceived by the child as earned. Children are incredibly astute at recognizing the phony, with-a-plastic-smile "good job" or the generic certificate that everyone receives just for showing up.

Over the years, my sons have received numerous certificates, trophies and awards for all kinds of academic, social and athletic endeavors. Every soccer, baseball, and basketball season produced the obligatory certificate and trophy. I was initially puzzled at the varying levels of importance my sons accorded each of these well-intentioned attempts to praise the young athletes. At the countless awards ceremonies, large gold trophies often warranted only a polite smile and respectful placement on their seat, quickly forgotten and retrieved by me at the end of the ceremony. Conversely, both boys have created shrines in their bedrooms where their most treasured items are displayed; not the shiny trophies or framed certificates, but items whose significance is known only to their owner: a baseball, dirty and marred from a full game's abuse, the coach's faded signature; the tiny newspaper clipping documenting the first points scored in a high school game; the golf score card and accompanying pencil stub; a dime-store medal placed with the care and prominence of Olympic gold. After years of watching these shrines fill up with treasured mementos, I finally figured out what the chosen items have in common. Each signifies an *accomplishment*; recognition truly earned. The trophies and certificates had no meaning, because in my sons' eyes, they had done nothing noteworthy to receive such a prize. Although they had fun and enjoyed playing the game, a trophy given to all participants just for showing up held no meaning for them.

It is the intrinsic feeling of competence that determines the degree to which a child appoints value to praise or recognition. The baseball that occupied center stage in my oldest son's shrine symbolized a performance representing his best skills and efforts. It marked his passage from one skill level to the next. He surpassed his limits and created new expectations for himself. Each and every item in both boys' shrines tells a similar story, with the common link being that they represent a level of competence achieved.

Based on their studies of the mechanisms for healthy youth development, Drs. David Hawkins and Richard Catalano of the University of Washington in Seattle developed the Social Development Strategy (SDS), a framework that explains the pathway from birth to healthy adolescence and adulthood[9]. The SDS helps us understand the importance of competence in healthy development. Hawkins and Catalano's research shows that in order to develop healthy behaviors in adolescence, children need to be immersed in environments that have and communicate healthy beliefs and clear expectations for their behavior. In other words, the adults in children's lives communicate clearly and consistently to them what behavior is, and is not, okay. However, for those expectations to have the power to influence a child's behavior, there must be a strong bond between the child and the adult holding the expectations. This means that when children have a strong attachment to an adult, when they have a stake in the future of that relationship, they will be more likely to follow that adult's expectations for their behavior, because they don't want to risk losing that relationship. Bonding provides the motivation for children to follow the healthy beliefs and clear expectations held by the adults in their lives. So the $64,000 question is "How is that bonding created?" How do parents, teachers and other adults build those attached, committed relationships with children? The research indicates that bonding is developed when children feel like they are a valuable and indispensable part of their family, classroom or other group. According to the Social Development Strategy, those feelings of competence are created by providing children with *opportunities* to contribute or be involved in meaningful ways. This means that children are given significant tasks and roles to play in their families, schools and communities. They are given opportunities to see themselves as *assets* to their families, schools, or communities, as important contributors, without whom those groups could not function as well.

Entitlement

For most of our country's history, this was a normal and natural occurrence in families. On the farm, even the youngest children helped by feeding the chickens. In the larger families that were common in earlier times, older children helped the family by caring for their younger siblings. Without today's modern conveniences, families simply couldn't survive without each family member pitching in to help. In contemporary American culture, however, children routinely live as virtual guests in their own homes, much as they would in a hotel. They expect meals to be provided for them with no effort on their part; they drop their clothes and toys wherever they land, trusting that someone else will pick up after them. Although this may sound like a dream come true to children, the consequence of this kind of lifestyle to family bonds is disastrous. Children who have no significant role to play in their family are left feeling that, not only are they not an *asset* to their family, when all is said and done, they are, in fact, a liability. In other words, rather than helping to shoulder some of the workload required to keep their family functioning, they, just like the hotel guest, actually *increase* the workload.

This same sense of entitlement permeates today's classrooms. As a teacher in an upper middle class school district, the view of teachers I routinely observe in students (and often their parents) is, "You are my servant, just another person put on this earth to focus on me and my needs." Rather than building strong bonds to teachers and schools, pandering to and allowing this behavior emasculates classroom teachers, stripping them of the respect needed to communicate clear standards and have students follow those standards. This lack of respect results in the palpable loss of connection and feelings of alienation that have become rampant among America's youth.

My parents' generation approached rearing of children much differently than we do today. Asked about what they wanted for their children, they would have replied that they wanted their children to get a good education, get a good job, and raise a family. They wanted their children to grow up to be independent and responsible adults. Because of the circumstances that shaped them—World War II, the Depression—they understood some important truths about parenting that their Baby Boomer children never learned. Their experience taught them that children are resilient, competent human beings. They recognized the importance of challenges, adversity, struggle, and hard work in building the significant characteristics that make up healthy, functioning adults. In short, they knew quite clearly that their job as a parent was to prepare their children for adulthood. They did not view their primary parental responsibility as making their children feel good, or be happy, or have high self-esteem. They knew that, even if those things might make life with children more pleasant in the short term, they were not the things that should be focused on to produce the kind of adults they wanted to be raising. They understood something that their Boomer children clearly don't: that the ultimate measure of their success as a parent was the kind of *adults* they produced. They viewed their job as raising children to successful adulthood, not as providing a protected, saccharine-sweet, perpetually happy childhood. With that as their goal, they could accept the inevitable moments of conflict, discomfort, inconvenience, frustration, and downright unhappiness that are a natural part of guiding a human being from the helpless, dependent, self-centered state of infancy to the independent, responsible, competent, other-centered state of adulthood.

Ask any parent over sixty-five how much time they spent promoting their child's self-esteem, and you're likely to get a laugh, a snort, or a "promoting what?" Without labeling it or consciously addressing it, our parents promoted our self-esteem by seeking out areas in which we could excel. They knew from their own experience that children feel good about themselves when they have opportunities to be successful. Unlike many of today's parents, who go to extreme lengths to manufacture artificial activities to promote self-esteem, our parents used the daily experiences of family life, school, and community as natural opportunities for us to learn skills and demonstrate competence, as well as to build the important qualities that would make us successful as adults—confidence, integrity, work ethic, responsibility, empathy, teamwork, etc.

My father was a master at using daily experiences to teach lifelong lessons. An electrician, he would often bring home discarded wire remnants from job sites. The value in the wire was the copper inside, but, in order to recycle the copper for money, the plastic sheathing had to be stripped. One day my father sat me down and explained to me that, if I wished, he would bring home wire, I could strip it, and he would recycle it, giving me all the profits. He carefully showed me how to complete the process, since it involved a razor sharp knife. As an eleven-year-old with few job prospects, I decided this was a good deal.

After several days of work, the blisters on my fingers and hands convinced me that I needed to find a way to do the job more efficiently. I designed a series of nails pounded into the workbench that would guide the wire's path. Placed securely in the middle of the series of nails was the razor sharp blade. Now all I needed to do was pull the wire through the nail apparatus and the wire would be sheared of its coating. I was working ten times more efficiently and, as a result, making significantly more money. Interestingly, my father never interrupted me or tried to help me. He allowed me to work through the process, first experiencing the hard work of stripping the wire by hand, then inventing a more efficient manner. It was my task and he was clever enough to stay out of the process. From that simple task, I learned to work hard. I learned that hard work was not fun. I learned to think about what I was doing. I learned that a difficult job could be made less difficult and more efficient by using my brain. I learned that I could solve problems. I learned to trust my ideas. I learned to think through procedures. And I learned that I would be rewarded for hard work, but that the reward would be greater if I worked more efficiently. That's a pretty good lesson from one relatively meaningless task.

My father found many such opportunities when I was growing up. I vividly recall the physical effort and attention to detail necessary to reach his expectations of a job well done. For many of these experiences, rather than money, gushing praise or a trip to the local fast food restaurant, my reward was often a sincere thank you or my father's proud grin. The greatest reward, however, was often the knowledge that I had done something successfully that I had been too young to do the year before.

Contributing

Taking advantage of children's natural desire to always be more grown up is a valuable parenting tool and an extremely effective and natural way to build children's esteem. Giving children legitimate, valuable tasks to master, and making sure that, as they grow older and demonstrate more competence, those tasks become more and more complex and skillful, allows them to feel that they are progressing in their movement toward adulthood. Children, in fact, often see more clearly than their parents that childhood and adolescence are temporary states. They often are the ones to push their parents to recognize their emerging maturity and skills by constantly testing the boundaries of their parents' perceptions of their limitations. I have consciously and deliberately mined this natural tendency to want to be more "manly" with my own two sons, using many types of chores as rites of passage for them. We frequently use a wood stove to heat our home, so there is a lot of work that goes into the chopping, hauling, splitting, and stacking of wood in our family. Knowing that this is something I needed my sons to help with as they got older, I deliberately structured their wood-related chores into a logical progression that culminated in the ultimate guy experience–using the chain saw! Obviously, when they were six or seven they couldn't yet use the chain saw, but I purposely set up the situation so that they knew there were increasingly important jobs they could learn to do that would prepare them to eventually be the "chain saw guy." Early on, their job was to stack the wood and to keep the wood box inside filled. When they were ready to move on, they learned how to use the splitting maul to split the rounds. Finally, at about age thirteen each reached the ultimate goal of using the chain saw.

I have adopted this technique extensively with my sons, with great success. Unlike many of their teenage friends, who couldn't put in a full day's manual labor if their life depended on it, my sons, at thirteen and fifteen, were experienced and capable laborers. One summer we painted our entire house inside and out. I had prepared them months in advance, letting them know that the job was difficult, physical, messy work and would take weeks to complete. It was already understood that they would receive no pay for their efforts. Of course, the usual questions had to be fielded, "Why do we have to do this?" They got the usual (and fully expected) answer, "Because you are part of the family." "None of our friends have to work like this during the summer, why do we?" "Because you are part of *this* family, and in this family everyone contributes."

Once we had gotten through their obligatory whining, I could then begin the process of esteem building. Rather than perceiving themselves as slave labor, my sons were involved in every aspect of the painting process. We discussed the colors for the exterior and interior paints. They were shown how to successfully complete each specific element of the job—from spackling to spraying. My older son was given tasks that fit his strength and skills, while the younger one was given equally labor-intensive tasks, but ones that were within his capabilities. This gave each of them the opportunity to take ownership of certain jobs and feel the appropriate pride when the job was complete.

Many parents are so obsessed with being fair that they ignore the fact that children of different ages have differing abilities. But matching the task to the age and ability of the child is critical to building children's feelings of competence and self-confidence. It is also an important part of motivating children to contribute, because, if a thirteen-year-old is given the same tasks as her ten-year-old sibling, she realizes that her increased maturity and skills aren't valued. On the other hand, when she is given a task that only *she* can do, because her ten-year-old brother is not capable of taking on that job yet, she will feel the pride of having her competence and maturity recognized and valued.

When selecting tasks for children, it's important to ensure that there is a realistic chance that they will be successful, given a reasonable amount of effort. That way you build in opportunities for children to both feel the personal sense of accomplishment that comes from a job well done as well as to provide the chance to earn well-deserved recognition from adults whose respect and acknowledgment they value. After my sons and I had completed our painting job, I called them together in one general viewing spot. Reflecting on the days of hard labor and teamwork, I told each of them that they could be very proud of themselves because they had done a man's job, and that I would choose them over most of my adult male friends when it came to selecting work partners. The look on my son's faces when they heard those words confirmed for me that no amount of gushy praise or insincere, "you're wonderful just because you're you," could ever have matched the esteem-building power of that experience.

There seems to be a consensus that young people today are increasingly spoiled, rude, and egocentric. Yet there seems to be little thoughtful attention paid to how they got that way! I find it amazing that people can't recognize the very logical connection between the way children are treated and the negative behaviors they exhibit. Is it surprising that children are spoiled when they are given everything they want with no expectations that they contribute in any way? How do we expect children to learn to behave civilly when they have never been told "no," when they are routinely allowed to disrupt adult conversations with attention-getting behavior that is labeled "cute" by parents trying to make their children feel special? Why should young people show concern for others when they have spent their entire childhood being the center of attention, their every whim satisfied, their every word or action gushed over? So, given this obvious cause and effect, why do so many well-intentioned, often well-educated, always loving and caring parents choose to follow a parenting pathway that is likely to lead to such unsatisfactory results? Because they are chicken. They want the easy, positive parts of parenting without having to deal with the messy, negative, frustrating, or difficult aspects.

Once again the experts lead us astray by not telling us the complete story of effective parenting. The positive parenting movement sounded like such a winner! In the name of promoting positive self-esteem, parents could avoid disciplining their children, avoid confrontations, avoid following up on imposed consequences. My mother once said that the best thing about being a grandparent is that you get to experience all the good things, without having to experience the bad. You get to be the good guy, showering the child with gifts, having fun experiences together, but, in the end, you get to send the child home with her parents. Unfortunately, in many American families, there is no one willing to be the parent to whom all of the good guys can send the child to learn life's tougher, but critically important, lessons.

Bad Stuff

A fundamental fallacy of the self-esteem movement is that only positive experiences are valuable in developing healthy, well balanced, productive adults. In fact, like everything in life, you can't have the good without the bad. You don't recognize pleasure if you never feel pain. You don't experience success without experiencing failure. In order to create a well-balanced child there must be pain with pleasure, criticism with compliment, labor with leisure, demands with choice, responsibility with freedom. Without this balance you have a personality off-center. Am I suggesting that for every compliment there must be an accompanying criticism? No, it is not a one-to-one correspondence. It is simply that some lessons are best learned through positive experiences, others are best learned through negative experiences. The important thing is that the child experiences a balance and that parents use *all* of life's experiences, positive and negative, to teach their children valuable life lessons. If childhood is preparation for adulthood, and if we all would admit that adulthood is filled with both positive and negative experiences, then it follows that children must experience both in order to be adequately prepared for adult life.

The experts also convinced us that negative experiences were somehow damaging to children, primarily through their negative impact on the child's self-esteem. But neither common sense nor the large body of research on self-esteem supports this theory. In fact, children are incredibly resilient creatures, and their resilience is bolstered by opportunities to successfully master new situations and conquer new challenges. When we remove the opportunities for children to overcome difficulties, when we protect them from the normal slings and arrows of childhood, we send a powerful message that they are too small, too weak, and too incompetent to handle these challenges. Contrary to what the experts would have us believe, it is this over-emphasis on eliminating bad experiences from children's lives that is the true threat to a child's positive esteem.

In my first year of teaching I fell into the same trap most rookies do. I wanted to be liked by the kids. It seemed to be the right thing to do. The students seemed happy. I had no problems with parents. The administrators enthusiastically reinforced congenial relationships between students and teachers, with their yearly evaluations of teachers reflecting as much. On the surface things appeared great, but what was missing was real substance in my teaching and genuine rapport with the students. Sure, if they needed someone to supervise a dance or participate in an assembly, I was their man. I was the cool teacher. True to the prevailing philosophy of positive teaching, I flooded students with canned compliments. It became second nature to me to just tell a kid "good job" for no real accomplishment; to praise a student for doing the bare minimum—for just showing up; for just completing the assignment. As a result of my adherence to this ill-founded philosophy, I lost the respect and the trust of the kids and they stopped believing anything I said—positive *or* negative.

I can still recall the moment I knew I was off track. At the end of each year I had the students fill out an evaluation, partly for the purpose of improving the program and partly because I needed the inevitable kiss-up strokes. I knew my classes were not as well-behaved as I would have liked them to be, but I passed it off as letting them do their own thing. As I reviewed the evaluations, I noticed that those students who I most respected were not as positive as I had expected them to be. Their feedback was honest but damning:

"You need to control the class better."

"It's hard to learn with all the students talking."

"Your class is fun, but I would have liked to learn more about..."

I realized I was missing the mark. The exceptional students were not pleased and were not learning in this semi-carnival atmosphere. It was time to look in the mirror and rethink my approach.

Then something marvelous happened—my sons were born. As they grew I began to see great differences between how I raised my sons and how I "raised" my students. In both cases there were similar goals and outcomes to achieve but my methods were quite different. In the classroom, I avoided any negative talk and refrained from raising my voice (or apologized if I did). I always took the time to explain every rationale for what we were doing in class and entertained every question asked. I fed my students' self-esteem regularly. I avoided the word "no" and rephrased statements in the positive form. "No yelling" turned into "Use your inside voice," "No fighting" turned into "Be respectful of others' feelings." I'm so embarrassed! Of course, all of these positive affirmations would build such solid student self-esteem that I would surely be the best teacher in the entire school. Wrong.

I began to study the methods I was using with my sons. Having reflected many hours on my own childhood, weighing both the positive and negative effects of my parents' child rearing practices, I immediately realized that many of the most valuable positive lessons

I had learned grew out of negative or painful experiences. Of course, there were many lessons that were achieved through reinforcing and rewarding experiences, but the ones that seemed to stick out in my mind and contain a power of their own were experiences that had uncomfortable elements.

Looking back on my own childhood through the eyes of a new father, I realized that my Dad had orchestrated many events specifically to teach me a valuable lesson. Without having read any parenting books or attending any parenting classes, his common sense and understanding of human behavior told him that one valuable way for children to learn important lessons is to experience or to witness the consequences of poor decisions first hand. I can recall as if it were yesterday the day my father decided to teach me about the evils of alcohol. It was the mid-sixties, a time when alcoholics could often buy their way out of a DUI or arrange to keep car accidents off the record. My uncle, an alcoholic who knew the police officers in his drinking territory quite well, had managed to keep both his license and his car through years of heavy drinking and driving. On an afternoon errand to the local lumber store, my father and I came upon a police car, lights flashing. A car had gone off the road and crashed into a telephone pole. To my surprise, my father pulled over just past the police car, got out and, before shutting the door, told me to stay in the car. After a few minutes, my father returned to the car, escorting a fully inebriated Uncle Bob. He gingerly placed Bob, head bleeding profusely from an abrasion that cut to the bone, in the back seat of our car. As I observed this scenario from my perch in the front seat, I was amused by the actions of my intoxicated uncle as he tried to drink out of a whisky bottle whose cork had been pushed inside. Every time he would lift the bottle to take a swig, the cork would block the flow of booze and create an unsolvable dilemma. However, my amusement came to an abrupt end when my father firmly directed me to get in the back seat. Panic, fear, and disbelief took over. Thinking that my lack of compliance would be enough to deter my father's request, I didn't budge. Undaunted, he sternly repeated, "Sit in the back seat." No explanation, no emotion, just a firm request to be obeyed. I had no way of predicting what my apparently out-of-control seatmate would do. The resulting fifteen-minute ride next to my inebriated uncle was an experience that was forever imprinted on my mind. I witnessed firsthand what drinking could do, as well as how humiliated a person can be in this situation. I learned an invaluable lifelong lesson through this uncomfortable experience.

Was my father mean for making me experience this? Was it abusive to expose an impressionable eight-year-old boy to such an unpleasant situation? Did it scar me forever? Surely the positive parenting gurus would say yes to all of the above.

Maximum Opportunity Moments

However, I believe that my father acted out of love and that he understood fully that this unique window of opportunity had the potential to be a powerful, life-changing experience. My father was not too chicken to take advantage of these valuable moments. He did not fear the effects of the temporary discomfort for me. Rather he understood the overwhelming benefits of this unique teaching opportunity. In fact, these slices of time are so important that I refer to them as *maximum opportunity moments (MOMS)*. These critical moments are splinters of time that shape the adults that our children will become. They shape the basic value system that our children will count on for guidance in the future. They have the capacity to influence their lives in dramatic ways. These moments can teach potent lessons about honesty, integrity, friendship, obedience, family commitment, or work ethic. However, these opportunities are only useful if the parent or teacher is confident enough and courageous enough to take advantage of them.

Think about your own actions with your children or your students. Are you brave enough to cross this line? Do you have the confidence to take advantage of these unique opportunities? Can you keep your focus on the end you have in mind even when it means moments of discomfort or confrontation? Can you tame the fear that prohibits you from orchestrating teachable moments? Can you accept the fact that the fleeting discomfort or pain your child will experience has the potential to pay back in immeasurable dividends? Are you strong enough to pay the price of the inevitable backlash–from your children, your students, your students' parents, your administrators, the community, etc.? Are you chicken or are you a mature adult?

The actions of my father were not abusive. As an educator I am well aware of the pervasive and devastating consequences of child abuse and strongly support efforts to stop it. However, like so many things in our society, a commendable effort has been distorted and taken to such an extreme that it becomes counterproductive. I believe we have distorted and twisted the definition of what "abusive" parenting entails, to include any experience that involves the slightest measure of pain or bad feelings. We have even gone as far as including voice decibel in this "abusive" classification. I've actually had students who have gone to the counselor complaining that I talked too loudly!

Yes, it is true that abuse can take the form of verbal attacks and manipulation. Certainly striking a child in anger and with the sole intent of causing physical harm is most definitely abuse. But imparting a lifelong lesson through a moment's annoyance or discomfort does not fall in the category of abuse. Conversely, it is my opinion, that to cross into this unsettling territory is an act of love and demonstrates to the child an honest caring that rings true. Think about the message that is sent to a child when a parent or teacher is willing to go to the wall with him, when that adult is willing to confront uncomfortable feelings, to be brutally honest, to risk the possible "I hate you!" from the child. When dealing with unruly teens, it is often this boundary-breaking maximum opportunity moment that is the catalyst for a very strong bond. Having used this confrontational approach hundreds of times, I have witnessed a clear pattern; the more intense and direct the critical moment, the stronger the bond. I have used the entire spectrum of responses in my teaching career, from the most sugary sweet sunshine positive statements to the most outrageous antics and I find it interesting that the most difficult students, with the most difficult attitudes, are quickly and profoundly reached with very direct and honest truths about what they did or who they are. Yes, it is unsettling to have to tell a student truthfully and directly that they are disliked by many of the other kids, that their behavior irritates and annoys people, that if they continue such actions their friends will be few and their future unhappy. It is unpleasant to say such things to an impressionable teen, but it is critical and necessary if you seek constructive change. If young people *only* receive positive feedback, particularly when that feedback is indiscriminate and insincere, they have no information to help them make constructive change.

I remember the moment when I realized that this brutally honest approach had its rightful place in parenting and teaching. I was teaching in the junior high school when I was assigned a student, Melissa, who had created havoc in another teacher's class. To prepare me to work with this student, the counselor shared Melissa's past experiences with me; they were more than any person should have to endure. Her parents had divorced because her father sexually molested Melissa at the age of six. A few years later, she was taken away from her mother because the mother had begun molesting Melissa. She was then placed in a foster home where she was molested again. As a student in my ninth grade Health class she was angry, confused, trusted no one, and acted out daily in outrageous ways. After tolerating her antics for a few days and giving her ample opportunity to comply with my classroom expectations, I decided it was time to be honest with her. I was ready to cross the line into that unsettling area of brutal honesty. Following yet another unacceptable outburst, I calmly but firmly requested that she leave class. After giving her a few moments to calm down, I joined her outside. I began the conversation by first telling her how sorry I was that so many horrible things had happened to her. I apologized for the adults who had hurt her and assured her that none of these things were her fault. My tone of voice was not soft or compassionate. Rather, it was the voice of a parent calmly presenting the facts non-judgmentally; a "this is real life" tone. I then explained to her that, even though all these horrible things had happened to her, she still needed to take care of business. She needed to come to school on a regular basis. She needed to participate in class and do the assigned work. She needed to refrain from doing things that annoyed or bothered students and teachers. If she wasn't sure what behaviors fell into that irritating category, we agreed that Melissa would ask me or I would remind her privately sometime during the class. When I had concluded this brutally honest and confrontational lecture, Melissa was speechless. The entire ordeal had lasted less than a minute but had a powerful impact that changed the course of Melissa's life. No one had ever told Melissa the truth. The adults in her life had either been predators who abused her or caring professionals who were so concerned about further damage to her self-esteem, that they allowed her to continue behaving in ways that prevented her from overcoming the challenges of her family life and building a successful life, despite the horrors of her childhood. My message to Melissa was different. By treating her as she knew I would treat any other student, I conveyed to Melissa that, despite her past, I believed she had just as good a chance as any other student at succeeding. By helping her see that, regardless of the reasons she behaved this way, her irritating and annoying behaviors were keeping her from having friends and being accepted at school. This gave her valuable information about how to improve her life, instead of the justification to continue her alienating ways that had been provided by the myriad of other adults who professed to help her. That year Melissa passed all of her classes for the first time in her entire junior high experience. At the end of the year Melissa wrote a farewell paragraph in the school newspaper, as was traditional for out-going freshmen. The only statement she made was a thank you to me for caring enough to be honest with her.

When I use this confrontational, honest approach with students, it amazes me how often students display something close to relief, as if a great weight has been lifted from their shoulders. They know they are being obnoxious but no one has ever had the guts to be honest with them and help them find ways to *stop* being obnoxious. I believe that it is this honesty that forges the bond between the student and teacher. An immediate trust is formed because they know that I will tell them the truth, even if it's ugly. Their initial response may be hurt or anger, which is a natural response to criticism. But, once they recognize that my behavior is the highest form of caring, the door is opened for a deep and powerful bond. I recognize that it is difficult for someone who has not had this experience to believe that this approach can be effective. It is only because I have seen it work, over and over again, with all types of students in all types of circumstances, that I am so convinced of its power. I stay in contact with many of my former students, some of whom are in their thirties and raising their own families. When we get together, they often sheepishly recall their own maximum opportunity moment with me. Many also tell me that they have successfully used the same techniques with their own children.

This philosophy has also passed the test in the Wong household. My experience has been that, as they mature, children move through a predictable emotional cycle. In the toddler years, this cycle seems to complete itself every six months, with the cycle getting progressively shorter and shorter as children get older, peaking in the prime adolescent years (fourteen through sixteen), when the cycle may turn over every few weeks. Like ocean waves, this constant ebb and flow serves an important developmental purpose—gradually helping the child establish her own understanding of the boundaries of acceptable behavior—helping her define her own standards and values. This discovery process prepares the child (and the parents) for the inevitable time when the child leaves home to establish her own adult life. Part of this cycle involves continually testing the boundaries, trying to discover what is, and what is not acceptable; teasing out what is *really* important to the parent and what is arbitrary or negotiable. In the calm part of this cycle, you and your child will be in sync, with a clear understanding of what is acceptable for the child at this point in her development. Then, as she gets older and develops new skills and capabilities, she, justifiably, wants to renegotiate the boundaries. However, most four-year-olds (or fourteen-year-olds for that matter) are fairly unskilled negotiators, so they resort to what they know—testing the boundaries again! It is at this point that the child expects, needs, and actually wants to be confronted. Children really do want to be set back on the right track. The astute parent will recognize the need for involvement and firmly realign the child so their values and standards for behavior are reinforced. Although this testing can be trying and exhausting for parents, it is a critical part of effective parenting. Your child is asking, "Do you really believe in these values? Am I important enough for you to stop and deal with me? Are your values and standards important enough for you to do the hard work of making sure I understand them and abide by them?" It is through this constant cycle of testing, confronting and affirming that children know that their parents truly care about their future. The cycle also helps students recognize that their teacher is committed to their long-term development as a human being, not just to controlling students' behavior for the nine months they are in the teacher's classroom.

I can tell you without hesitation that my sons are fully convinced that I would not hesitate to firmly reinforce our family's priorities. My students are totally convinced that I will step in when behaviors are not meeting my expectations. Both groups know that I will do *whatever it takes*, regardless of personal sacrifice, regardless of the difficult feelings or conflict that might result, to ensure that they are on the right track. That is how both my sons and my students are convinced of my genuine devotion and love for them.

Forced Success

Human behavior is always full of surprises. A gaping hole in my teacher preparation program was that most of what I learned was theoretical and ivory tower, while what I needed was the real truth about teaching and some practical, effective strategies for promoting positive change. It's a shame that, like most teachers, I had to learn my lessons the hard way, by trial and error in the classroom. It took years of experimentation before certain clear philosophies began to emerge. One of these real truths is the concept of *forced success*. In certain situations kids literally demand that you force them to do something right. This method works for children who, for some reason, aren't succeeding at the level at which you know they can succeed. The child may lack confidence or be afraid of failing and they demonstrate this through avoidance behavior.

This strategy requires you to be willing to accept and endure the repercussions of your response. It's important to remember that children, like adults, don't generally *like* having someone make them do something they don't want to do. But our job as parents and teachers is not to make decisions based on what children *like,* but on what they *need* to grow up to be responsible, productive, successful adults. So, don't expect the child to react positively, happily, gratefully or quickly. Expect the opposite. This technique takes time and sacrifice on your part, so don't start it unless you are willing at that moment to finish. In some ways you are challenging the kid to a contest where you are their teammate and the opponent is the task.

The following example illustrates how this technique worked with one of my students. Sherry was a chronically truant ninth grader who had more pressing issues in her life than my Health class. Although it was clear that she was very smart, Sherry did not use her time in school to her benefit. She managed to do just enough to pass all of her classes, but rarely put forth any more than the minimal effort. One day she arrived fifteen minutes late, as the rest of the class was taking a test. I knew she was prepared because she had been in class the day before and I had seen her paying close attention to the review. I gestured to her that she could begin taking the test. She shook her head no and sat down. Thinking she didn't understand or see the gesture, I walked to her desk and quietly said she could begin the test and would have ample time to finish. She loudly declared that she wasn't going to take the test because she "didn't know anything." Given what I knew about this student, I decided to employ forced success. I forcefully told her, within clear earshot of her classmates, that I was tired of her thinking and acting like she could do anything she pleased. I demanded that she get up from her chair and go to the back room, where I followed her. Now remember, the entire class was taking a test as I focused all my energy and attention on this one girl. We sat down at a table in the back office and I read the first question to her. My tone of voice made it clear that I expected an answer from her. She gave an answer and wrote it down. I then firmly requested that she read the next question out loud, which she did, then wrote down the answer. This pattern continued for half of the questions, after which I got up from the table and told her to finish the test. As I returned to the class, I could tell the students were a bit perplexed at my actions, but I could also tell that they were convinced that I was not going to stand for sub par performance or poor pitiful me excuses. Sherry earned a "B" on that test, her best test score to date that trimester. I didn't need to lecture Sherry on what had happened. She had experienced forced success and understood my point. In fact, my only statement to her upon returning her graded test was a sarcastic "Oh, I guess you didn't know anything?" and an accompanying smirk.

Like so many effective techniques, forced success can also have secondary effects on other students. The entire class witnessed the episode and learned some important lessons. First, they learned that I wasn't about to let someone just give up because they wanted to. Secondly, they learned that Mr. Wong is a little crazy and that will always work in my favor. And finally, they learned that I truly care about their future; that I won't let them undermine their own success. Unlike the false praise and constant efforts to make students *feel* good that so many believe are the hallmarks of a caring teacher, this episode illustrates behavior that actually communicates to kids that someone is willing to go to the limit with them, to go to an uncomfortable and unpleasant place with them, to refuse to take the easy way out. A very clear message was sent to each student in that classroom about what I expect. They realize these actions demonstrate that I fully believe in them, that I am totally convinced they are smart, capable human beings worthy of my efforts. By forcing them to be successful, I communicated my complete confidence in them. How can that not be a powerful message?

Although I'm sure some of you are, once again, saying, "Gee, this guy is so mean. How can children possibly withstand this level of pressure to succeed?" In reality kids are pretty tough, much tougher then we give them credit for. As long as the actions of adults are well intentioned, with the child's welfare truly at heart, kids will see that and respond favorably. I will caution you about the use of this technique. If your motivations for using forced success *aren't* guided by a genuine desire to get the child over a self-imposed barrier to achieving her potential, then this strategy will backfire. Teachers and parents get into trouble when their expectations for the child are really a smokescreen for projecting their own desires and goals onto children. Kids know the difference. If a parent is using his child to feed his own ego, the child will pick up on this and react unfavorably. Parents who push their children to excel can lose sight of their child in the process and create the very opposite of the outcome they desire. The child begins to hate the activity instead of developing a love for it.

I don't believe kids are fragile or weak. I don't believe they are emotionally traumatized by hearing the word "no." I don't believe students are forever scarred if I raise my voice to them. I don't believe the players I have coached have been harmed by the honest feedback I have given them. I don't believe my sons have suffered as a result of being raised by a father who truly believes in them enough to let them fail. I don't believe the pathway to a self-sufficient offspring is through pampering and obsessive protection of her self-esteem. I do believe kids need to be challenged often to achieve greater heights. I do believe an adult who shows kids that they have their best interests at heart can motivate and focus students to be better. I do believe a child who doesn't hear the word "no" will grow up with glaring inadequacies. I do believe the only way to efficiently bring about improvements is to honestly present the problem, followed by clearly stated solutions. I do believe my sons are stronger individuals, not because of the glorious things they have experienced, but because of the struggles they have endured and overcome. I do believe the way to nurture a child to healthy adulthood is to truly trust in her abilities, in easy times and tough times.

As adults who care about children, whether our own children or our students, we need to constantly remind ourselves that we are not raising children, we are, in fact, raising adults. Nurturing a child from birth to healthy, well balanced, productive adulthood is a long-term process. It requires adults who are willing to invest their time, energy, and commitment in the child's emotional, intellectual, physical, and moral development. It requires adults who recognize that children need to *learn* appropriate behavior, just as they need to learn the alphabet or math facts. And it requires adults who have the courage to *teach* children these lessons, even when those lessons are difficult and cause painful or uncomfortable emotions for children, and often for adults. It calls for adults who realize that true self-esteem is not a gift that they can bestow on a child, but a hard-won treasure that is earned through countless, day-to-day opportunities for the child to learn new skills and demonstrate his growing emotional, intellectual, physical and moral competencies. Children need adults who will take charge.

CHAPTER 5: THE PRICE WE PAY

The results of our overindulgence in the positive parenting and self-esteem at all costs philosophy are logical and predictable. They are also pervasive, devastating and far-reaching. Excessive, artificial praise and a plethora of undeserving rewards have had a very real detrimental effect on our families, schools and communities.

It seems like such an innocent thing to give constant praise to a child. It appears so logical that frequent reinforcement would be beneficial. It feels good to be positive and to have all of our interactions with children be happy and conflict-free. It certainly can't do any harm. It must be the right thing to do. If the experts say it's so, then it must be the pathway to being labeled a good parent.

Wrong.

We pay a great price for such selfish behavior. Selfish because, as the adults who are supposed to be in charge, we are taking refuge in a cocoon of irresponsibility, conveniently avoiding those duties that carry the burden of taking on the job of the limit-setting adult. The role of authoritarian is a difficult one for parents to play. Being a grown-up involves taking responsibility and making tough decisions. Instead, we snatch the opportunity to shirk our responsibilities under the auspices of a parenting and teaching strategy that lets us be the good guys. Unfortunately, this fear and immaturity has created a generation of egocentric offspring.

Previous generations of parents had clear goals for their children. For example, going to college was one goal that was unambiguously articulated by many parents when I was growing up. Focusing on that long-term objective helped them make daily decisions that would help move their child closer and closer to that goal. Whatever situation arose, whatever difficulty presented itself, their response was dependent on the effect it might have on their child going to college. In order to go to college, our parents knew it was imperative that we learn certain essential lessons. These lessons would ultimately enable us to reach the goal.

However, unlike our parents, today's parents bought into a philosophy that was faulty from the outset. We developed a lopsided approach to the raising of our children. The experts certainly played a role in sending us down this unproductive pathway, but we were more than willing to let it happen. With the experts preaching their self-esteem gospel and parents and schools blindly following the trend, the self-esteem craze quickly became a snowball rolling down a steep hill, gathering momentum and supporters as it traveled. Despite the preponderance of scientific evidence debunking its effectiveness, this fad has contaminated every institution we depend on to shape our youth. The message has been communicated loudly and thoroughly—be positive, only say positive things, only use positive tactics, there is always a positive way, etc. Fully integrated into the home, school, children's programming, extracurricular activities—everywhere children go they experience this bombardment of well intentioned but ineffective positive pabulum. So is anyone surprised that children have come to expect it? Should we be shocked at the unpleasant repercussions of those expectations? Having spent their lives immersed in this culture of positivism and self-esteem promotion, we should not be surprised that children now expect every aspect of their lives to abide by the rules of this unrealistic model.

Preparation and Training

The negative effects of being blanketed with insincere, unearned praise and reinforcement are pervasive. First, if our job as parents and teachers is to prepare children for well balanced, productive adulthood, then we must prepare them for the full range of experiences they may encounter as adults. We all know that it is impossible for a person to live a life drenched only in positive experiences. The total absence of pain or struggle is absurd.

Think back over the last several years of your life. What painful, difficult or negative experiences have you had to cope with? Perhaps it was the loss of a job, a divorce, the death of a loved one. Of course, these are the biggies. The everyday frustrations of dealing with difficult bosses or co-workers, traffic, trying to make ends meet, or dealing with the constant demands of children are an equally omnipresent part of most of our lives. When parents shield children from negative, frustrating or painful experiences, they deny them the opportunity to learn the skills and therefore gain the confidence required to meet the challenges that surely await them in life.

If you had to train for a 10-K foot race in two months, how would you train? Would you begin your regimen by sitting on the couch every day, hoping your energies would accumulate for the big day? Would you find someone to tell you over and over again what a good runner you are? Of course not. The only way to prepare oneself for a race is to run. You might begin the training by running just a few blocks each day. Then, as your body reaches a certain level of conditioning, you increase the distance. You run a mile each day. After a couple of weeks you begin running two miles each day, progressively increasing your body's endurance. At the end of the two months you are ready for the 10-K race, having endured the daily workouts and developed the confidence needed to finish the distance.

How can children build true self-esteem just sitting on the couch? How can they develop confidence without having put in any effort toward mastery? They can't and they don't. Just as in the training for a foot race, children must begin with small, achievable tasks. Then they can progressively build their confidence and competence with increasingly difficult challenges. If we expect our children and students to survive the hard knocks of life, we must train them just like runners. The only way to get in shape to finish the race is to run. The only way to learn to survive the painful or difficult events in life is to experience smaller frustrations and challenges that will act as the training ground for the inevitable biggies that each of us ultimately must confront.

For some children, their daily existence provides sufficient opportunities to practice coping with challenges: poverty, abuse, family conflict, learning disabilities, or the host of other difficulties that plague our country's highest risk youth. They desperately need the support of parents, teachers and other adults to teach them the social, emotional, intellectual and physical skills they need to cope and survive, and to provide encouragement and guidance as they struggle. However, for many of our country's children, the adults in their lives have carefully constructed an artificial, "Disneyland" world, stripped of any of the normal challenges, frustrations, conflicts, disappointments, and suffering that accompany, and are necessary for, the process of growing up.

Just as they need to learn how to ride a bike or brush their teeth, children need to learn how to cope with the full range of human emotions. Most of us are quite comfortable helping our children cope with positive feelings, but many parents struggle with their child's negative emotions, such as frustration, anger, disappointment, or envy. Even parents who have learned about the importance of "I messages" and acknowledging feelings often give only lip service to this important concept. In other words, even though the parent may *say* the right things in response to their child's anger or disappointment (e.g. "It sounds like you are really frustrated about that homework."), they *behave* in ways that constantly either protect their child from situations that may induce negative feelings or rescue them from struggling with those negative feelings. What does this protective or rescuing behavior look like? It may be the parent of a six-year-old who is whining and complaining because he is frustrated with his homework. "This is stupid!" "Math is boring!" "My teacher never explains anything!" Uncomfortable seeing the child upset, and worried about his self-esteem, the parent rushes in and says, "Oh, it's not so hard, let me help you," and proceeds to do the problems for the child. Or it may be the eleven-year-old baseball player who comes home from practice stomping through the house and pouting. "It's not fair. I always have to play outfield. The coach just likes Tommy and Alex better than me. I want to pitch, too." Rather than calmly stating, "That may not be fair, but many things in life aren't fair," or "Well, if you want to be a pitcher, let's go out in the back yard and practice your pitching," his father says, "Well, I'm going to have a talk with that coach tomorrow. I pay good money to have you on that team and you have just as much right to pitch as any of those other kids!"

The bottom line is that life is full of frustrations, disappointments, conflicts, and other difficulties. Life is *not* Disneyland! No matter what we do, we cannot build a protective bubble around our children that will shield them from negative experiences and the negative feelings that accompany those experiences. There will always be some child who dislikes, teases, or rejects our child; there will always be some teacher, coach, Scout leader, or ballet instructor that treats our child unfairly; there will always be something (math, music, sports, drawing, public speaking, dancing, spelling, playing chess) at which our child will either fail or be less than successful. At some point in their young lives, most children will be excluded from the cool group, do something for which they are totally embarrassed or humiliated, fail to win the spelling bee or the football playoff or the drawing competition, experience the loss of a friend who moves away, have to sit through a class that is boring or too easy for them, get in a conflict with another child or an adult, or make a decision that has poor consequences. Not only can we not build that protective bubble around our children, we shouldn't *want* to even if we could. Because, at some time in their life, our children will have to cope with even more difficult situations–the serious illness or death of a close friend or family member; their parents' divorce, dating or remarriage; the loss of a beloved pet, being dumped by a boyfriend/girlfriend, a parent's job loss and resulting changes in the family's economic situation. Without the opportunity to gradually learn coping skills, practice using those skills successfully, and develop the confidence that comes from coping successfully, children become overwhelmed when these more serious difficulties arise. It's like putting someone who has never played baseball into a professional baseball game, with the score tied in the bottom of the ninth inning and saying, "It's up to you. If you hit a home run, we win and go on to the World Series. If you don't, we lose."

In my teaching experience, I have seen countless examples of teenagers whose well-meaning parents had tried to protect them from any negative experiences and feelings. Suddenly, at age sixteen, when Susie's steady boyfriend dumps her for another girl, Susie's parents can't fix it for her. They can't make the boyfriend take her back. They can't talk her out of her feelings of rejection, embarrassment, jealousy, and loss. Having had no experience dealing with even minor difficulties, Susie has no idea how to cope with these very powerful feelings that are now confronting her. She swallows a bottle of her mother's prescription antidepressants.

Or take the case of Jonathan, who, at age fifteen, had never received anything less than an "A" grade in his entire school career. All of his life, his parents had told Jonathan how special and gifted he was. Although he did not qualify for his district's gifted and talented program, from elementary school on, Jonathan's parents actively lobbied the principal to have Jonathan placed with certain teachers, because Jonathan didn't do well if he wasn't challenged enough; he tended to be disruptive when he was bored. On the couple of occasions when Jonathan had a teacher in whose class he had trouble, his parents intervened and had him transferred to another class. In one situation, they transferred him to another school, where there were teachers who would be more supportive of Jonathan's free spirit and need to learn in his own way. When Jonathan entered a prestigious private high school as a freshman and received two "C's" and two "B's" on his first term report card, he was devastated. When he realized that his parents' intervention would not be successful in this new environment, he became severely depressed, began cutting classes, and eventually dropped out of school.

When we formulate an artificial existence for our kids, we produce young adults who have not had the essential experience of suffering through hardship and realizing that they are, indeed, strong enough and competent enough to get through it. We convey to them that they are too fragile to be trusted to deal with difficult experiences; they are too weak to cope with feeling bad; they don't have the resources to overcome frustration, or boredom, or disappointment.

The last several decades have seen a rash of highly visible, emotionally charged incidents, to which children have inevitably been exposed through the media. Beginning with the Challenger space shuttle explosion, escalating with the spate of school shootings, and reaching its pinnacle in the attacks on the World Trade Center, we have all struggled with how to help young children and adolescents cope with these tragedies. I'll never forget the "expert" response to the Challenger Shuttle explosion. My son was a first grader at the time. Immediately following the accident, counselors were mobilized to all of the city's schools to help children cope with this tragedy. Teachers were instructed to tell students that, "We know you're feeling very sad about what has happened and that's okay." Counselors went around to each class, encouraging the children to talk about their feelings. My son didn't know anything about the shuttle. He didn't know anyone who was on the shuttle. He may have seen television coverage of the explosion, but it was not particularly real or significant to him. This is an event that happened three thousand miles away to people he didn't know. *He wasn't feeling sad.* Mind you, this child was not a callous, unfeeling child. He has always been a sensitive, empathetic child. But this situation was *not* part of his daily life as a six-year-old. But here were all of these adults, including his trusted teacher, telling him that he *should* feel sad. What message was being sent to these children? That they were so fragile and so incompetent, that they needed special counselors to help them deal with something they saw on television.

Over the years, I have seen numerous parents respond to their teenager's failed love affair by sending the child to a therapist. Come on! Do you really think kids are so weak that they can't even cope with getting over their 2-month relationship with their girlfriend/ boyfriend without expert help? I witness students on a weekly basis confused as to how to deal with the normal emotional bruising of adolescence. The smallest aggravation can send them into a tailspin that manifests itself as the end of the world. How horribly ill prepared they are for real life.

Learning

Rather than shielding and protecting children from negative experiences, the wise parent will ensure that children are deliberately and gradually allowed to experience, cope with, and triumph over difficulties. These experiences should be appropriate to the age, abilities and personality of the child. For a toddler working on building a tower with blocks, allowing the child to work through the frustration of having the tower fall and having to rebuild is an invaluable learning experience. For the school-age child whose best friend has suddenly found a new best friend, allowing the child to experience and feel the pain of rejection and loss and to martial her own resources to find a new best friend will pay great dividends in self-esteem and self-confidence. For the teenager who gets in a fight at school and comes home suspended, allowing the child to experience the school-imposed consequence of missing a school dance or basketball game teaches him the valuable lesson that actions have consequences, and that sometimes the consequences seem unfair. But then, life's not fair.

In conversations with both my teaching colleagues, as well as other parents, I know many people share my observation that a particularly insidious change has occurred in kids in the last ten to fifteen years. Too many children are growing up without experiencing the logical consequences of their actions, creating a generation of young adults who don't take responsibility for what happens to them. With chicken parents and chicken schools cowering behind the smokescreen of positive self-esteem, children are regularly allowed to escape the consequences of their negative behavior. Rather than learning to do the right thing, simply because it's the right thing to do, they learn to do the right thing only when someone else is watching or when there is a reward at the end. In other words, they never reach what moral development expert Lawrence Kohlberg describes as the highest stage of moral development, in which moral decisions are made based on an internal sense of right and wrong, rather than an external system of rewards and punishments.[10] According to a survey of 12,000 high school students by the Josephson Institute of Ethics, the number of students who have cheated on an exam at least once in the past year increased from 61% in 1992 to 74% in 2002.[11]

Compounding the delusion of positive self-esteem, overworked teachers and stressed out parents are often unwilling to put in the effort required to follow through on consequences. It just seems *so* much easier to let it go, just this once....

My students constantly tell me that being late to class is not their fault—their friends made them late. They don't have their homework done because their parents forgot to get them paper or didn't take them to the library. Middle school students failing a class tell me it's because a teacher doesn't like them. The disturbing thing is that these examples involve the *good* kids! The price we pay is far more serious when we look at those young people whose belief that they are immune from the consequences of their actions takes the form of violence, crime, or drug use. The young man who says to society, "It's not my fault I shot that kid. He was picking on me!" Or the young woman who says, "It's not my fault I sell drugs. I'm poor." When asked about their experience with the juvenile justice system, young offenders around the country pronounce, "Juvie's a joke." These kids are telling us the answer! Give us consequences! Make the consequences mean something! If we don't learn from that consequence, give us a more severe consequence. In fact, research indicates that the most effective way to prevent first-time young offenders from progressing to more and more serious crimes is to ensure that the first time they offend, they receive a swift, appropriate, but severe enough punishment that they know the system is serious about changing their behavior.[12]

Research also shows the devastating impact of inconsistent consequences in families. Children whose parents fail to set clear guidelines for their children's behavior, who don't monitor whether or not guidelines are being followed, and who provide either excessively severe consequences, no consequences, or inconsistent consequences are at greater risk for substance abuse, delinquency, early sexual activity, school dropout and violence.[13]

It's always someone else's fault. Well, of course it *must* be someone else's fault, because, after all, they've been told all their lives that they are great kids doing a fantastic job in a terrific school. A lifetime of undeserved superlatives develops a personality that shirks responsibility–being a child is much easier than being an adult.

We have brainwashed children into thinking they can do no wrong. The ever-present undeserved applause is a constant reinforcement to this erroneous perception. There is a huge difference between appropriately reinforcing actual effort and achievements and smothering a child with vacuous approval. The price our children pay is that, at some point in their lives, they *will* have to take responsibility for their actions; they *will* run head on into the realities of the adult world. They *will* have to suffer the consequences if they break the law, fail to pay their bills, or tell off their boss. Unfortunately, learning to face those consequences as an adult is infinitely more difficult and usually has far more devastating and life-changing effects.

The price we pay as a society is that our prisons are overflowing with young adults whose first exposure to any consequence in their lives is the one imposed on them by the judge. Unfortunately, using incarceration to teach these young people the lessons they should have learned years earlier has wide-ranging negative consequences. In addition to gobbling up an ever-increasing percentage of our scarce public dollars and threatening to bankrupt several states who can't build prisons fast enough to keep up with the demand, prison has not proven to be a particularly successful environment for teaching young inmates responsibility and preparing them to be productive citizens on the outside. On the contrary, prison is generally viewed as a breeding ground where young offenders can develop and hone their criminal skills in preparation for even more serious offending once they are released.

Losing Trust

Another price we pay for our unquestioning adherence to the fallacy of self-esteem is that young people have lost their trust in the adults around them. Children raised on a steady diet of positive experiences, whose every waking moment is celebrated by an unending stream of esteem-building cheerleading, inevitably find out that not everyone thinks they are so special. In fact, they *aren't* as good a pitcher as Bobby; everything they do and every word they utter is *not* wonderful and acceptable. Somewhere along the line they realize that they are *not* the center of the universe. The later in life they come to this realization, the more devastating the impact. I have witnessed countless times the overwhelming pain that accompanies a child's realization that they have been lied to by the people they counted on to tell them the truth. The discovery of this treachery quickly nullifies all of the previous praise or accolades that were heaped on the child. Children are bright and perceptive. They quickly learn that, if you are not willing to confront them when their behavior is inappropriate, if you tell them that they are wonderful when they know they are misbehaving, if you praise them equally for something that is mediocre and for something that took great effort or talent, your feedback is useless. If we want children to trust our feedback, we need to tell them the truth.

I recall a junior high girl who had been the victim of such false praise. Ashley came from a very wealthy family. Trained in ballet and exposed to many different things through her family's travels, she felt very comfortable in adult surroundings. Ashley was her Daddy's princess and she had been told she was special from the day she was born. She was the smartest, the prettiest, and the most talented. She was also a pain to have in class because she had a difficult time understanding that the class didn't exist just for her. Empathy and sympathy were not a part of Ashley's makeup, not a big surprise, since she had been treated all her life as though the world, and everyone in it, existed solely to meet her every need. As a result, Ashley hung out with the popular crowd, but was disliked by most of her classmates.

After having many run-ins with her over her constant socializing and egocentric behavior in class, I finally decided it was time to be honest with Ashley. I backed off my usual behavior control tactics for one day, allowing her to show her true self and the accompanying obnoxious behaviors. Taking advantage of this opportunity, she sat on top of her desk, ignoring her assignment and holding court with the few students who felt forced to listen. She chattered so loudly and incessantly that, at one point, another student finally told her to shut up. Ashley continued this behavior until she was summoned to the office. As she left, she chose to exit out the back door of the portable, which had been off limits to students all year long. Throughout the class period, I had been documenting Ashley's behavior, preparing for the parent meeting that I was sure would ensue. Ashley returned from the office near the end of the period. As she gave me her office pass, I requested that she stay after class for a few moments. She protested and challenged the request, her behavior quickly escalating into a full-blown tantrum. She was calling me out. With the whole class watching, she was counting on my backing down. She pulled out her best manipulative tactics and she did so with great expertise.

I spoke to Ashley in an honest and firm tone. I informed her that she had been lied to by her parents. They had told her that she was special and that was simply not true. I proceeded to inform her that, in fact, she was just like all the other students. She needed to abide by the rules and adhere to civilized manners. This class was not here for her entertainment and she was not the only student in the room. Ashley was visibly shocked. For the first time in her life, her manipulation attempt had failed, and, on top of that, she had received a healthy dose of honesty in front of her peers. Speechless and shaken, her eyes filled with tears and she sunk into her seat. After class, I explained to her, again very honestly, how other students perceived her behavior. We then discussed how she could change her behavior to benefit herself. The next day I was called into a meeting with Ashley's parents and the Principal. Ashley's parents were angry, vehemently disagreeing with my methods and approach. I patiently listened to their concerns and waited for them to finish. I began my response by relating the list of inappropriate behaviors that Ashley had demonstrated the previous day. Initially disbelieving, the parents gradually softened their position as the truth of my words sank in. Within a few minutes the father admitted that Ashley often behaved similarly at home and it had been the cause of conflict for the family for years.

Ashley's parents were well-educated, loving, caring, responsible parents. Like all parents, they wanted the best for their daughter. Unfortunately, they had succumbed to the pied piper of self-esteem and had willingly adopted the unfortunate practices that had produced Ashley's egocentric, obnoxious behavior. Ashley paid the price.

False Praise

Part of telling young people the truth is ensuring that we don't, in the name of promoting their self-esteem, smother them with insincere, untruthful praise. Most of us are familiar with the story of the boy who cried wolf. Just like the boy who cries wolf too often, as parents or teachers we must avoid the use of insincere or undeserved praise or face the probability that, when we do offer sincere feedback, it will be ignored or disbelieved.

I remember vividly when my oldest son learned this lesson about an adult. At his cooperative preschool, a variety of centers were set up for children. A very kinesthetic and active child, my son routinely bypassed the arts and crafts center and headed directly for the climbing toy or the block area. His teacher, however, was determined that he should experience all of the centers. On this particular day, he tried to sneak pass the table where this teacher was waiting to encourage him to create a project with Styrofoam blocks and all kinds of items that could be stuck in the Styrofoam. No such luck. The teacher, with a syrupy smile on her face, grabbed his arm and suggested that he come to the crafts table. Not wanting to cause trouble, he complied. He quickly took a small block of Styrofoam in his hand, grabbed the nearest item, which happened to be a pegboard hook, and proceeded to stab the hook into the center of the block. He then put it down in front of the teacher, said, "Okay, I'm done," then waited for an indication from his teacher that he could escape. Of course, she began to gush over this masterpiece, as she did for each of the children's creations. His art project received the same accolades as others who had worked on theirs for hours! Later that day I asked my son what he really thought of his art project. He told me that he had just wanted to get it over with so he could return to the activities he enjoyed. At four, he already understood the game. But my son paid a price for this teacher's blanket kudos. From that point on, he clearly ignored her feedback, good or bad.

Insincere or undeserved praise gradually results in children distrusting any feedback they receive. Why would my son trust his teacher's positive feedback about the building he created out of Legos when, just a few minutes ago, she had praised him for thrusting a peg into some Styrofoam? When children distrust the feedback they are getting from adults, they become confused about the standards for quality work. We all have a human need to feel good about what we do, but we can only truly feel satisfied when we trust the sincerity of the person who is giving the recognition.

As you were growing up, whom did you trust to tell you the truth? If you were lucky, it was your parents. It certainly was for me. I knew that my parents would tell me, show me, or force me to see the truth, even if telling the truth hurt my feelings, made me mad, or caused me to feel bad in some way. They would take the time to tell me the truth and help me to learn from the truth. As a result, I learned to trust their thoughts and advice. Often I didn't like it, but I *did* trust it.

When positive, earned praise is balanced with corrective feedback or criticism, children view both types of comments as valuable and honest. They are reliable. One price we pay for our over-reliance on unearned praise is a fundamental lack of trust by kids for their parents' or teachers' advice and opinions. The bottom line is that someone needs to be there for them, to tell them the bad stuff and the good stuff, to tell them the truth, even when the truth hurts. Wouldn't you like to be that person?

Kids Pay

Without a mechanism for providing valid and useful corrective feedback to children, an over-dependence on unearned praise and rewards sets up a system that distorts, and often inflates, children's true abilities. Kids are convinced that they are all stars, when, in reality, all children have varying degrees of ability in different areas.

By magnifying their skill level, we damage children by allowing them to become complacent. If a child is told she is a great writer, why should she work hard to improve? If she is told that she is the best goalie, what's the payoff in trying to get better? After all, best is as good as it gets. Children are satisfied with their level of performance because we convince them that they have reached a mastery level, even when their skills are lacking. Rather than giving kids an honest assessment of their skills, then working with them to improve those skills, we take the chicken pathway and lie to them. After all, it's so much easier than dealing with their disappointment, or hostility, or frustration. Unfortunately, our lies carry a price—their natural hunger and drive to be better is squelched. Their motivation to work harder is diminished.

Different children will pay different prices for our chicken behavior. Some will grow up convinced that everything they do is special. Every picture they draw, every statement they utter, every thought they have, and every effort they make is worthy of special recognition. Egocentrism, here we come! Will you want these people living next door to you? Do you want them working for you or with you? Do you want them making decisions in the voting booth?

The price to be paid is lowered standards for all. The kid who turns in the paper half done gets rewarded because at least he did something. The student who arrives to class on time looks for his reward after being tardy every other day that week. The baseball player who can barely throw the ball wants to know when it is his turn to pitch. The child who lives in filth wants to know how much money she will be paid to keep her own room clean. All are expecting to be reinforced for sub par performance. Each time we lower the bar in the interest of protecting a child's self-esteem, we do a disservice to all children, who lose the motivation to achieve their potential. And, don't forget, decades of research have shown that doing it in the name of protecting a child's self-esteem isn't good for the child either.

Some children will fail to reach their true potential because, when excellence and mediocrity are treated equally, the truly exceptional child is unlikely to get the valuable feedback or the contingent reinforcement he needs to improve and achieve his potential.

I see the results of this damaging practice daily in my students. Students who feel entitled to success without the effort; who believe they should be exempt from the struggle that is required for progress. There is no bell curve with these young people! Everyone's a winner. They think they should get an "A" just for showing up and doing the work. Just completing the project or assignment should be enough. Simply attending class is their standard for passing. Give a student a "B" or, Heaven forbid, a "C" and you're likely to hear, "But you can't give me a "B," I've never gotten a "B" before." What does that have to do with the grade they *earned* in my class?

When their whining, complaining, threatening, or tears don't produce the desired result (my changing their grade), they waste no time looking for a more sympathetic ear, from their parents or from a counselor or administrator. Unfortunately, they often find it. They are certain that they won't *really* be forced to live with the consequences of their actions. They are convinced that they have the unalienable right to feel good about themselves at all times at school. My, how well we've taught them. Anything that threatens their precious sensibilities is certain to draw the attention of an administrator, counselor, or over-protective parent.

One natural consequence of this absurdity is that it becomes difficult for parents to trust feedback from the school. Is your child really an "A" student or is the teacher just trying to avoid conflict? Are his abilities truly exceptional or is the school just convinced that everyone should be a winner? Is your child progressing as he should be or is the school inflating grades and test results so that they look good to the public? When teachers and other educators can't be trusted to give honest, sincere feedback, how can students be expected to learn? Feedback, both positive and negative, is critical to the learning process.

The noxious effects of our misdirected practices find their way onto our playing fields, as well. After a childhood of playing on community teams that mandate equal playing time regardless of skill, commitment or talent, high school students join sports teams fully expecting this practice to be continued. They seem to believe that their skill level or their suitability for the position are secondary to the fact that they showed up, so they *deserve* to play and they deserve to play whatever position suits their fancy. The kid who can't throw wants to pitch; the kid who can't hit wonders why he isn't batting clean up; the kid who can't catch the ball demands to play first base.

The ultimate irony is that, as parents, we pay the price by espousing a philosophy that we don't fully support. What do I mean by that? Well, as much as we pay lip service to everyone being a star, we don't *really* want everyone to be a star, because if everyone is a star, then *our* child is not really going to be special! We want our own children to be exceptional. We want our sons and daughters to be the best. We want them to excel. We want them to be set apart from the crowd. Our kids know that; they feel it when we help them make their science project just a little more impressive; when we get just a little too excited about the math test they're taking the next day. Their small ears hear the boasting of the proud parent bragging about his child. Their eyes see the disappointment in the faces of the frustrated parent. They understand thoroughly the judgments we parents can't help but reveal in our every gesture. They understand that, despite our protestations to the contrary, we're a lot happier when our kids are winners than when they're losers.

We pay a high price for wanting our child to be special, to be exceptional, to be the perfect child. The financial cost of over-involvement in a myriad of activities can be a real burden: weekly piano lessons, ballet three times a week, and, just to fill the remaining few free days, they join the community soccer team (even though you really wanted them to take karate.)

Participation in these types of activities is great, but at what emotional cost is this over-participation? The quest to build a child's confidence and esteem may actually contribute to tearing it down. The potential rewards are numerous, but the stress children feel can be overwhelming. As adults, many of us experience stress and difficulty trying to balance our busy lives, yet too often we burden children with the same frenzied schedule. When do you allow your child the luxury of just being a kid? Do you schedule time for frivolous play? I bet not. Like so many parents who want the very best for their kids, you're probably worried that they might miss out on something that's really important. So your child is wound so tightly that he is likely to explode.

Children are seeing therapists in record numbers. The Washington Post, citing a recent study by Dr. Julie Zito at the University of Maryland, says "the number of American children being treated with psychiatric drugs has grown sharply in the past fifteen years, tripling from 1987 to 1996 and showing no signs of slowing down."[14] Over-involvement and pressure have taken a toll. Children have been pushed too hard and deprived of the simple joys of childhood. In the quest to make children feel good about themselves, to make them feel special, parents are often blinded to the very real needs of children.

Parents intervene in children's activities where their presence is not necessary or welcomed. Adults have taken children's activities and twisted them into vehicles to satisfy their own self-serving needs.

Some of my most treasured childhood memories are of timeless summers, meeting my friends at the neighborhood park in anticipation of another day of pick-up baseball. Makeshift bases were made from whatever discarded material could be found. Rules were dictated by the number of players and the available playing field. Teams were chosen by the first to yell "second captain, first choose." Winners and losers were determined by the score. Arguments were solved by the intricate, unwritten code understood only by young boys. And at the end of the day, we felt an undeniable craving to return the next day for more of the same. The quantity and quality of lessons I learned about life in those lazy summer days could fill volumes. What role did our parents play in teaching us those lifelong lessons? They butted out. They made us breakfast; they washed the clothes coated with dust from the baseball field; they listened to our tales of home runs hit and bases stolen.

As I pass the same park today, the scene is different. I see fields overrun with organized teams. Kids seem to be more concerned with who has the latest style of shoes, uniforms or equipment than with playing the game. Adults run the show. They set the rules, decide who plays on which team, run the drills, make the call about whether or not the tag was good, determine who plays which position, set the practice schedule and keep the stats. Is this activity for the kids or for the adults?

When adults take over activities, children often lose. As we orchestrate the many details and roles inherent in these activities, kids are removed from the natural lessons and development involved in these activities. They lose out on the lessons of cooperation, compromise, responsibility, determination, creativity, etc., they would normally experience. I spent sixteen years coaching in the schools and as many years coaching community teams and I've seen firsthand the negative effects of adults taking over children's "free" time.

We wonder why kids have trouble filling their own time, why they're always bored. How do we expect them to learn how to entertain themselves when we fill every waking minute for them? We don't understand why so few kids are able to take on leadership roles. When do they have an opportunity to learn to lead? We do all the leading for them. We are puzzled at their lack of ability to resolve conflicts. How could they have learned this valuable skill? We have voluminous rule books spelling out every conceivable situation and adult umpires to make the calls. We wonder why kids don't pay more attention to their athletic performance, why they don't seem to spend the time practicing on their own to perfect a certain skill. Why should they? We do it for them, with every movement recorded, charted, analyzed, and reviewed. We wonder why kids just don't trust their natural abilities. How could they? We convinced them that there's some magic, five-step formula for hitting a baseball, or fielding a grounder, or sliding into second. We wonder why kids aren't having any fun, why we often have to drag them to practice. Well, we're too busy screwing it up. Naturally, the adults all claim that they are doing it for the kids. But, in fact, it is the kids who pay the price.

Another unfortunate result of the cult of self-esteem is that we fall victim to a never-ending inflation of expectations. If you had bought a toy for your child each and every time you went to the store, what do you think your child will expect when you go to the store today? Of course, he'll expect a brand new shiny toy. However, it won't take long before your child tires of the cheap trinkets that used to suffice and begins demanding something bigger and better.

Overuse of praise sets up the same dynamic, particularly when the praise is insincere and unwarranted. It teaches children that for every action, they should expect a reward. A term has actually been coined for kids who are conditioned this way. They are referred to as "praise junkies." You may know kids like this; I know thousands. I particularly like this term because it so clearly articulates the serious and damaging aspects of the overuse of positive affirmations. Like Pavlov's dogs, we have trained these children to require a reward after each action. So, should we be shocked when kids won't do anything unless they are rewarded? No, that's how they have been conditioned;

they have learned our lessons well. Should we be surprised when kids won't do things for their intrinsic value? Of course not, we created these self-centered individuals by assuming that children won't do anything without praise or rewards. Should we be puzzled when children have trouble persevering to achieve challenging goals? No, we trained them to believe praise would come no matter what amount of effort they expended. Have you ever asked your children or students to do something and the immediate response is "What do I get if I do it?" "How much will you pay me?" or from students "Do I get points for this?" "Will this be graded?" "Can I get extra credit for this?" The praise junkie's efforts can only be stimulated by the extrinsic reward at the end. Remember, these are the future adults who will be supporting our Social Security system. What kind of society will we need to create to support their habit?

Another interesting spin-off of our devotion to positive self-esteem is the validation of every thought or feeling a child has. Of course, when children are very young they have yet to learn that there is a world outside of them and that they are not the center of the universe. One of the key developmental tasks of the toddler and preschool years is to recognize that other people exist outside of their relationship to the child and that those people have needs and feelings. This is the beginning of the development of empathy and should appear in the second year of life. However, this normal period of egocentrism seems to have been extended in the name of helping children feel good about themselves. This constant reinforcement of children "just for being" confirms the notion that their opinion always counts and that they have the right to be heard. Although children may get away with this exalted impression of their importance in their early years, their needs will eventually collide with the needs of the teacher, other students, their employer, or the community. The collision is likely to be an unpleasant one.

It seems we have convinced young people that, simply because they exist, they have the right to participate in the decisions of the family, or the school, or other groups in which they participate. I don't get it. When did we decide that children should become equal partners in running families or schools? On what basis was that decision made? What are their qualifications for the job? As a parent, I have more experience, information, and maturity than my child and am, therefore, better equipped to make many of the decisions required in our family. As a teacher, I have five years of college and thirty years of experience to inform my decision-making about how my students should be educated. Certainly, there are areas of family life or school in which young people's input is extremely valuable. There are family and school decisions that young people should be given the skills and opportunity to make, and these opportunities should be increased as young people mature and approach adulthood. But children and adults are not equal! Neither families nor schools should be run as democracies. We know that one of the cornerstones of democracy is an educated populace and an 11-year-old does not have the information, experience, or maturity to participate effectively in a democratic process.

In this process of listening to children's every minute utterance or complaint and accepting them as valuable and legitimate input, we have relinquished our position as the grown ups and become desensitized to disrespectful language and behavior. What our parents viewed as back talk, we perceive as children expressing their opinions.

"Why do I have to eat this? "Why do I have to do this homework?" "Why do I have to set the table?" "Why can't I take the test tomorrow?" "This isn't fair." "You treat me like a slave." "Mrs. Smith doesn't care if we come in late." The constant barrage of questions and challenges set up by this imbalance of power can be exhausting and, ultimately, weakens the family or the school. It frustrates parents and dilutes the authority of the teacher. In addition, the ease and righteousness with which young people give their opinions is disturbing. They seem comfortable confronting their parents, teachers, principals, police, grandparents, almost anyone at almost any time.

Why would adults fall for this usurping of power? Why would we give up our rightful place as the grown ups in our families and schools? Well, there's that term again—grown up. Being the grown up is too hard. It's too much work. We're too chicken.

It's interesting to note that many schools have begun to require community service as a graduation requirement. When you see a young person volunteering at your local park, shelter or food bank, there's a good chance that he is there, not because he believes it is important to help others, but because he *has* to. The only way to move these narcissists out of their self-absorption is to "pay" them with credit.

Communities Pay

American communities are currently experiencing the egocentric backlash of the first generation of young adults who were raised with the fallacy of self-esteem. Involvement in politics or other community or neighborhood life is diminishing dramatically. Why should they care about others when their focus is on themselves? I see examples of this self-centered attitude on a daily basis in my own neighborhood. My pet name for minor illustrations of this self-absorbed behavior is the "Costco Syndrome." If you shop at Costco, or a similar large warehouse store, you have undoubtedly witnessed, or been the victim of, the Costco Syndrome. See if this sounds familiar. As you push your cart around the corner you encounter a person whose cart is positioned such that it effectively prevents anyone from passing in either direction. There are people waiting on both sides, glaring at the oblivious shopper, whose only concern is which size can of chili to purchase. When he finally makes his chili choice, and realizes that his inconsiderately placed cart is blocking the aisle and that people are being inconvenienced, the true test of egocentrism begins. If he apologizes and hurries out of the way, looking embarrassed, this person was just preoccupied for the moment. This could and does happen to anyone. But the true Costco syndrome offenders actually look you in the eye with absolutely no acknowledgment of their inconsiderate behavior. In their minds, they deserve to be in that aisle; they can put that cart anywhere they like; they are paying customers who have the right to get their needs met. Are they intentionally being mean? No, they just don't have the capacity to put the considerations of others first in their thoughts. They are remarkably oblivious to how their actions affect others. But is it actually that remarkable? Not really. It is, in fact, quite logical. A child who is raised to be the center of the universe is unlikely to magically turn into an adult who demonstrates empathy and consideration for others. We reap what we sow.

Schools Pay

A truly tragic price we have paid is the gradual erosion of authority in the home and schools. My first year of teaching was in 1977. I remember receiving a copy of the school rules that first year. This single eight and a half by eleven-inch page consisted of less then ten specific rules. As directed by the administration, I reviewed them with the class on the first day of school. Within a period of fifteen years, this single page had evolved into a booklet containing over seventy pages. The print was small and every rule and regulation was spelled out with the pomposity of a legal document. The expectation was that the booklet was to be read from cover to cover by the student. A separate card was to be signed, indicating that the student had read and understood the contents of the booklet. It would have taken an entire trimester for junior high students to read and comprehend the contents of that booklet! So, the typical practice of the classroom teacher was to pass out the booklets, have the students blindly sign the cards and collect them a few seconds later.

How was one page of rules transformed into a seventy-page booklet? In the early eighties Washington State passed legislation that required schools to officially inform students of their rights under the law. The school district in which I taught decided to print a document listing students' rights and distribute a copy to be taken home and kept for reference. The document was entitled "Student Rights and Responsibilities." Not only did we distribute copies to each and every student but there was also a day designated for school administrators to review and explain specific parts of the document. Remember that students already *had* these rights. We were just *informing* them of their rights.

As time passed, certain rules and regulations came under attack. It began with polite questioning and peaked with long, drawn out, contentious court battles. As parents realized how easy it was to manipulate the school and its employees using their students' newfound rights, they began to challenge established policy. For many parents, their goal was to have their child absolved of any wrongdoing and to have any assigned punishment revoked, regardless of who was right or wrong. Why would these parents behave so irresponsibly? Well, you know, kids will be kids, and, after all, punishment would make their child *feel* bad! What would that do to the child's self-esteem?

Attorneys were hired by parents to punch holes in the language used in the booklet. Finding loopholes in the rules became routine.

Students escaping the consequences of their behavior because their parents' attorneys got them off on a technicality became as commonplace in schools as it was in the justice system. As each challenge or lawsuit was settled, another detail would have to be added to the Rights and Responsibilities document to protect against each and every possible eventuality. Johnny, who had been suspended from school for setting a fire in his locker during lunchtime, challenged the suspension on the grounds that nowhere in the document did it specifically state that he could not do so. "Show me where it says I can't start a fire in my locker." The result? Arson was directly addressed in the ever-growing booklet. What price does Johnny pay? He learns that criminal behavior goes unpunished. Next time, he's probably going to need a bigger kick to get his thrills. Why not? His parents will protect him from any consequences.

Susie, who was suspended for smoking, questions the definition of the word smoking. Did the Vice-Principal really see her in the act of smoking, cigarette in hand? If not, then how can the smoking rule apply? After all, she has rights, doesn't she? Seeing a pile of cigarette butts at Susie's feet and the last puff of smoke exiting her mouth is certainly not adequate grounds for risking the potential damage to her self-esteem that would result from her suspension. Suspension revoked. Another paragraph is added to fully define the exact conditions under which a student can be charged with smoking. Susie pays the price because nobody seems to care that she is doing something illegal and unhealthy. She learns to look for every loophole possible to excuse her behavior. Schools pay because they must now either waste precious administrative time skulking around in the bushes trying to catch students with the lit cigarette in their hands, or give up their attempts to protect their students from unhealthy and illegal behavior.

Eric brings a lead pipe to school, armed for the bashing of a well-known rival. A fight ensues, fortunately interrupted before any major harm is done. When the school threatens to expel Eric in accordance with the district's zero tolerance policy for weapons, his parents hire an attorney. Eric's attorney argues that the lead pipe was not a weapon, but an item for his shop project. Eric stays in school. Another whole chapter is added to the document, detailing every potential object that could be considered a weapon. Who pays? Next time, instead of using a pipe, maybe Eric will use a gun. Maybe my child or your child will be caught in the crossfire. Maybe next time, Eric's uncontrolled anger will be turned against a teacher; maybe against me or against one of my colleagues. Sadly, any veteran teacher could regale you with stories like these.

As the legal challenges continued, so did the number of pages in the Rights and Responsibilities booklet. Judgments about attendance had to be made. Tardies were questioned, requiring official definitions that pinpointed the exact placement of the body when the bell rang. (When the bell stops ringing your body has to have broken the plane of the door to the classroom.) Challenges to what the school could issue as discipline had to be outlined. Result? The only consequence we could impose was to take away their time, meaning detention. Even that was subject to challenge, however, with students negotiating to serve their detention when it was convenient, because, after all, we couldn't expect them to miss their soccer practice, or the big sale at the mall, could we? Nailing a student on the use of profanity became an absurd and exhausting exercise. Was the cursing directed at the teacher or was it just a general adolescent outburst? If it was an outburst, was the word or phase used semi-acceptable (e.g. "damn") or was it a downright vulgar word? Was the student provoked in any manner or did he just lose control for a moment? Is this language often used at home? If so, then perhaps the child just doesn't know any better. If the profanity was directed at the teacher, was the student's demeanor one of being upset or did it have an angry characteristic? If it had an angry quality, was the anger self-directed or outwardly aggressive? Did the aggressive tone have any violent quality to it or is it the student's typical emotional intensity? Do you see how ridiculous it becomes? Schools have become so paranoid that this sort of dissection is customary.

Thousands of these challenges later, the document reached the status of a seventy-page volume of students' rights (and responsibilities, although that part seems to have gotten little attention). I recall an incident that is a perfect illustration of how new pages are added to the ever-growing booklet. I was teaching a required eighth grade Health course in the junior high. We were on a quarter system, which allowed nine weeks to cover the curriculum. A very good student, Justin, came to me before class and requested work for the remaining five weeks of the quarter. I inquired about his lengthy absence and he explained that he was attending a family reunion on the east coast. Justin's flight was leaving the next morning and he needed the work that day. I informed him that it would be impossible for me to assemble all the work in the few minutes before class started. I signed the request sheet and wished him a pleasant trip, suggesting chapters he could read in the text on his excursion. He returned to school with three days remaining in the quarter. We frantically put together all the basic work and, to Justin's credit, he completed the majority of the work and took the required tests. Having missed more than half of the scheduled classes, Justin was able to earn a "C" grade for the quarter. Days later, I was paged to the office where a parent was waiting to see me. It was Justin's mother. She demanded an explanation for the "C" grade. A little bit shocked at the inquiry, I reviewed the situation, emphasizing the fact that Justin had missed more then half the quarter and that I found it somewhat remarkable that Justin was able to earn a "C." Justin's mother argued that it was not Justin's fault that he had to attend the family reunion and he should not be penalized. She believed Justin deserved an "A." In fact, she suggested that I shared the blame for not providing the required materials before his departure. At the conclusion of our discussion, having failed to reach her objective (an "A" for Justin), she went directly to the Principal and argued her case again. Result? The "C" grade stood, but another half page was added to the booklet outlining in detail the procedures for an extended absence from school. The entire faculty was called to an emergency meeting just to design the specifics of the policy: number of days' notice required for the teacher to gather the work that will be missed, number of days allowed for make-up work when the student returns, maximum number of days a student could miss per quarter, types of alternative work or projects equivalent to the established curriculum, and on and on and on.

Did this stop parents from challenging the policy? No, but it did provide the necessary "cover your rear end" documentation for teachers and administrators to deal with the challenges.

Each change in policy, each sentence added to the booklet manifests a much deeper problem. With each modification, the authority of the school slowly erodes. In the attempt to be fair to each individual, in every situation, we gradually dilute the influence and control we once had over the student population and our own school environment. School decisions could no longer be made solely by the professional educators. Committees were formed, with parents, students, and community members sharing decision-making power with teachers and administrators. Although input from key stakeholders, including parents, students and the broader community, can be valuable to school decision-making, many school decisions are best made by those individuals who have the experience and training needed to make those decisions–the professional educators. When you go to the doctor, do you expect her to convene a committee of other patients, local business owners, etc. to help with your diagnosis and treatment? Would you expect it from your attorney? Your accountant? Your electrician? By giving up our power and influence in this way, educators devalued our position as the experts who have the training and expertise. We slowly relinquished our power until we finally lost it altogether. We were no longer in control.

As schools lost their stature in the community, the public's trust in those institutions diminished. Administrators are no longer trusted to make decisions for their schools. Teachers are not trusted to make decisions for their own classrooms. Legislators, most of whom have no formal training or expertise in education, blithely initiate educational restructuring initiatives that are untested, under-funded and often doomed to failure from the onset. Virtually everyone has a hand in changing the face of education.

How did teachers control students in the old days? The best teacher I ever had was Mrs. Brown, my Junior High Language Arts teacher. She commanded respect and personal responsibility like no other. What I didn't appreciate at the time, but learned to admire after spending numerous years in the classroom myself, was her superb ability to choose the correct response for each individual in each unique situation. Her repertoire was vast. One minute she would be gently soothing the frustrations of a troubled reader with her deeply caring manner; the next she would hush an entire auditorium of fourteen-year-olds with a stare that would intimidate a drill sergeant. Her bag of tricks included physical tactics to grab the attention of a distracted student or intimidate a physically imposing ninth grade boy.

Mrs. Brown made an impression on you, both academically and emotionally; few students forgot her or the important lessons she taught. I recall one particular episode when I hadn't quite finished my homework for that day. Demonstrating her uncanny clairvoyance, Mrs. Brown positioned herself next to me and gently pinched the short hairs above my ear between her fingers as she asked me if I had completed my homework. I had no choice but to answer truthfully. With my head completely still and Mrs. Brown exerting varying amounts of pressure to emphasize certain key points, I listened intently as she told me, in a soft but stern voice, that it was necessary for me to complete my homework each day. She followed with a short lecture on personal responsibility.

Mrs. Brown was a small woman in her mid-forties. As an eighth grader, I could have picked her up and pitched her across the room. But, on that day, she may as well have been a six-foot-four, two-hundred fifty pound linebacker. She had my attention. Her influence on me was unmatched. I learned a lot about Language Arts from Mrs. Brown. But, more importantly, I learned about being a responsible person. She influenced her students through strength and kindness.

Unfortunately, to employ some of Mrs. Brown' tactics in today's classroom would immediately result in reprimands. Being physical with a student is out of the question, even if the student is out of control (lawsuits and all.) Teachers' choices of disciplinary tactics are constantly second-guessed and challenged. In addition, had Mrs. Brown' methods failed with a given student, she could have turned for support to the Vice Principal, who unfailingly backed the teacher. In many schools today, however, the Vice Principals are victims of the self-esteem philosophy. Rather than being disciplinarians, Vice Principals act more like counselors, interested more in students' feelings than in changing inappropriate and uncivilized behavior.

If Mrs. Brown had not been satisfied with the response of the Vice Principal, she could then have played the ultimate trump card—she could have called the student's parents. In those days, parents and teachers were allies in the battle to civilize children's behavior. My father never questioned the school's actions or motives. The school was sole ruler of the academic kingdom and he was a faithful supporter. If I got into trouble at school, I got into twice as much at home. The allegiances were clear—teachers, administrators, and parents versus students. Although this may sound unfair and harsh in today's world of students as equal partners in their education, doesn't it make sense that the adults who have the increasingly difficult job of guiding young people to successful adulthood should be allies, rather than adversaries?

As the power slowly shifted from administrators and teachers to students, parents, and legislators, a productive classroom environment, and the learning that it supports, suffered. Hamstrung by new prohibitions and regulations, the classroom has become a daily battleground and the teacher rarely emerges the victor. Handcuffed by restrictions that Mrs. Brown would have found ludicrous, the options for today's teachers are virtually nonexistent. Direct criticism and honest corrective feedback are thought to be too harsh for students. Their fragile self-esteem might be compromised. Sarcastic remarks or pointed humor can't be used, because the student might be embarrassed. Students cannot be forced to do chores around the school (e.g. clean the lunchroom or pick up trash) as punishment. Confronting a student's behavior in front of the class may be too humiliating. The student might feel unjustly singled-out. We certainly can't hurt the child's feelings! Teachers are discouraged from lowering a student's grade for misbehavior. Body language that was used by past generations of teachers to communicate authority is now considered to be too intimidating for students. Teachers shouldn't be feared. Students should view teachers as caring and accepting. Negative comments by the teacher destroy the nurturing climate of the classroom. In fact, teachers, like parents, are encouraged to banish the word "no" from their vocabulary. Unfortunately, in order to learn, students need to know what they are doing wrong as much as they need to know what they are doing right. If no one identifies and corrects their inevitable mistakes, whether those are errors on a math problem or inappropriate behavior with a classmate, then students cannot be expected to learn academics or social/emotional skills.

After decades of legal challenges and amplification of students' rights, schools have been reduced to a handful of methods for dealing with inappropriate behavior. Teachers try to reason with students, lecture them about inappropriate behavior, and, of course, try to, "catch them being good," (which can take a long time with some students!). They may take away special privileges, such as free time, or special activities. They can send students to the office, but administrators have few options for disciplining them. The most frequently used method, keeping students after school (detention) is ineffective, even when used properly, as a swift, sure punishment. Unfortunately, the whining of parents and students has eviscerated even this option. In my school district, students cannot be forced to serve their detention on a day specified by the teacher. They get to choose! Imagine the judge asking a convicted felon when he's available to serve his prison time. He can serve his time at his convenience!

Teacher's Pay

If you think this sounds absurd, you're right. This shifting of power has left the classroom teacher stripped of any viable methods for controlling the behavior of students. The authority of today's classroom teacher is so limited that it is no surprise that classrooms everywhere are out of control. Put thirty-two hormone-crazed teenagers in a thirty by thirty-foot room, strip the adult of virtually any useful methods of maintaining control, and you have a recipe for disaster.

At the same time as the range of discipline methods has narrowed, the need for classroom discipline has increased exponentially. Many of today's students come to school lacking the basic social and emotional skills required for getting along in the classroom. Such basic skills as taking turns and listening when someone else is speaking, not to mention self-control, empathy, conflict resolution and anger management, are shockingly under-developed in today's students. This may be understandable if I were referring to kindergartners; but I'm talking about high school students who lack these skills! How many times should a teacher have to ask a student to stop talking before further action can reasonably be taken? Mrs. Brown would have said once. Not likely under today's guidelines. Strip classroom teachers of the full array of behavior control techniques, support them with "feel-good" administrative philosophies, take away parents as allies, and the very children we were trying to protect are the ones who pay the price.

I have had the eye-opening experience of working with thirteen

116

teacher interns. Fresh from college campuses, armed with the latest educational theories, they came ready to take on the world. Their enthusiasm was contagious and their energy enviable. All were literally months away from graduating, already sending job applications to school districts of their choice. Working with these aspiring teachers, I found them completely unaware of the reality of today's classrooms. They had been fully indoctrinated in the "self-esteem at all costs" philosophy and had been exposed only to those teaching methodologies that supported that approach. My first intern was a man who adapted quickly to the real classroom jungle, which may be because his internship came before the onset of the self-esteem period. As subsequent interns arrived, I noticed a deeper indoctrination into the positive-only techniques. These aspiring teachers lacked the strategies necessary for surviving, and certainly for thriving, in the real world of the classroom. Over the course of the teacher preparation program, none had reviewed or role-played any of the more challenging situations that occur on a regular basis in today's classroom. Sadly, my second intern had to be removed from the intern program because he just couldn't handle the demands of the profession. He had wasted years of college taking classes that did not properly prepare him for the realities of the classroom.

After that unfortunate experience, I decided to adjust my approach. In the initial meeting with my interns, I now emphasize two things. First, I tell them that it isn't too late to get out. They can go back to school and get another degree, prepare themselves for a job where they can earn more money and be respected for what they do. I purposely paint the most gruesome picture possible, highlighting every disagreeable aspect I can think of. Having been thoroughly immersed in the culture of the positive approach during their teacher training, most interns are shocked at my approach. However, at the conclusion of their internship, all have been grateful that I told them the raw truth. The second thing I tell my interns is to forget everything they learned in their educational theory classes. I tell them we will be starting from scratch, because those theories are just that–theories. Their internship is going to be about surviving and thriving in the *real* world.

If teacher preparation programs continue to focus on educational theories that are unrealistic and/or ineffective in the everyday classroom, new teachers will be forced to learn their real lessons on the job, a situation that plays a significant part in the current high failure rate of new teachers. To combat this problem, many school districts have instituted mentoring programs in which first year teachers are paired with experienced teachers to help them through their first year on the job. How much more logical it would be to prepare teachers for the real world of the classroom *before* they get their first teaching job, rather than wasting years of college learning theories that will be useless with real students.

One particularly amazing example of the extent to which the fallacy of self-esteem has invaded teacher preparation programs comes from a young intern at my school. I happened to be chatting with a colleague whose intern was grading papers when my colleague said, "We should ask Roland what color of pen should be used for grading papers."

I quickly realized what was happening and replied, "Please don't tell me they taught you in your education classes that you shouldn't use a red pen to grade student papers because it might be perceived as too hostile or angry by students?" The intern said, "Well, yes, of course."

When valuable teacher training time is spent worrying about what color of pen to use to grade students' papers, is it any wonder that new teachers are unprepared for the *real* challenges they will face in the classroom? Does anyone really believe that the color of pen used on a student's paper is going to be a significant factor in that student's success? Do we really believe the solutions are so trivial and elementary? If new teachers are not honestly told what to expect and given the tools to be successful, it's no wonder so few survive. Another price paid.

Those who do survive their trial by fire often pay a staggering price for the stress that bombards them on a daily basis. It's difficult for "outsiders" to understand how stressful teaching is, because most of us remember school as it was in an earlier time, before the inmates took over the asylum. However, health statistics reveal that teaching is, indeed, dangerous to one's health. According to a large study done with over 130,000 educators in California, teachers had higher than expected rates of breast cancer, ovarian cancer and endometrial cancer.[15] This is validated by my own experience; roughly 20% of the female teachers with whom I have worked in the last seven years have been diagnosed with breast cancer. Mental breakdowns and incapacitating disabilities are not uncommon. Just in my small circle of colleagues there are plenty of examples. I taught with a man who experienced a catatonic episode during class. He stopped functioning in the middle of a lecture, could not speak, and was reduced to a mental stupor. No medical explanation could be found. He believes it was his mind escaping from the torture of the daily stress. A very good friend and colleague for twenty years suffered a brain hemorrhage, coinciding with a highly stressful period in his teaching career. Doctors also failed to find a medical reason for this event.

The field of education is littered with rookie teachers leaving before completing their first year as well as mid-career educators finding it necessary to take an extended leave, all testimony to the damaging affects of the profession.

The breakdown of control in schools across the country has led to increased incidences of physical injury to school employees. Assault of teachers by their students is on the rise. Between 1995 and 1999, teachers were the victims of approximately 1,708,000 nonfatal crimes at school, including 635,000 violent crimes.[16] School employees who have been punched, kicked, slapped, pushed, and attacked with makeshift weapons are far too commonplace. Aggressive, intimidating, and confrontational student behavior is seen with greater frequency. We once would have dismissed the angry threats of a disgruntled student, thinking it was just normal teenage overreaction. Teachers today know better. A student who had flunked his class threatened a colleague's son, who was a first year teacher. The student claimed he was going to, "get a gun and shoot him." In the wake of Columbine, the threat was taken seriously and the police suggested that the teacher disappear for the last week of school. This young teacher was literally forced to go into hiding, his location known only to my colleague and his wife. Welcome to teaching!

When school violence erupts, a teacher is often among the victims, sometimes the target, sometimes just a casualty of a system that has lost control. They pay the ultimate price.

For those of us who spend our days in schools, each new horror story about a school shooting has altered forever the way we look at the young people in our classrooms. Could that sullen young man be the next student who goes on a rampage because I imposed a consequence for being tardy? Is the look of alienation and anger in that student's eyes the normal angst of a teenager who doesn't quite fit in, or could he be the next student to take revenge on everyone who has ever made him feel bad? Who pays the price when teachers begin to look at their students as potential killers?

Families Pay

As damaging as this redistribution of power has been to schools, its effects are even more catastrophic in families. The self-esteem propaganda machine has cast its spell on today's parents, leaving them powerless and ineffectual. Unfortunately for children, home and school are their world, so they pay double the price. Parents have been made to feel that the tools once available to their own parents are no longer acceptable. In today's positive parenting culture, parents worry about how their parenting behavior will be judged by others. The fear of child abuse lingers over any aggressive disciplinary action. Savvy children have even resorted to threatening their parents with calling child protective services when parents impose consequences. Punishment involving physical labor, a standby of previous generations of parents, is now considered inappropriate and, potentially damaging to the child's esteem. Preschool children can be heard telling their parents, "You can't make me." They're often right, because the positive parenting crowd views making your child do something as a Gestapo-like tactic that is certain to cause irreversible trauma to the child's fragile self-esteem. No harsh language, no demands, no raised voices, no decisions made without the child's input, on and on, the same rhetoric.

Every parent has experienced that uncomfortable moment when your parenting skills are on display for the whole world to judge. At the grocery store, your child begins to make a fuss over the new cereal he wants for the prize it contains. You are certain that every other shopper in the aisle is just waiting to see how you will respond to this opening volley. You quickly set your goal—just avoid an embarrassing scene. If you can just keep the kid quiet until you get out of the store, then your parental face can be saved. You tell your child "We have plenty of cereal at home." Good move, firm but positive. But since your child long ago learned her parent badgering tricks from Bart Simpson, she continues to escalate her demanding behavior until you are eventually battered into submission. Just before she breaks into a full-blown tantrum, with the attention of shoppers from four aisles down now riveted on your ineptitude, you concede, "Okay, but just one box."

Our need to be seen as a good parent is so powerful that we lose sight of the greater objective—The Big Five. We forget to ask ourselves the most important questions, "What will my child learn from this? And is that a lesson that will be beneficial in the long run?" In the episode recounted above the child learns that she can manipulate and control her parent by being demanding and persistent. She learns that her parent makes different decisions depending on who is watching. She learns that her parent is so afraid of appearing to be a negative parent that she gives up her power to her child. She learns that her parent is chicken.

The pervasiveness of the positive parenting philosophy creates even greater pressure for those chicken parents. The small amount of assertiveness required to deal with the tantrum is too risky a venture. It becomes more important to present a phony positive front than to suffer the temporary embarrassment of a public family spat. Thus begins the loss of power and control in the family.

Although the loss of authority and control in schools carries substantial consequences, the risks are even more serious for families. The individual teacher's time with a student varies from 45 to 80 minutes a day in middle and high school to six hours a day in elementary school. Students rarely have the same teacher for more than a year. In secondary schools, exposure is often limited to a quarter or semester. Parents, however, have a lifetime investment in their children. Decisions made in a child's early development will have repercussions, positive or negative, for years to come. Parents, therefore, have much more to lose by abdicating their responsibility and authority in the name of being positive and protecting their child's self-esteem.

If you lose the small battle in the store with your three-year-old, how do you expect to fare when that child is fourteen years old and a foot taller than you? The character of the relationship between a parent and a child is established early in development. Long before a child reaches school age, he has conducted an ongoing series of experiments to determine how each of his parents will react in a variety of situations. He learns that if he keeps bugging him long enough, Dad will always cave in when other people are watching. If he asks Mom for something when she's getting ready for work, she'll usually say yes. Dad finds it tough to enforce a consequence when his "little princess" looks at him with those big eyes filled with tears; awfully crafty for a six-year-old kid. They learn fast and they learn well. As they get older, their manipulation skills increase, the games become more complex, and the stakes get higher. Allowing a five-year-old to get away with throwing a tantrum in the grocery store because she doesn't get the candy she wants may not seem too serious. By the time that same child reaches fifteen, her tantrum might involve sneaking out to a party and getting drunk or high; it may involve unprotected sex with the "bad boy" that she knows you don't approve of. As the saying goes, "There's no free lunch." At some point, children need to have rules and they need to learn that there are consequences when those rules aren't followed. You can either pay the price when your child is young, by doing the sometimes difficult, seldom positive work, of teaching your child this valuable lesson, or both you and your child can pay the price of your being chicken.

An astonishing number of parents are at the breaking point, unable to control their preteens or teens. I remember an eighth grade student who simply refused to attend school. When asked by the school counselor why the student wasn't attending school, his mother, an intelligent, professional woman, said, "I can't *make* him go to school." I remember being perplexed. What did she mean she couldn't make him go to school? Why didn't she just push him out of bed in the morning? Why didn't she dump a bucket of cold water on his head each morning he refused to get out of bed? Why didn't she systematically begin taking away his privileges and luxuries as the days absent stretched into weeks? Why couldn't this mother come up with a better solution than simply allowing this fourteen-year-old to do exactly as he pleased, regardless of the impact of his behavior on his future? After fourteen years, patterns of behavior had been established and his mother had lost control years ago. She felt helpless in this situation and her son knew it. The cute toddler who had once snuggled on her lap had grown into a massive teen, fully capable of using his superior strength to intimidate her. In fact, he had hit her once and she knew he would do it again if she tried to assert her parental authority. So, she conceded. He continued to miss school, failed his eighth grade year, and, to my knowledge, never graduated from high school.

Unfortunately, this story is played out in countless families around the country. It happens in single parent and intact families, in wealthy suburban families and in poor, urban families. Parents become paralyzed by the very parenting strategies that they so enthusiastically supported. No parent walks out of the hospital with their newborn in their arms thinking, "I want my child to grow up to be a juvenile delinquent, or a drug addict, or a teen parent." Most parents want the very best for their child. Unfortunately, when a child's day-to-day experiences fail to gradually teach him the skills he needs to control his emotions, to follow guidelines and expectations, and to treat others with respect, parents' dreams for their child are unlikely to come true. By the time they realize the consequences of their chicken parenting, it's often too late. The critical early childhood years, when a parent's influence is so easily wielded, have been wasted. The opportunity to take advantage of a young child's innate desire to please her parents to shape desired behavior has passed. Any effort the parent makes in the preteen or teen years to gain control will be far more difficult, much more unpleasant, and considerably less likely to produce success. So what do many parents do? They deny, they rationalize, they gradually retreat into their parenting bunker. Uncivilized behavior and rampant disrespect flourish. Foul language and poor manners go unchallenged. Chores go undone, schoolwork uncompleted, and curfews disregarded.

If you put a frog into a pot of cold water and slowly bring the water to a boil, the frog will stay contentedly in the pot until it dies. If you drop a frog into a pot of boiling water, he will struggle to get out. The gradual acceptance of inappropriate behavior from children works in a similar way. The slow unfolding of a child's increasingly disrespectful or disobedient behavior lulls the parent into thinking that today's behavior is just a little bit worse than yesterday's behavior. However, if you had asked such a parent five years ago if it was okay for a thirteen-year-old to call his mother a f.....ing whore, she would have answered with a resounding, "No." But, when he was nine, he got away with calling her a dummy. When he was ten, he told her to shut up. When he was eleven, he slammed the door in her face. When he was twelve, he got mad and called her a bitch. By the time he was thirteen, being called a f....ing whore didn't really seem all that bad. Parents tell themselves that this out of control behavior is just a teenage phase, that "boys will be boys" or "it's so hard being a teenage girl these days."

Poorly behaved children exert an influence on all aspects of family life. When parents lose control, families pay a huge price. Ongoing conflict between a parent and a child has a ripple effect throughout the family. Marriages are strained as parents blame each other, a strategy often used by the manipulative child. Seeing the amount of attention that their misbehaving brother or sister is getting from their parents, siblings quickly learn the rules of the game.

Parents rearrange their schedule so that they can go shopping when the kids are in school because they can't control their child's behavior in a public place. Grandparents or other relatives are suddenly "busy" when asked to baby-sit. One mother I knew couldn't leave her fifteen and seventeen year old children at home together because they would routinely get in fights and either hurt each other or damage something in her house. She actually changed her work schedule so that she could be home after school to play referee for these two teenagers. Do you have friends that you have purposely pulled away from because you couldn't stand to be around their kids? Are there families that you hesitate to invite to your home because of their unruly children? What a sad price to pay.

These parents may find it hard to believe that they are to blame for their children's poor behavior. After all, they did all the right things! They were very conscientious about building their child's self-esteem! They were their child's best friend. They kept the lines of communication open—their child could tell them *anything*, even if what the child chose to share was disrespectful, mean or inappropriate. They used lots of praise and studiously avoided being negative or saying no.

Unwilling to look in the mirror, parents inevitably find someone else to blame—the school, teachers, television, rap music, those other kids, etc. They may rationalize their child's behavior by finding examples of other children who are even more out of control than theirs. All because they were too chicken to forcefully assert themselves early in their child's development; to take on the adult responsibility of setting and enforcing guidelines; of teaching their child that behavior has consequences. They continue to pay a great price.

One of the saddest prices paid in families where children's behavior is allowed to run rampant is that eventually the parents often find themselves not liking their children. Sure, they *love* their children, but they don't *like* them. In their misguided attempt to be chronically positive, to be their child's buddy, or to raise the perfect child, they rob their children of one of the most valuable gifts they can possibly bestow; parents who delight in their child, who want to spend time with their child, who truly *like* their child as a human being.

The final irony of the cult of self-esteem is that the message we send our children is shockingly inconsistent with the kind of adults we hope to develop. Our goal is to develop young people who are confident in their actions, competent in their performance, satisfied with themselves, and independent in life. But what we tell them through action and words is just the opposite. When we praise too often and reward too soon, we allow them to avoid paying the price for excellence, and, by doing so, we show a lack of confidence in their abilities. When we protect children from the bad feelings that are a normal part of life, the real message we are sending is that we don't truly believe they are capable of coping. When we falsely design success for children, we are telling them that they are not really capable of excellence. When we orchestrate activities so that our child can be the center of attention, we demonstrate that their success is dependent on our involvement. If we are afraid to have our children push themselves to the limits of their talents and experience failure, then we prove to them that we don't love them enough to risk bad feelings, suffering, and pain. Every time we save our child from the natural consequences of life, we are telling him we don't have faith in him; we don't see how he can possibly ever grow up to be a competent, confident, responsible adult. The price we never expected.

CHAPTER 6: FEAR ITSELF

With the price tag so high for adults' failure to take responsibility for guiding children to healthy adulthood, we need to ask ourselves why. Why do parents find it so difficult to control their kids and schools their pupils? It really shouldn't be this way. Adults are bigger, stronger, and smarter. Parents control the money and other resources; they have veto power over most of the decisions in a child's environment. Teachers have the power to assign grades. Their decisions can impact a student's ability to play on sports teams or participate in other school activities. They can influence older students' futures through recommendations for college.

So what's the problem? Why do these powerful adults so often find themselves at the mercy of children? The problem lies in a society drowning in fear; a fear that has left far too many adults paralyzed, confused, and emasculated. We flounder in a sea of philosophical uncertainty, stripped of the confidence and conviction required to successfully guide young people to adulthood. We are unsure and confused. We are afraid. How did we get to be such weenies?

Failure

First of all, we are afraid we won't do it right. The experts convinced us that our experience and instincts were untrustworthy, that parenting was a complicated, treacherous journey that required their guidance at every turn. This constant brainwashing twisted our reality and drove us to question our every decision. Are we doing the right thing? Are we being too assertive? Are we being too tough? Are we being abusive? Are we damaging children's delicate self-esteem?

Fear paralyzes us and inhibits our natural reaction to situations, crippling our ability to make sound, appropriate and timely parenting decisions. It makes us second-guess the common sense solutions that we may have experienced in our own childhood. We are so enmeshed in finding the "right" solution that we often hesitate until it is too late, the *maximum opportunity moment* gone.

The pervasiveness of this fear really hit home for me during a conversation with a very good friend. I have known John since elementary school and I hold him in the highest regard. I truly admire and respect what he has accomplished. He is a very powerful man, a sought after high tech executive whose career has advanced at a rapid pace, due to his extraordinary intelligence, confidence, emotional intelligence and leadership abilities. His success can be measured both in his wealth and his family, a beautiful, intelligent wife and two children. One night he approached me with some reluctance, obviously not used to being in such a vulnerable position. He had just talked to his wife, who had finally put the kids to bed, after becoming totally frustrated with their antics. She was fed up. Irritated with the increasing inability of he and his wife to deal with their children, John began pumping me for solutions to his dilemma. Being the high-powered, solution-oriented person he is, it was clear to me that he believed there was some almighty answer to his dilemma that, once discovered, could solve the problem and get his family back on track. After probing for some more details, I led him to his own discovery. It was clear to me that John knew the solution to his problem, but he lacked the confidence to even suggest it in front of me. When I finally got him to articulate how he *really* thought the situation should be handled, he admitted that he wanted to take care of the situation the "old fashioned way," but he didn't think that was acceptable. He clearly feared he would sound like a mean parent in front of a man who works with kids for a living.

I reminded John of his own childhood, growing up with a police officer father who personified the parenting practices of that era. I said to him, "Remember how your father handled situations like this?" With a smirk, he described the firmness with which he was raised. When I asked him if his father's old fashioned, tough approach had been a bad thing, John quickly answered, "No." He went on to say that he believed that the combination of fear and respect he had for his father had been instrumental in making him the successful man he was today. Given the fact that he felt his father's parenting practices were so effective, I didn't even need to ask him why he had so readily given them up and adopted such a wimpy parenting approach. He had already come to that conclusion on his own. All he really needed was the affirmation, from someone whose opinion he trusted, that those old fashioned, politically incorrect techniques were okay to use. The unsettling thing about this conversation was how this very confident and powerful man felt he needed to be given permission to do what he knew was right. He knew he had to be the bad guy at times, using methods that seem to have become extinct with our parents' generation. He realized, that, if he wanted his kids to grow up to be the kind of adults he wanted them to be, he needed to trust his instincts and tame his fear. In order to prevent problems in the future, he needed to act swiftly and decisively now. These are lessons he had learned long ago in his professional life and practiced on a daily basis, with routinely successful results. We talked a few more minutes, discussing specific things he might try. But, knowing that he could rely on his common sense, intuition and the practices he had observed in his own family, he was well on his way to being the kind of father he knew he could, and should, be.

Like so many parents, the experts had led John astray. Previous generations learned how to parent in a natural way, by observing their own parents' child rearing practices, as well as through exposure to the parenting techniques used by other relatives and friends. The professionalization of child rearing in today's culture has distorted this natural process and produced a generation of parents who spend more time thinking about and worrying about parenting than they actually spend nurturing, guiding, and enjoying their children. The result is parents who are *afraid* to parent.

Damaging Our Kids

Convinced by the self-proclaimed authorities that our parent's child rearing methods were archaic and destructive, we have become willing disciples, discarding those antiquated and ineffective techniques to adopt the new, enlightened trends. We were quickly indoctrinated into a parenting philosophy that viewed positive self-esteem as both the end goal and the pathway to healthy child development. With "feeling good about themselves" as the new mantra, parenting and teaching practices were revised to accomplish this new goal.

Among the myths perpetuated by the experts' focus on positive parenting is the view that children are delicate, fragile creatures whose healthy development can be compromised at any moment by the uninformed decisions of their parents. Parents' every word and gesture has the potential to permanently influence children's progress, for good or for bad. Each moment with the child is fraught with the possibility of irrevocable scarring if we make the wrong choice, if we use the wrong words. Without the constant vigilance of adults to shield them from the big, bad world where life is not always happy and positive, children will crumble. Given the countless decisions made by parents and teachers in any given day, the potential for disaster quickly becomes overwhelming. With this degree of pressure, it's no wonder that so many adults end up deciding that it's far safer to abdicate responsibility; to avoid making decisions; to pick the safe, easy, pleasant pathway. However, this fear is not supported by the facts of child development. In fact, children are remarkably resilient creatures. Throughout history, in all kinds of cultures, children have survived and thrived in spite of exposure to conditions far more difficult than those facing most American children today.

However, today's parents are afraid to let their children's development run its natural course. With little faith in their child's capability and an abundance of arrogance about their own influence, they are afraid to give up their role as protector; they are afraid to let their child learn life's valuable lessons the hard, but effective, way. As a result, parents consider it their duty to shield children from negative experiences and feelings. The slightest hint of discomfort or pain brings parents racing to the rescue. Difficult tasks that might create frustration are eliminated or diluted. Standards and expectations that previous generations had successfully reached are lowered to ensure that all children can reach them, thus eliminating any feelings of struggle or "different-ness." The firm discipline that had been successfully employed by generations of parents is dismissed in favor of interactions that are positive and make the child feel good about his or herself. Even the word "discipline" itself has been banished due to its incorrect association with punishment. In fact, the root of the word is "disciple," meaning "to teach."

Too many parents believe that socializing a child to healthy adulthood can occur without frustration, anger, disappointment, sadness, or conflict. They have swallowed the myth that a good family is one in which everyone is perpetually happy and interactions are always positive. When they are faced with the inevitable reality that negative emotions and conflicts are a normal and natural part of the human condition, particularly for young people who have not yet acquired the social and emotional skills of mature adulthood, fear creeps in and common sense and resolve fly out the window.

Giving Up

While some parents respond to their fears by attempting to structure their child's existence to avoid pain, frustration, discomfort, sadness, and struggle (a task that could not be accomplished even if it were desirable); other parents are so overwhelmed by the scope of this responsibility that they become paralyzed. With every parenting decision carrying so much power to impact their child, they simply give up and adopt a laissez fair approach.

This parental fear has far-reaching and devastating conse-quences—for families, for children and for society. From the disappearance of common decency and civility to horrendous crimes being committed by younger and younger children, the effects of parents' failure to set clear guidelines and expectations can be seen in all types of communities across America. Baby Boomer parents, whose own teen years may have been influenced by the "whatever feels good" culture of the sixties, are afraid to set guidelines for their children around alcohol and other drug use. They are terrified that, if they do so, their child might ask, "But Mom, did you ever smoke marijuana?" and they won't know how to reconcile their own youthful behavior with the behavior they want for their child.

The same parental paralysis seems to occur with respect to teen sexual behavior. Parents who spent their own teenage years in the pre-AIDS, free love, sixties and seventies are reluctant to try to influence their teen's sexual decisions. They may ensure that their children have adequate *information* about sex, but they shrink from drawing a line in the sand about what is and what isn't acceptable behavior. Despite overwhelming evidence to the contrary, they are afraid that their influence can't compete with the influence of their child's peers or the media. So they say nothing. They do nothing. They cross their fingers and hope that their children make the right decisions. But why should they? If their parents don't have the guts to set guidelines for them, why not just go with what feels good, what's easy, what's cool?

Despite a steady decline in the last several decades, teen pregnancy remains a serious problem, with consequences that reverberate throughout society and negatively impact generations to come. However, when we look more closely at the problem of teen pregnancy, we find that the problem has its roots not in the behavior of teenage girls, but in the behavior of adults. Eighty percent of the teenage girls who become pregnant are impregnated by an adult male, who is, on average, six years older.[17] That means when you hear about a thirteen-year-old girl getting pregnant, the father is likely to be a nineteen year old man; for a sixteen-year-old girl, the father is likely to be a twenty-two-year-old man. So, the problem of teen pregnancy is not one of teenage boys and girls having sex and getting pregnant. The problem is one of adult males using all the advantages of their age and power to lure young girls into a sexual relationship.

The other culprits in this situation are the parents of these young girls. What are they thinking? Do they believe that a grown man is looking for love and companionship from a sixteen-year-old girl? Wake up and smell the roses! Are they giving their blessing to their daughter's relationship with a grown man? Are they unaware of the potential danger and the negative impacts of a relationship in which the balance of power is so skewed? Or are parents aware but simply unwilling to step in and do their job? Are they afraid of sounding like the parent they once cursed in their own teenage years? Are they afraid that their daughters will hate them? Whatever the reason, it's not good enough. A teenage girl dating a grown man is a disaster waiting to happen.

Jackie was a very popular and attractive ninth grade girl. One day as I looked out my classroom window I saw her standing alone. She appeared to be crying. As I approached her she quickly wiped away the tears that rolled down her face and insisted that nothing was wrong. After some probing, I got her to tell me her story. Jackie, who had just turned fourteen, was in a relationship with a senior at the local high school. He was a popular athlete and, at first, she had been flattered by his attention. However, things had been getting progressively more serious (surprise!) and Jackie found herself in over her head. She tried to end the relationship nicely, but the boy refused to accept it. He started stalking her, calling her at home, following her around town, and sitting outside her house in his car. After enduring this for a while, she made the decision to confront him and try to convince him to accept the fact that it was over. She agreed to meet him after school. After hearing Jackie's insistence that she didn't want to see him any more, the boy attempted suicide in front of her. He was unsuccessful and was taken to the hospital, leaving Jackie shaken and confused.

At this point in her story, I asked what her parents' response had been and what they had done to help her get out of this unwanted and unhealthy relationship. She told me they hadn't really gotten involved except to arrange for her to see a therapist after the boy's suicide attempt. I then asked what the therapist had suggested. In a somewhat disgusted tone, Jackie told me that the therapist just kept asking her what *she* thought should happen. I couldn't help but feel that the entire adult population surrounding this girl had failed her. Her final poignant comment summarized the failings of the adults on whom she had counted, "I just want to be a regular fourteen-year-old. Why doesn't someone *help* me instead of expecting me to solve these big problems myself? I'm just a kid." Jackie was right. She shouldn't have had to deal with this situation. The adults should have stopped this tragedy-in-the-making before it got started. Jackie longed for someone to tell her what to do. She was clearly over her head and needed an adult to step in. The seriousness of the situation was overwhelming and the guilt she felt for not being able to handle it ran deep. Unfortunately, Jackie was surrounded by chicken adults.

How might Jackie's life been different if her parents had stepped up to the plate and told their barely fourteen-year-old daughter that she couldn't date an eighteen-year-old man? Did their fear of saying no to their daughter overpower their common sense? Did appeasing the flattered ego of a young girl take precedence over making sensible decisions to keep her safe and protected?

This reluctance to take a stand on certain issues is a serious problem for Baby Boomer parents. Do you allow your underage child to drink in your home? Do you feel it's better that your child drinks under your supervision than to be off somewhere else drinking? Do you just accept the fact that your teen will experiment with alcohol and cigarettes, breathing a sigh of relief because, after all, at least it's just alcohol, not drugs? Do you let your child spend the night with a boyfriend/girlfriend in your home? Do you let your child smoke at home, despite the fact that it is illegal for minors to be in possession of tobacco? Do you allow your daughter to date a man six years her senior? Have you given up on your ability to influence your teenager's behavior? What absolutes do you have?

Feelings of hopelessness can also fan the fires of parental fears. Although most parents are reasonably confident in the degree of influence they have over their toddler and preschool children, as children enter the school-age years and move toward adolescence, parental confidence wanes. Parents fear the power of the media to shape their child's attitudes, beliefs, and behavior. They cringe at the vulgar speech, sexual overtones, and violent behavior that permeate so much of the music, television, video games, and movies to which young people are attracted. And yet, they let their fears prevent them from setting standards and guidelines for their children. They fear that such guidelines will make them seem un-cool.

Unwillingness to set and enforce guidelines and expectations is a direct retreat from parental responsibilities. The refusal of parents to accept their responsibility to guide and shape their children's behavior through clear, non-negotiable expectations has created a generation of kids who are insecure and unsure of where their boundaries lie. How can our kids be strong and sure, if we are not? How can we expect them to make sound decisions if we waiver at the slightest challenge? How can they do the right thing if we are afraid to set the example? How can they choose the correct path if we are still standing at the crossroads undecided? Our children are being crippled by our own indecisiveness. The longer we shun our duties, the more they suffer. Children need adults in their lives. They need adults who are willing to stand up and be the grown-ups; adults who are willing to make tough choices, to take a stand and not back down, to set the boundaries against which children can push and test themselves.

Teens need parents who will ask invasive questions when they suspect possible problems. They need parents who insist on knowing where they are and with whom they spend time. They need parents who pay attention to the subtle changes in their behavior. Are you waiting up for your child when he returns from an evening out? When your teen is going to a friend's home, do you call the parents to make sure there will be adult supervision? Are you afraid this type of investigation will show distrust? Are you fearful of the potential confrontations? Are you worried that your child will think you're not a cool parent? Are you willing to sacrifice your child's health and safety?

Buddies

In order for us to intellectually handle this chicken approach to parenting, we may choose to camouflage our irresponsibility under a blanket of parent/child friendship. If we're too afraid to be their parent, why not be their buddy? Why not be the cool mom or dad? We welcome this role because it fits our Baby Boomer mentality. Convinced that we're certainly not the old fogies that our parents were, abdicating our parent status to become one of the kids allows us to continue our Peter Pan existence. We get all kinds of compliments from our kids' friends ("Your mom is so cool to let you have parties at your house when she's not home!"), which feeds our needy egos. We are cool and hip. We feel young again. We might even be satisfying some unfulfilled need from our own adolescence. We are making up for lost time and opportunity. Of course we reassure ourselves that this kind of "parent and child as best friends" relationship is really much healthier for children. It will improve communication because we will be so much more approachable than our stodgy, authoritarian parents. Unfortunately, we've got the equation all wrong. Our kids don't need us to be their best friend. There are a lot of other children out there who can play the role of best friend to our children. They need us to be *parents*. We're the only ones they've got.

Jim arrived at Sunday morning basketball, moaning and groaning and looking more rumpled than the eight a.m. starting time could explain. When I asked about the source of his obvious discomfort, he explained that he had gotten very little sleep the night before because his girlfriend's daughter had a seventeenth birthday party at their house. He began to describe what was involved in this high school girl's birthday bash. Twelve teenagers had been invited, with boys outnumbering the girls. Their rural property included a large barn-like building that had been transformed for the party, with areas set up for dancing and eating. Jim had been asked to help with food preparation and general party needs. The party was an all-nighter, with all the kids expecting to sleep overnight in the barn together. Being a cool, hip mom, Jim's girlfriend had promised to limit her visits to the barn, so as not to interrupt their festivities. She had also agreed to provide ample amounts of beer for the teens, confident that she had done her duty as a responsible parent by requiring the teens to surrender the car keys to her when they arrived.

As the party moved into the early hours of the next morning, Jim's role changed. With most of the beer consumed, Jim found himself nursing the intoxicated teens as they vomited repeatedly in the barn, in the yard, and throughout his house. As soon as he finished cleaning up after one guest, he would quickly find another one retching violently and looking for solace. This went on all night, explaining his total lack of sleep.

At the end of Jim's story I was so profoundly appalled that the only response I could muster was to ask a question that would illuminate the incredible stupidity of this event; "Does the word *litigation* mean anything to you?" I proceeded to rattle off multiple scenarios that could easily have taken place—kids hurting themselves or each other, or the many other natural by-products of the disastrous combination of teenagers, beer, and co-ed sleeping arrangements. I explained to Jim, who has no children of his own, that the laws pertaining to adults supplying alcohol to underage drinkers are very clear; he and his girlfriend could be held liable for anything that happened as a result of those kids' drinking.

A little embarrassed at his own participation in this totally irresponsible fiasco, Jim tried to salvage some of his personal pride by reiterating that all car keys had been surrendered. Good, they had eliminated one problem out of potentially thousands they had created. I then asked how his girlfriend had gotten permission from the guests' parents for an overnight beer blast. Jim sheepishly informed me that she had not. Most of the parents didn't know beer would be provided and many of the kids had lied to their parents about the sleeping arrangements. The potential repercussions were endless, both legal and personal.

So why would this mother, a well-educated, intelligent professional woman, plan such an event? What could possibly be gained? The answer's not hard to divine in this case. She would surely win the award for the coolest mom in the world. She would be so hip no other parent could possibly measure up. She would be the greatest best friend a daughter could have.

This woman risked everything. All of her belongings and wealth, the physical well-being of each child, the trust and respect of the guests' parents, her reputation in the community, Jim's respect for her as a parent; all to be the cool mom.

I Hate You

Unfortunately these kinds of stories are far too frequent. Chicken parents have a whole host of reasons why they refuse to be the grown-ups in their families. A variation on the, "I want to be my child's best friend," theme is the parent who cowers at the threat of an, "I hate you," escaping from his child's lips.

Children of all ages gain control by playing on their parents' fear of being unloved. From the four year old who says, "I hate you!" to the teen who grumbles, "You suck!" many parents crumble under these declarations. Rather than seeing these outbursts as either a young child's temporary tantrum or an older child's skillful manipulation, we allow our most immature and insecure self to respond, caving in to the fear that we will lose our child's love forever if we make him unhappy, angry, or frustrated. Previous generations of parents would be appalled at the degree to which today's parents submit to their children's blackmail techniques simply because they want so much to be liked by their children.

Best Kids

Personal insecurity and lack of confidence drive many unproductive parent behaviors. In a warped attempt to replay their own childhood with the hope of more successful outcomes, some parent behaviors are really a way to mask their fear that their child will not measure up. In our highly competitive culture, having the best kid is as important as having the best house, the best car, or the best job.

Our child's success, or failure, becomes a powerful extension of our own self-worth. Over-involvement in a child's schoolwork, athletic pursuits or other activities is often an attempt to ensure that our child doesn't fail, because his failure is our failure. Our stake in our children's success is often far too great and far too personal. We help them with their homework because it's important for them to get good grades and be successful in school. I can't tell you how many student projects I've seen over the years that were clearly done almost exclusively by the child's parent. After all, how would *we* look if they failed in school? We force them into sports, squeezing every ounce of fun out of the activity until it resembles junior boot camp, because, after all, if they're going to be a star, they have to start training early. We schedule every hour of every day with activities and lessons so they can be the best kid on the block. If our child isn't the most popular kid in class, we buy friends for them by making sure that our house has the coolest video games, the best toys, and a never-ending supply of junk food. Not content with our child being the best in a group of average kids, we put them on select teams and in elite academic programs. Under the guise of giving our child the best possible chances for success, we feed our own need for approval and status and attempt to banish the fear that our children will not be as good as the others. In the end, if they aren't the best kids, then we aren't the best parents. We fear our own shortcomings. So we push them even harder.

Sacrifice

One fear that is difficult for most parents to admit, but that shows itself clearly in their behavior, is the fear that being a grown-up parent is just too much effort. Sacrifice, a word that conveyed a noble and worthy effort to previous generations of parents, is a dirty word to many of today's parents. Sacrifice means that we don't get our needs met and, to a generation brought up to believe that our needs are paramount, the concept is as foreign as it is distasteful. We are unwilling to adjust our lifestyles or postpone personal goals for the betterment of the family. We allow our jobs to command more of our time than our kids. We justify missing our children's activities or dinners together as a family by telling ourselves that we need to work hard because it costs a lot to raise a child these days; or that it's important for us to have a fulfilling career because "a happy parent is a better parent." We are afraid of the sacrifice it would require to actually have the family life that we visualize in our heads. So, we rationalize our fears away. We cling to the myth that we can have it all. After all, the experts told us we could! We fear the pain and hard work involved in doing the job right. We fear the loss of status and income we might suffer if we made career decisions with our children's needs in mind. We continue to replace activities, lessons, and material things for time we should be spending with our kids. We soothe our enormous guilt by buying our kids things and hiring surrogates to take on the time-consuming, mundane aspects of parenting. Nannies and babysitters fill our child's days with classes and lessons, sports and activities, so that we don't have to be distracted from our "real" job. The beauty of this approach is that, when something goes wrong, it won't be our fault. There are plenty of other people to blame.

This chicken attitude by so many parents has resulted in other painful repercussions. The number of teens referred for professional help has increased. Once virtually unheard of, parents are sending their children and teens to counselors, therapists, psychiatrists, and psychologists in record numbers. Problems that were once handled at home are now dealt with by "specialists." In our professionalization of child rearing, we have created diagnoses and labels for behavior resulting from poor parenting. There are no bad parents, there are simply children who have conduct disorder, or oppositional-defiant disorder, or the ubiquitous attention deficit hyperactivity disorder. Parents seem unwilling to sacrifice the time or energy required to set guidelines for their children, follow up to see if those guidelines are being met, then either reinforce children when guidelines are met or follow up on consequences when they aren't met. Then they turn to the experts when their kids get into trouble. The reluctance to get involved with the dirty work of parenting is providing a very lucrative living for the expert community.

The drive-through parenting approach is a perfect fit for today's parents. Rather than doing the tough work of examining our real values and beliefs and figuring out the best way to ensure that those values and beliefs are the foundation of family life, regardless of the sacrifices that may be required, we take the easy road. We convince ourselves that the quality time we spend is equivalent to the day-to-day experiences that parents and children share only as a result of a considerable *quantity* of time together. We cram parenting into the spare moments of our over scheduled lives. We substitute the difficult job of guiding and shaping our children to responsible adulthood for the much easier, and certainly more fun, role of being our child's best friend. In a nutshell, we avoid growing up. We continue the self-indulgent behavior to which our generation has become accustomed and allow the experts to reinforce our immaturity. We succumb to our fears.

CHICKEN TEACHERS

The best human beings I have ever met are teachers. As a group, they are the most well-balanced and responsible professionals with whom I have ever been associated. They take their responsibilities very seriously, routinely sacrificing time, effort, and their own money for the good of the school and classroom. They care deeply about their students and willingly provide support for their colleagues whenever requested. Their manner is generally kind, patient, and non-confrontational. Having chosen a profession with few opportunities for advancement and paltry compensation, they learn to live without extrinsic rewards and realize that intrinsic rewards may be few and far between. They are nurturing by nature and have the best intentions at heart. Their quest is to continually improve and their goal is perfection. Honesty and integrity are constant companions. They understand the importance and responsibility that accompanies being a role model for their students. Creativity, cleverness, quick wit, and efficiency are tools they use daily. They are laborers who wear more hats in one given day than most people do in an entire career. They are strong, enduring individuals and I truly salute and respect all that they do.

The above-mentioned traits are what make good teachers effective in working with students. However the very characteristics that allow teachers to be successful in their professional lives are also often their Achilles' heel, leaving them easy prey for all aspects of the educational system. Because teachers are nurturing and non-confrontational, they are constantly being asked to sacrifice "for the kids." Teachers routinely accept additional work without pay, because, after all, they can't let the kids down. They obediently swallow the ever-changing policies that usually make their jobs more cumbersome.

Teachers can be powerful, impassioned advocates for their students, but their zeal and commitment flies out the window when it comes to their own needs. Why? The American public has certain expectations of teachers. We expect teachers to be compassionate, nurturing, and self-sacrificing. We expect them to be free from the self-serving need for recognition and respect afforded to other professionals. We expect them to do whatever it takes on behalf of their students. We get what we expect. The profession attracts individuals who are unwilling to rock the boat; individuals whose tentative attempts to assert themselves are easily quelled by the mantra, "Do it for the kids." But filling our schools with teachers who so willingly subjugate their own needs exacts a heavy price. Despite their outward willingness to accept the status quo, teachers pay a price for the relentless stress of working in an environment where they struggle daily against overwhelming challenges. Despite very little control, few resources, and no recognition, they live with the knowledge that their daily interactions with students have the power to influence those children's lives forever. This constant pressure of life-changing responsibility without significant support or control gradually eats away at teachers' physical and emotional health. Demoralized, disenfranchised, powerless teachers are not likely to buck the educational establishment that fails teachers as often as it fails students. They are not likely to fight for the respect and dignity that their profession deserves. They abdicate responsibility for educational policy to distant lawmakers, politicized school boards and educational experts with limited exposure to the realities of today's classrooms. Bombarded with the unrealistic demands of the job, teachers are forced to exhaust their energy on fighting the daily battles they face in their classrooms.

Trapped in a Catch 22, teachers know how to solve many of the persistent problems in schools; but, because of the kinds of people they tend to be, they are the least equipped to fight the necessary battles to ensure that those solutions are adopted. Teachers are crippled by their own caring, giving temperaments. They are afraid to endanger their image and are even more afraid of the actions needed to bring about change. They are chicken—chicken teachers.

Truth

What are teachers afraid of? Teachers are afraid to tell the truth. Whether the truth needs to be told to a student, colleague, administrator, parent, or community member, they are afraid to speak the honest truth. They fear repercussions from parents if they tell them the truth about their child's behavior or academic performance. They fear that they will damage students' precious self-esteem if they speak honestly. They fear the judgment of their colleagues if they speak out against the latest educational fad. They fear a backlash from the school or district administration if they challenge policies. They fear the loss of public support if they assert their demands strongly enough to force change. Their environment breeds compliance because every honest statement produces conflict and increases demands on them. Issues aren't addressed; problems aren't solved. So they go along to get along.

Disrespect

Teachers are afraid that people will think poorly of them. In addition to the inherent personality traits that prevent teachers from speaking honestly and clearly, they are also hampered by a firmly entrenched inferiority complex. Society's message is made clear to teachers every day—teachers are not valued. Of course, few people at any level of society would say they agree with this message. When people find out that I am a teacher, they often say, "Boy, I really admire you. What a tough job that is." Polls routinely report that the American public thinks education should be a high priority. The majority of Americans think teachers should be better compensated. We *say* that we value and respect teachers, but our actions are painfully inconsistent with our words.

Teachers' salaries are lower than almost any other professional with similar training and expertise. Joining teachers at the bottom rung of the compensation ladder are other human service professionals, such as social workers. I wonder what that says about our society? The respect given teachers by all levels of society has been gradually eroding for decades. In other countries, teachers are held in great esteem. Their position in society is one of prestige and honor. A colleague of mine related an incident that occurred on a trip to Mexico to visit a friend who was living there. One night they went out for dinner at the best restaurant in town, where they encountered a long line that signaled a significant wait. His friend, understanding the cultural differences in Mexico, went to the front of the line and informed the hostess that my colleague was a "professor." He and his party were immediately seated. Imagine how far that line would get you in the U.S.!

Over the course of my almost three decades in teaching, I have seen respect for teachers diminish each year. I am appalled at some of the statements made to teachers by students. I think most adults would be shocked at the types of things students feel perfectly comfortable saying to, or in front of, a teacher. The use of profanity in classrooms and hallways is so widespread that schools have thrown up their hands. But it's not just students whose outward disrespect for teachers has mushroomed. Like so many things, the attitudes of students toward their teachers are highly influenced by the attitudes and behavior they witness in their parents. The level of disrespect shown by parents for teachers is sometimes beyond belief. Surrounded by this climate of total lack of respect, it is very easy for teachers to believe that they don't deserve any better.

Confrontation

Teachers are afraid to be confrontational. As pointed out earlier, the prototypical teacher temperament is one that prefers consensus to conflict, possibly because the teaching profession has historically been a female-dominated profession. Few teachers have the stomach for confrontation. In meetings with aggressive or assertive parents, teachers often back down, intimidated by behavior that is so foreign to their professional world. Despite the fact that teachers have a level of job security that is unusual in today's economic climate, teachers are terrified of challenging their superiors, whether a building principal or a district administrator. Students learn early in their school career that most teachers are easily intimidated by assertive or aggressive behavior and many use that knowledge to their benefit. Confronting inappropriate student behavior and telling students the truth can be unsettling and uncomfortable for teachers because they are so focused on keeping students happy and making everyone feel good. With a profession so steeped in a philosophy of nurturing, peacekeeping, and consensus building, it is no surprise that teachers are woefully inadequate when it comes to confronting and following through on tough issues.

There is an interesting game played in the educational world that I like to call, "Who can suffer the most?" In a system that treats all teachers as equals, in terms of compensation, status and recognition, teachers have very few avenues through which they can compete and distinguish themselves. In the absence of legitimate avenues for achieving recognition, many teachers turn to self-sacrifice. Who stays the latest on campus? Who spends the most of their own money on school-related expenses? Who works more hours preparing lessons? Who grades the most papers? Who has the hardest classes? Rather than demanding legitimate avenues for professional advancement and recognition, they settle for martyrdom. To ask for more money would be greedy. It's easier to rationalize that, "We should be willing to sacrifice for the kids." To ask for the supplies they need to do their job would seem gluttonous. Instead they make do, spending their own time and money to make sure that the students don't suffer. To demand lower class sizes would be an admission of failure. After all, shouldn't a *good* teacher be able to handle just one more kid? To ask to be paid for extra hours worked seems arrogant and self absorbed. After all, most teachers didn't get into teaching for the money. Once again, it takes very little guilt-induced prodding to find a teacher who will say, "Sure I'll supervise the Math Club." We are a group of incredibly well intentioned people who suffer by our own hand.

My brother is a firefighter for the Port of Seattle. In that position, he is given the respect of society for the important job he does. As a sign of that respect, voters willingly ensure that he and his colleagues have the most technologically advanced equipment and supplies available to keep them safe and to ensure they can do their job successfully. If the breathing masks used by firefighters were found to be faulty in some way, the public would have no qualms about immediately replacing that equipment. One of my brother's duties is to operate the crash truck in the event of an airplane fire. The cab of this truck is specifically designed to keep the firefighter alive and safe under extreme conditions. The cost of each crash truck is approximately half a million dollars, with four active trucks deployed at the fire station. During his twenty years as a firefighter, these trucks have rarely been used to fight an actual airplane fire resulting from a crash. Yet the voters are willing to support the cost of these little used trucks in case they are needed. We feel this way because lives are at stake and firefighters deserve the best we can provide.

Unfortunately, we seem to forget that, every day, in classrooms across America, millions of children's lives and futures are at stake. Don't America's children deserve the best we can provide? If your child were having brain surgery you would surely insist on the surgeon using the most sophisticated and up-to-date equipment, regardless of the cost. Well, the teachers who work with your child each and every day are, in effect, performing surgery on your child's brain, too, because when your child is learning, her brain is physically changing. Yet, America's teachers are performing this life-changing role in dilapidated buildings, with outdated equipment and a deplorable lack of resources.

Wouldn't it be wonderful if the American public's much-touted concern about schools were turned into the financial support that is required to do the job well? Unfortunately, if we are relying on teachers to demand these changes, our confidence is misplaced. One of my sage colleagues has a saying that crudely, but appropriately, describes how teachers feel when they are once again asked to do more for the kids, but also at their own expense, "Not only do they tell us to bend over, but we have to supply our own Vaseline."

Teachers are afraid to demand the respect their profession deserves. There have been moments in my life as a teacher when I have been almost paralyzed by the absurd inequities and miserable conditions plaguing the profession. Society and the educational establishment count on teachers to continue to roll over and take whatever is dished out. Whether it's having our work responsibilities increased or our benefits decreased, teachers have demonstrated a clear pattern of refusal to maintain a solid front and hold the line until their demands are met. They may speak out initially, but when action is needed in the form of a lengthy strike or bold action, teachers have a history of folding soon and often. Once again, teachers' natural tendency to avoid conflict is the source of the problem. We don't want people upset with us for any reason. If we were to strongly stand up for our demands, students might view us in a poor light; the community would be inconvenienced; our reputation as the caring, nurturing martyrs of society, willing to do anything for the kids, would be tarnished. The notion that teachers are role models for civilized behavior is great, but at what cost? Do we really want our children to aspire to be society's doormats? We may very well be the best group of individuals to serve as role models for America's youth, but why should we have to pay such a heavy price for taking on this role? Shouldn't a position like this be rewarded instead of taken advantage of?

Adding to teachers' belief that their time, talent, and expertise are not valued is the fact that working conditions have gotten consistently worse over the last several decades. Each year more is demanded of teachers, with no commensurate change in compensation. When I started in the profession, my job was to teach my subject matter, covering pretty much the same basic content each year, to pretty much the same types of students. This process allowed teachers to gradually build their experience and expertise, mastering their craft with each passing year. Today's crowded classrooms are filled with such a diversity of student needs that teachers are forced to individualize the curriculum to meet each student's unique needs, exponentially increasing the workload. With curriculums changing every couple of years, teachers are never able to achieve the mastery that comes with teaching the same thing over and over again, refining and improving each year. In addition, each new curriculum requires substantially more of the teacher's time to learn than the few days often provided as professional development. That time, of course, most often comes at the end of the teacher's working day, at the expense of personal and family time. Each new school year brings new technology that teachers are expected to master, usually on their own time. With the high risk student population mushrooming, teachers are increasingly expected to meet the emotional needs of their students, as well as their academic needs. The recent rash of school shootings by alienated students has prompted cries for teachers to connect with each of their students every day, not an easy task for a secondary teacher who sees 150 students each day. In an admirable effort to meet the needs of all students, the number of activities and clubs in schools has expanded. However, each of those activities and clubs requires a teacher, who, if she *is* compensated for this additional work (which is not always the case), is paid at a level far below her hourly rate. How many $40,000/year jobs can you think of where employees are consistently expected to work overtime for no additional compensation, or at a rate less than their normal hourly pay? This and more are the daily reminders to teachers that they are not valued.

Trusting Judgment

Teachers are afraid to trust their own professional judgment. Education has a history of jumping on every bandwagon that comes through town. New educational philosophies and approaches are adopted and discarded constantly. Veteran teachers know that nothing is really new, it is simply an old idea recycled and repackaged. The educational system, however, has an astonishing propensity to disregard evidence of effectiveness, whether that evidence is based on research or on personal experience. We routinely throw out the baby with the bath water, rather than identifying which parts of a specific approach are working well and keeping those components, while improving the areas that are not effective. This constant change for change's sake puts teachers in the position of always being at the beginning of a learning curve and prevents them from ever reaching true mastery of a given curriculum. Having experienced this many times, I can attest to the fact that it often takes several years before an individual teacher feels confident with a new curriculum. In the first several years, we are learning the new material and determining what does and doesn't work with our particular students. Confidence in the program takes time and practice. So, if a new program is being introduced every five years, several years' worth of students are guinea pigs. Once the teacher reaches a level of mastery, he may deliver that curriculum effectively with a couple of year's worth of students, then, bam, the cycle starts all over again. Imagine if the medical profession worked this way; if every few years cardiovascular surgeons were forced to discard everything they knew about bypass surgery technique and learn a completely new way of performing the surgery. Would you want to be the first patient on whom your surgeon tested his or her new technique? Wouldn't you feel more comfortable knowing that your surgeon had performed that particular technique over and over again and gotten really good at it, only changing the technique when there was overwhelming evidence that the new method was superior? We should want the same thing from teachers, the opportunity to achieve mastery with a given curriculum. The current system, however, values innovation over mastery.

This ridiculous process astonishes me. Wouldn't it be much more logical to identify those things that are working well in the current system and replace the ineffective parts only? Wouldn't it be more efficient to start with a program that has merit and reinforce the weak spots? Wouldn't it make more sense to tweak the existing program, keeping the strengths and adding the enrichment? One of the best teachers I have ever known, my son's exemplary first grade teacher, a 20-year veteran, stated it well when she said, "There's nothing new in education. Good teachers try out a number of techniques, keep what works for them and their students, and, over the years, they integrate all of those effective strategies into their own unique teaching practice." Although this is a common sentiment expressed by veteran teachers, those making educational policy decisions clearly fail to see its wisdom.

It amazes me that so many intelligent, educated people can so blindly ignore the facts. There is a large and growing body of research that tells us what works in education. Although new research over the last several decades has added significantly to our understanding of how the developing brain functions and how learning occurs, this new research simply serves to explain *why* the time-tested teaching strategies used by effective teachers for generations work. It *does not* steer us toward radically different strategies for managing student behavior and promoting learning.[18] Research tells us what is effective. Practice shows us it works. But we continue to choose to ignore it. We are afraid to do what is right for ourselves and for the good of our students.

Independent

Teachers are afraid to act. Being an independent thinker, asserting those thoughts, and acting them out are not well accepted in the educational world. In the typical school environment, where teamwork and collaboration are the mantra, teachers who rock the boat generally find themselves overboard. As one of my colleagues says, "You're either on the train or on the tracks." Conformity is rewarded in education; independence is squelched. I learned this lesson well during my first year teaching high school. I was teaching mostly math classes but also wanted to teach a senior health class, my area of expertise. I got my opportunity the next year. I was summoned to a meeting with the other health teachers. Having heard a considerable amount of negative feedback from students about the way health was taught by these other teachers, I proceeded to explain to my colleagues how I would teach the class. It's important to note that, of the three health teachers, I was the only one whose degree was actually in health. I had also taught health successfully at the junior high for nineteen years. I was told in no uncertain terms that I would teach the material as it had been taught for years. Needless to say, I ignored the decree and proceeded to teach the class for many years with resounding success. However, my two colleagues have not spoken to me since.

One of today's most pervasive educational philosophies is "team-building." Patterned after similar approaches in the business world, the goal is to have all departments and disciplines working together as one unit. Unfortunately, like so many fads adopted wholesale by the educational system, there is too little attention paid to whether this process actually leads to better teaching and better learning. Whether by students or by staff, teaming in schools is fraught with the same problems that have been found in the workplace. Ask any good student how he feels about working in teams and he will quickly tell you the problem: the good students on the team end up doing all of the work. Those students who would be unlikely to do their work in an individually-based classroom are just as unlikely, if not more so, to do it in a team-based situation. It's a lot easier to hide in a group. The other innate problem with the education system's total buy-in to a team-based approach is that it ignores the fact that teachers and learners are all different, with diverse teaching and learning preferences. In other words, when teamwork becomes the accepted norm, individuality is often the victim. A team approach to teaching requires ongoing consensus. This may work well for some teachers. However, most of us have experienced wonderful teachers whose unique approach, though unconventional, was highly effective. Some teachers work best solo, just as some students work better alone than in groups. To deny this individuality is to contradict the vast body of research on multiple intelligences and diverse learning styles. The best measure of a teacher's effectiveness is *not* how well they work in a team or whether or not they use the same teaching strategies as their peers. The best measure of a teacher's effectiveness is how well their students learn. There are as many ways to produce good learning as there are teachers and students. Unfortunately, today's consensus-based dogma makes it difficult for the maverick teacher. Those who play fair, who go along with the group, who are willing to compromise their individuality for the sake of the team, are rewarded. The "art" of teaching disappears, because art requires creativity and individuality. Great works of art are not created by consensus.

Taking Responsibility

Teachers are afraid to make decisions. In the educational world, the buck stops nowhere. Everyone from the custodians to the superintendent skillfully shakes off responsibility. Just as with the students, it's always somebody else's problem or somebody else's fault. This occurs because the system, itself, is dysfunctional. The never-ending finger pointing follows a cyclical pathway, with teachers blaming parents, parents blaming the school, the school blaming "the system," which is made up of the teachers—right back to the beginning. Because of this cyclical process, teachers become discouraged trying to make meaningful changes. I have been involved in numerous attempts to address a variety of problems, everything from changing district curriculums to redesigning rules for assemblies. It didn't take me too long to realize that these efforts never result in substantive change because nobody really has the power to make changes. The reason nobody has the power to make changes is that, in order to exercise power, you have to be willing to take responsibility for your decisions. In the dysfunctional school system no one is willing to take responsibility for decisions. Teachers, particularly, are afraid to make decisions because they have learned that when decisions are challenged, the teacher is often left hanging out in the breeze, vulnerable to the slings and arrows of students, parents and the community. The educational climate in many schools, where the customer is always right, too often means that the teacher is always wrong. Some teachers are fortunate to have strong principals who support them, but they are few and far between, an unfortunate result of the dysfunctional system that rewards principals who keep their customers happy. Ultimately teachers fear being the "tallest nail" because they know it is the first to be hammered.

Challenge

Teachers who challenge school policies are labeled as troublemakers. Teachers who dislike or disagree with the current spate of teamwork approaches are denounced for not being team players. Teachers who have the audacity to challenge the status quo are deemed radicals. Teachers who point out long-standing, serious problems in the system are dismissed as cynical. Teachers who speak honestly to students and parents are said to be lacking in compassion. Teachers who refuse to spend increasing numbers of unpaid hours on schoolwork are branded as burnouts. Teachers are afraid to act assertively because they experience the real consequences of those actions. Passivity and compliance are rewarded. Challenging the status quo is punished. The result is predictable. You end up with a work force that is cooperative and malleable. And the ones who pay the price are teachers themselves. How effective do you think a fearful workforce can be?

CHAPTER 7: TOO MUCH

It was the Friday afternoon before the ultimate high school event. My senior health class was buzzing with anticipation. Only one more day until Prom! Since it was obvious that the students' attention was hopelessly distracted by higher priorities than my lesson for that day, I decided to go with the flow and find out a little more about how this adolescent rite of passage had evolved since my high school days. A simple question quickly unleashed a frenzied reciting of itineraries and plans. As the details of this event unfolded, I couldn't help recalling my own Prom night. I found myself stunned by how much this time-honored tradition had changed in a quarter century. Prom is no longer a single event, the dinner and dance that I remember capping my high school career. Rather, Prom has grown into a multi-day, multi-event extravaganza.

If my students' experience is typical, it begins with the girls getting together early in the day, often meeting for a late breakfast. Apparently this meal needs to suffice for the entire day, to ensure that dresses will fit without undue discomfort. The remainder of the morning is typically filled with shopping, manicures and makeovers. Afternoon activities often include the dates, with informal activities being the norm–visits to local tourist attractions, hikes, or a movie or theater matinee. To my astonishment, several couples' plans included a short trip by seaplane. As early evening approaches, girls and boys split up again to begin the Prom night metamorphosis (although most of the boys told me they planned to just go home and watch the baseball game). After adequate primping, it is time for the next step, dining at one of the city's many elegant (and expensive) restaurants. Of course, the trip to the restaurant couldn't be made in a regular old car, even though many of these students have very luxurious cars available to them. Some travel by limousine, many by stretch limousine, and others by novelty vehicles, such as Hummer or SUV limousines. Once they reach their dining destination, no expense is spared as their young palates sample multi-course meals. They linger over their meal, knowing that it would be an unforgivable faux pas to arrive *on time* to the dance. Next stop–the Prom–where they dance, take pictures, and enjoy their final formal event with their high school classmates. But the evening doesn't end when the band stops at 1:00 a.m. That's when the post-prom plans begin. Many students move on to hotel suites that have been reserved by their parents. The rooms are furnished with hors d'oeuvres and refreshments. Some parents provide alcoholic beverages. Other students head for the family cabin to continue the festivities.

What does such an outing cost? According to my students, well over $1,000 is the norm. In addition to the expense, countless hours are spent orchestrating this event, with planning that would rival Oscar night. Am I the only one who thinks this has gone way too far?

This is a perfect example of how a simple, albeit significant, adolescent ritual has been distorted to the point of ridiculousness. If you are wondering who is responsible for this distortion, parents or kids, just ask yourself the question, "Who has the power to say yes or no?" I'm sure my high school friends and I would have thought it was pretty cool to burn through a thousand dollars doing everything we ever wanted to do in one weekend, but our parents would have either laughed or responded with a resounding "No!" The teenager's role is to push the limits, and the adults' role is to reinforce reasonable parameters. Maybe I'm crazy, but spending over a thousand dollars on a single event for a teenager pushes the boundaries of reasonableness and flirts dangerously with insanity.

Prom has become the ultimate expression of competition for status among high school students. Who can put together the most memorable and amazing Prom extravaganza? Who can raise the bar a notch higher so future prom goers will have to pull out even more stops to top it? It's easy to see what's in this competition for students, but what's astounding to me is that this gluttony is fully supported by eager parents. So, why do parents agree to such lavishness? What could they possibly gain from such overindulgence? Do they do it because money is no object and spending $1,000 on a single event seems perfectly normal to them? Do they do it because they feel it is an appropriate expression of love? Do they do it so their child can win a competition? Do they do it to soothe their own guilt? Do they do it to fulfill their own needs for the perfect prom night they never had? Do they do it because they are afraid to say no? Whatever the reason, it's not good enough. The potential consequences aren't worth the risk. The normal pressures and stresses associated with this milestone evening are tough enough, but to have the standards raised to such an unrealistic level is unnecessary and damaging.

If Senior Prom were the first or only time this excess occurred, I wouldn't feel the need to write this chapter. However, for many students, prom is the culmination of eighteen years of chronic overindulgence that has left them woefully unprepared for productive, responsible adulthood.

It may seem absurd to be talking about "too much" in today's world. One only has to pick up a newspaper or listen to the evening news to be reminded that there are many children around the world, as well as in our own country, who suffer daily from not having enough—not enough food, shelter, love, education, or safety. The needs of these children are real and must be addressed by neighborhoods, communities, and society as a whole. However, hidden behind the headlines is another group of children whose needs may be less visible or acute, but whose futures are being compromised by a culture of too much. How do these children suffer?

In their book *Kids Who Have Too Much,* Drs. Ralph Minear and William Proctor, describe a condition they have dubbed the "Rich Kid's Syndrome."[19] This condition arises when kids are given too much of a good thing, given too much too soon, given things in the wrong way, or given things with the wrong messages attached. According to Minear and Proctor, with the best of intentions and often without realizing the negative consequences of their behavior, parents give too much, do too much, push too much, plan too much, butt in too much, protect too much, and rescue too much. As a result, their children move through childhood and adolescence without really maturing in any kind of meaningful way and they enter adulthood devoid of the skills and character required to be successful. These children have missed out on some very important life lessons.

One of the lessons they fail to learn is one my parents taught me well—that you'll appreciate something more if you earn it yourself.

You probably remember learning this lesson yourself. For me it was a baseball glove I purchased with my carefully saved lawn mowing money. I remember the picture cut from the catalog and placed strategically near my bed as a constant reminder of my goal, the anticipation of each week's earnings, the careful calculation of the precise day I would have enough to purchase my ticket to baseball glory. I recall the excitement I felt the day I finally reached my goal and marched purposefully into the store to claim my hard-earned, much dreamed of treasure. Almost forty years later I can still remember the pride of my first grounder cleanly caught with that glove. I remember the daily cleaning and oiling, the meticulous care I gave this new prized possession. As I watch little league games today and see expensive gloves carelessly forgotten on dugout benches, exposed to the elements and potential thieves, I am convinced that none of their young owners were given the gift my parents gave me—the chance to feel the joy that comes from wanting something, figuring out how you can earn it, setting yourself to that task, anticipating the day your dream will come true, then finally seeing that wish fulfilled through your own hard work and effort. How sad for them.

Beyond denying children a valuable and wonderful experience, the symptoms of "too much" are manifested in many ways. Headaches, nausea, stomachaches, hypertension, muscle tics, and eating disorders can all plague children who suffer from "too much." Lack of motivation, depression, withdrawal, aggression, panic or anxiety attacks, drug and alcohol use, and early or promiscuous sexual activity are also consequences of too much. Let's take a look at each of the "too much" areas in greater detail.

Too Much Stuff

The good news is that you have plenty. The bad news is that you have plenty. Even with recent economic slowdowns, our nation is blessed with an abundance of wealth and resources. With the spread of dual-income households, more and more families find themselves with more money than time. In the adult world how much money you make is a well-established form of competition. The visible trophies in this contest are fancy cars, grandiose homes, designer clothes, exotic vacations, expensive electronics and other "toys." This competition has rapidly trickled down to kids. Name brand clothing, shoes, and accessories have become the preferred currency in the game of adolescent popularity. Although this phenomenon is certainly not new, its intensity has increased and the stakes have risen dramatically. In many communities, whole groups of young people can't even get in the game, due to the tremendous disparity between resources available to rich and poor families. The life and death nature of this game reached its zenith in the late eighties and nineties, when the news regularly reported on young people being coldly and callously murdered by other teens for a pair of tennis shoes or a jacket.

However, the losers in this dangerous game are not just poor children. In a phenomenon I call *perceived poverty*, children who attend schools in very affluent areas often view themselves as poor, even though their families are middle class, upper middle class, or even wealthy. Using an alarmingly distorted yardstick, these young people compare themselves to their super-rich peers and inevitably come up short. The truly unfortunate result of this warped perception is that, rather than building a sense of self that is dependent on their own character, talents, and competencies, their self-worth is measured by their *parents'* wealth, possessions, and status. Not only does this encourage young people to judge each other by shallow and superficial characteristics, it means that when they inevitably leave their parents' home, they are forced to leave behind the very things from which their self-worth is derived. It's not hard to see why many of these young adults seem to remain in a state of arrested adolescence well into their twenties.

It's natural for parents to want everything for their children that they didn't have themselves growing up. So what harm can come from buying kids the things they want? Especially when it can make life so much easier. Well, let's look at it from the child's perspective. Imagine that, throughout your entire childhood and adolescence, experience has taught you that you pretty much get whatever you want. There may be a certain amount of effort attached to these acquisitions–kissing up, whining, threatening to withhold your love, the silent treatment, or persistently annoying behavior, but you are still relatively confident in your ability to ultimately get what you want. You have a closet full of clothes that you seldom wear, a playroom full of toys that were cast aside after a few uses, every trinket, gadget, and doodad that ever caught your fancy was yours for the asking. Few of these items have meaning to you because, unlike the baseball glove whose value was directly proportionate to the amount of time I spent *wishing* for it, none of your possessions required waiting, wanting, or working.

Think about what your child is learning from this consumption-oriented, want-it/get-it lifestyle. He learns that things are disposable. Anything can be replaced with something newer or better. Quality becomes less important than novelty. Lasting power is not a priority. Items that stimulate thought or imagination rarely survive in this shiny new world because they require active engagement by the child. Activities that challenge thinking or promote problem-solving skills are exchanged for games that think for the child or entertain her with state of the art technology. If this is your goal for your child, fine. If not, you may want to reconsider the way you handle this aspect of child rearing.

Savvy marketers promote this latest, greatest mind set. Children and teens view their possessions as inherently disposable. Today's favorite toys, clothing, and electronics are only acceptable until the new, improved model becomes available, which can happen with lightening speed in today's fast-paced world. Few things are viewed as long-term investments. When I was young my parents regularly reminded me that my shoes had to last all year long, my clothes had to last throughout the school year, my spending money had to last for the week, and breakfast had to last until lunch. With that information, I was given the responsibility for rationing or budgeting my resources. I learned to choose items for their quality as well as for their style. Once purchased, I needed to take appropriate care of things so that they would last the intended period of time. These are valuable lessons that prepare children for responsible adulthood.

I often think that our parents had it much easier in this regard. It was easy for my parents to deny me the things I wanted because they could say, "I can't afford that." I knew that was true and, therefore, didn't think my parents were being mean or stingy. I actually believed that, if they could have afforded it, they might have given it to me, although I now know better. For many parents today, with considerably more disposable income than previous generations, the "I can't afford it" excuse simply doesn't fly. Rather than hiding behind,

"I *can't* get it for you," we have to take the tougher stand of saying; "I *choose* not to get that for you." This position is made even more difficult when your child is surrounded by other children whose parents give them everything they want.

The "too much" philosophy is not confined to material excess. The river leading to the Rich Kid's Syndrome is fed by many tributaries; each adding to the deluge that gradually erodes the development of a healthy adult personality.

Too Much Non-parent Time

Early in my teaching career I began asking my Health classes a simple question, the results of which have illuminated the dramatic changes in family life over the last two and a half decades. The question is, "How many times a week do you eat dinner together as a family in the kitchen or dining room? Every day? At least three times a week? At least once a week? Never?"

During the first ten years of my career, the average response I got from students was between four and seven days a week eating dinner together as a family. This was consistent with my own experience growing up in a traditional, working class family in the sixties, where I knew that dinner was at 5:30 each and every day. In my family, you didn't miss dinner and you were *never* late. I don't recall this being a particularly big issue in our household; it was simply the expectation. Dinnertime was family time and everything else came second.

In the late seventies I began to see a subtle shift in my informal survey. Although most students still ate dinner with their family the majority of nights, a growing percentage reported that, rather than eating together in the kitchen or dining room, their families ate dinner in front of the increasingly omnipresent television. The eighties and nineties brought further erosion of the family dinner ritual. With more mothers working and the increasingly activity-filled schedules of kids making a regular dinner schedule difficult, more and more kids began reporting that their dinners consisted of fast food eaten in the car between music lessons and soccer practice. If dinner was prepared at home, it was often each man, woman, and child for him or herself, meaning that Mom and Dad may or may not eat together, with kids eating whenever their schedule permitted, usually alone, often in front of the television.

At this point you may be asking yourself, "What's this guy's obsession with eating at the dining room table?" There is nothing sacred about the dining room table, or, for that matter, about families eating together. What's important is that families have regular, consistent, *daily* opportunities to spend time together, to talk with each other and to share the high and low points of their day with each other. The family dinner table provided that opportunity for many of us. Although there may have been times that I resented having to leave a pick-up baseball game mid-inning, the message communicated to me by this family standard was that the family was important and spending time together as a family was an expected behavior, just as getting good grades and going to college were expected behaviors in my family.

Few disagree that parents are the first and most important influence on a child's development. Through observing their parents, children learn their first lessons about what is normal behavior for adults. Parents can spark their child's curiosity and shape their interests. They can stimulate learning and communicate the value of education. They can set moral standards and support family values. They can reinforce personality traits and mold political opinions. They can teach skills and develop competencies. They can model physical and emotional health and balance. Of course, children can also learn many undesirable behaviors from their parents. What is indisputable, however, is that children are constantly watching and learning. You are your child's example of what an adult should be like. You are the standard for their behavior. You are their role model. But you already know that.

Despite the rhetoric about the big, bad influence of peers and the media, study after study shows that the greatest influence on children's behavior is their parents. So, the question for you becomes, "What kind of influence are you having on your child?" Studies show that the average amount of time an American teenager and his or her parents spend communicating each day is less than six minutes, with most of that communication being parental commands or interrogations: "Pick up your clothes!" "When will you be home for dinner?" The number isn't much higher for younger children. So you need to ask yourself how much influence you can expect to have on your child in six minutes a day? Even more importantly, if your influence on your child is dependent on six minutes a day of contact, who or what is influencing your child the other 954 waking minutes of each day?

The statistics tell the story of who's really raising America's kids. Three-fourths of mothers of school-age children in the U.S. work outside the home.[20] The number of children in daycare has grown steadily over the past fifty years. Once the preserve of only the wealthiest families, live-in childcare has become a widely-accepted practice for upper middle class working families, often providing mothers of very young children the surrogate they require to feel comfortable leaving their infant or toddler for eight or more hours a day. Consider this. If your child enters daycare nine weeks after birth, then spends nine hours a day being cared for by others until he starts kindergarten, he will have spent 11,250 hours being influenced by another adult. Assuming you spent eight hours with your child each day of the weekend and four hours every weekday, you would have spent 9,000 hours influencing him. Of course, we all know that even the most dedicated parent has to deal with cooking, laundry, shopping, housework, bill paying, etc. during those hours. If this is your situation, I certainly hope you have a childcare provider who embodies the kind of adult you want your child to grow up to be, because that person will be the adult role model your child sees for the majority of his or her day. If you do, you are fortunate—and rare. Due to the often prohibitive cost of high-quality childcare, particularly for infants, the sad reality is that far too many American children are cared for in sub-standard environments, by poorly trained, undereducated adults. Turnover rates in the daycare industry are frighteningly high. This means that, rather than the consistent, dependable, long-term relationship children need with the primary adults in their lives, they often have new caregivers every three or four months.

According to the Census Bureau, one fourth of parents are parenting alone. Almost two thirds of kids will spend some part of their childhood in a single parent family. In a family with only one adult to shoulder all the burdens of family and household, it's more difficult to ensure that children receive the time and attention they need than when there are two adults to share the load.

Full-day kindergarten classes have mushroomed in the last

decade, as parents increasingly demand this free alternative to extended day care for their young student, regardless of the readiness of the child for this transition. After school programs have expanded to fill the gap between the end of the school day and the end of the workday. For millions of "latchkey" children, some as young as five, after school care is self-care. The vast majority of American teens come home to empty houses every day, a situation fraught with risk. Researchers have dubbed the hours between 3 p.m. and 8 p.m. the "critical hours" because this is the peak time period for delinquency and other antisocial behavior. Research has shown that the most likely place teenage girls will have their first sexual experience is in their own homes.[21] Do you think their parents are there?

A rare phenomenon during my childhood years, parents absent for days or weeks on business trips is now a commonplace occurrence. Pick up any women's magazine and you can be assured of finding an article extolling the importance of "couple time," regular outings and vacations without the kids. The lazy days of summer have been replaced with a myriad of structured activities–sports camps, computer camps, horse camps, and science camps. Some parents use these activities as childcare; others believe that they are important enrichment for their children. And let's not forget the parents' non-work activities that take them away from their children; working out, socializing with friends, volunteering, etc. The last time I checked, the number of hours in a day hasn't increased since the time I was a child. So, given all of these changes, how can we expect kids to get the parental time they need and deserve? Answer—they don't.

I know what you're saying about now, "But the time I spend with my child is *quality* time." Do any of us *really* believe the world works that way? Do *you* really believe that the few hours a day you spend with your child can possibly make up for the nine hours you're not there? Even the so-called experts have begun to renege on this ludicrous concept. Noted pediatrician and child development expert Berry Brazelton explains that children need their parents' time on the child's own schedule, not when it's convenient for the parent.[22]

How much time do you need to spend with your child? More importantly, how much time does your child need to spend with you? The answer to both questions is simple—more.

If you're not there, who will be? That is the question that should be asked by every parent who sends his children off to daycare or allows hours of unsupervised time after school or at night. Unlike most other species, human children require a long period of protection and nurturing before they are ready to strike out on their own. The human family, with two parents available to care for a small number of children, provides the kind of one-to-one adult interaction needed to prepare young children to function in our complex world. The important early tasks of learning language and the social skills necessary to function effectively in the world outside the family are best taught through this kind of consistent, one-to-one, daily, interaction. When young children spend large parts of their day in institutional daycare settings, with typical adult to child ratios of one adult for every eight children, they are growing up in an environment where they are learning these critical developmental tasks from other young children, rather than from caring adults. Two-year-olds learning social skills from other two-year-olds! Should it surprise us that kindergarten teachers (or middle school teachers for that matter!) are having to spend a significant portion of their time teaching children such basic social skills as waiting their turn, asking for rather than taking something they want, and listening when someone else is talking?

Psychologists have long told us that one of the strongest human needs is the need to belong. Children and teens will go to great lengths to find a way to meet that need for belonging. Ideally, the adults in a child's life work together to ensure that children get their sense of belonging from adults and peers who have a positive influence on the child's development. These lucky children feel connected to their families, their schools, their coaches, their minister, or their employer. They get their sense of belonging through involvement with adults and peers who share the core values that their parents want them to develop. However, if that fails to happen, kids are left to their own devices, and, all too often, the results are not what we would want. Youth gangs provide a chilling example. Young people involved in gangs speak of their fellow gang members as their "family." The lengths to which they are prepared to go for this family speak volumes about the strength of those bonds; they are willing to steal for, do time for, and sometimes die for, this family. For them, the gang provides the acceptance, support, and stability they need in a confusing, often frightening, and lonely world.

If parents' influence is so important, why are so many American children left without this vital ingredient for successful development? Do parents today really want this influence over their kids? Do they really understand the sacrifices involved in being an effective parent? Do parents today have what it takes to be a confident example for their children and the leader of their family? To be truthful, I'm not convinced that they do. Maybe some parents prefer a more hands off role so that if something bad happens, they can rationalize it as someone else's fault. Maybe parents think they don't know enough or they are afraid to be proactive for fear of making a mistake. Maybe they are confused about the best way to address difficult situations with their children. Maybe they are too immature to confront the real truths and responsibilities of being a grown-up, which is what an effective parent needs to be. Maybe parents are just too spoiled and egocentric. Maybe they are too preoccupied or overwhelmed to pay attention. Maybe their priorities have become skewed and their children are not the focus. Maybe parents are afraid of the hard work and effort involved with active parenting. Or maybe parents are just plain chicken to do what they need to do.

American families have devised a childcare option for every conceivable situation. There is day care for working parents, neighborhood babysitters for movie nights, nannies to bring along on family vacations, older brothers and sisters watching their siblings after school, grandparents to fill in the holes, preschools that give a few days of relief to stay-at-home parents during the week, supervised play areas in large stores so parents can shop unburdened, and hospital drop-ins for sick children. It seems that some parents will do just about anything to avoid spending time with their children.

Regardless of the reason, too many children are being raised by "absentee parents" and the consequences are devastating for children, their families, and for society. As your child's parent, you have a stake in his future that no one else has. You are the keeper of the vision for the kind of adult your child will become. Even the most dedicated childcare provider, or teacher, or after school program leader doesn't care about your child the way you do. As a result, it's unrealistic to expect that person to do the tough work that is often required with children and teens. Sure, if you're lucky, they may provide the hugs and praise and fun activities that are an important part of your child's life. That's the easy part. But will they have the investment in your child's future that motivates them to tackle the less pleasant aspects of molding and shaping a young child into a mature and responsible adult? After all, if parents are running scared, why would we expect a poorly paid, under-respected, daycare provider to stand up and take the challenge?

Many balls get dropped when parents aren't around. As we discussed earlier, if you want to cushion your child against the inevitable difficulties they will face in their lives, they need the layers of protection provided by consistently communicated healthy beliefs and clear standards. They need the strong bonds developed through opportunities to be active contributors in their families, schools, communities, and peer groups. As a parent, you are the best person to ensure that this protection is built. That requires time, energy, and effort.

What are the effects of all this childcare on children? The experts are once again being proved wrong in their position on daycare kids. The rhetoric that saturated the popular media, proclaiming the benefits of daycare and denouncing any negative impacts, served its purpose (to placate guilt-ridden working mothers), but we are gradually coming to the realization that the emperor isn't wearing any clothes. The hype just doesn't ring true. How can we possibly swallow the logic that an often undereducated, always underpaid person, who is caring for children as a way to put food on his or her own table, is the best person to shape our own precious child's future? How can we believe that individual will put the love, commitment, and hard work into raising our child that we, as the child's parent, would? Shame on those who convinced a generation of parents that taking care of their children was such an unimportant and insignificant job.

You are unquestionably the most important person in your child's life. During discussions of human reproduction and sexuality in my Health classes, I always take the opportunity to convey to my students the ultimate importance of parenting; not just the techniques of parenting, but also the overriding concept of what it is to be a parent. I want every student who comes through my class to know that parenting is the most important job they will ever do; that the responsibility of parenting is 24/7; that it can bring the greatest rewards, as well as the greatest challenges and the greatest heartaches. Being responsible for another human being is an awesome task. I have solicited opinions from students on many topics but the one that always inspires intense conversations is the subject of parents and parenting. Despite all the other changes I've seen in students over the last twenty years, their opinions on this subject are clear and consistent. What they most want from their parents is their time. Whether it's quality time or just time spent in the same house at the same time, my students invariably want more time from their parents. They speak of the benefits of sharing dinnertime as a family and the talks that naturally ensued from that ritual. They talk about the "loss" of being shipped off to daycare. I was taken aback during one class discussion on daycare when an insightful young man shared his experience. He said that when he was younger, he hadn't thought that being sent to daycare every day was a bad thing. But, as he got older and reflected on it, he said he had "lost respect for his parents" for making that choice. His statement stopped the class discussion; it was one of those moments when you feel the discomfort of the truth in the silence.

I know that, for some families, childcare is a reality that simply can't be avoided. The safety net for poor parents has vanished; they are expected to go to work regardless of the quality of care their child will receive while they are at work. Single parents don't have the luxury of one stay-at-home parent. Our society needs to recognize this and ensure that *all* children have access to high-quality childcare.

But, if you don't fall into one of those categories, then you do have choices, and the choices you make will have real and long-lasting effects on your child. I know what you're thinking. "I have a *career,* and I just can't take five years off to be a mommy." Or, "We can't afford to live on one income. How would we pay the mortgage?" Well, if parenting is the most important job you'll ever have (and I certainly hope you believe that), you can find a way to make it work. Will it require sacrifice? Absolutely. Perhaps you decide that each parent will work a different shift, so that there is always a parent at home with the child. Will that be hard on your marriage? Yes, but you and your spouse are grown-ups, better equipped to handle the stress than a toddler or preschooler expected to spend nine hours a day in childcare. You may need to get rid of that mortgage and move to a home that you can afford on one income. You may need to forgo the vacations and the fancy new car and the dinners out, but are you really willing to say that your child isn't worth it?

The women's liberation movement of the sixties told women they could have it all—the great marriage, the fulfilling career, the wonderful children. After all, men had it all for centuries. Why shouldn't women get the same opportunity? Unfortunately, in the battle for equality between the sexes, we seem to have forgotten that these warriors are continuing to produce children, and children can't raise themselves. The bottom line is that you *can* have it all; you just can't have it all at the same time. Life is about making choices. When you choose to have a child, you need to make the needs of that child come first, before your personal needs or your professional needs. Sometimes sacrifices have to be made in order to bring about desired results. Be creative. Be painfully honest with yourself about what is driving your choices. Are the needs of your child coming first? Are you behaving like the grown-up in your family?

Too Much Guilt

I'm convinced that many of the destructive parenting practices I see on a regular basis are caused by parental guilt. Today's parents are hurried and frustrated. Hurried because they don't have enough time to do all that the world expects of them or that they expect from themselves. Priorities are dictated by forces beyond their control (at least that's what they believe) and demands on them are always increasing. They need to be in multiple places at the same time. When they're at home they're worried about work; when they're at work they're worried about home. Their energy is stretched to the breaking point. They are frustrated because they feel they *should* be able to meet all the demands of work, family, home, and self. Sadly, the area that is too often sacrificed is the family, because the consequences of neglecting work are more visible and more immediate than the consequences of neglecting children. So, time with children dwindles; dinners are missed, only the last few innings are seen, dinner table conversations are cut short with urgent phone calls, outings rescheduled, only to be rescheduled again, play time dissolves, and the excuses for missing important family events due to important meetings or business trips pile up.

In the precious few moments that parents do have available for children, energy levels are so low that family time can become more of a chore than a joy. One thing I learned quickly in the classroom is that kids are very perceptive. They can spot half-hearted effort and phony enthusiasm a mile away. When your body is there but your mind and attention are at the office, your child will know it and his behavior will soon begin to show it. Much of the acting out behavior that children exhibit is really a desperate attempt to gain their parents' attention. When that attention is chronically focused elsewhere, attention-getting behavior escalates.

But what's a busy parent to do? It can seem as though you are caught between a rock and a hard place. You can't just quit your job, but you instinctively know that the problem behavior you're seeing in your child is related to his need for more attention from you. With no easy answers on the horizon, parents often choose to rationalize their behavior; "I'll be able to spend more time with him after this big project is finished," or "Once I get to another department things will change," or "He's having a great time in daycare. It's the best daycare in the city."

The problem, of course, is that you can't have it all, at least not all at the same time. So, in order to make up for lost time and missed events you give them more money, more gifts, more special toys, and more enrichment experiences through classes and lessons. A new standard is born. The parents who foot the bill for Prom night *must* be the ones who love their children the most. The child with the most toys has a tangible measurement of her parents' love.

Too Much Instant Gratification

There is no question that we live in a world where fast is good, faster is better, and no one is willing to wait for anything. Too many parents fall into this trap with their children and choose the path of least resistance, the path that leads to the most instantaneous solution. Rather than focusing on the long-term consequences, or the lessons their child is learning from these choices, they opt for solutions that solve the problem for now. How often have you caved in to whining demands just to have a moment's peace? How many times have you purchased items to bribe, cajole, manipulate, or pay off your kids for not bugging you? Not for cooperative or helpful behavior, but simply for not causing trouble? How many times have you offered toys or goodies if your child behaves while you're shopping or running errands? These counterproductive parenting strategies seem to be the norm. I sometimes wonder if the problem is really one of maturity, the parents' that is! One well-established test of young children's emotional maturity involves putting them alone in a room with a piece of candy and telling them that, if they go three minutes without eating the candy, they will get two pieces of candy. I'm beginning to wonder how many parents would pass this test. Parents must know that this bribery process will lead to more serious problems in the future. It's much more difficult to deal with a demanding, materialistic teenager than it is to set limits with a five-year-old. Yet parents seem to consistently shirk their responsibility to teach their children lifelong lessons in favor of the quick win, the easy out.

Solving the problem for the moment doesn't solve anything. All it does is create a bigger and more complicated web of issues. A child who receives a toy for not causing a scene has just learned an important lesson. "I can manipulate my parents!" It doesn't take long for the child to establish a long and dependable list of strategies he can employ to get whatever he desires, whenever he desires it. He learns that in public places, parents give in. He learns that crying, whining, or being loud will reap rewards. He learns that asking for more or verbal badgering will bring desired results. He demands, instead of asking, because that strategy has always produced results. So it's not long before you are preparing special meals for little Johnny because he doesn't like what's being served for dinner. Or maybe it's costing you a toy every time you go to the store with your child, because otherwise you're subjected to continual harassment and badgering. Or you have accepted the fact that when you go out to eat with your child you will be sitting in the most remote corner of the restaurant. In other words, you are a chicken parent being abused by a powerful child.

Too Much Technology

Technology has infiltrated all aspects of American society, including the lives of America's children. When faced with a technology problem, adults often jokingly suggest finding the nearest ten-year-old, who can usually solve the problem in a few minutes. Technology is a reality in today's world and it should be an important part of young peoples' preparation for their future in that world. However, as in so many aspects of parenting or schooling, balance is the critical, but often missing, factor.

For example, the calculator is a wonderful device when properly used. It allows for very quick calculations and makes large cumbersome numbers much easier to deal with. When students are practicing complicated new math concepts, the calculator can simplify the process so they can concentrate on the concept, rather than struggling with the calculations. Unfortunately, calculators are over-used in most classrooms. As a result, students' understanding of the building blocks of mathematics has been compromised. For many students, calculators have taken on a frighteningly eerie sense of power. Rather than using the calculator to solve complex problems, students are tied to this device to do even the simplest calculations. My students routinely grab their calculators to multiply five by three or add thirteen and nine.

Years ago in my ninth grade physical science class I decided to make a bet with my students that would determine the use of calculators in class. The deal was that if half the students who had calculators could do a simple problem correctly, I would allow calculator use in my class all trimester long. Anything less than half would mean no calculators. I assured them that the problem would be one that fifteen-year-olds could reasonably be expected to solve. The class took the bet with confidence. After all, they had been using calculators since first grade! Twelve students had calculators with them that day. I asked them to find 37% of 83, write their answer on a piece of paper and bring it to my desk. They feverishly started pushing buttons. When I tabulated their answers, with a student witness standing guard to make sure I didn't pull a fast one, I found that *three out of the twelve* students got the answer right. Needless to say, I didn't bother to ask the class what percentage the correct answers represented! The truly depressing part of this demonstration was that many of the answers weren't even in the realm of possibility. How can 37% of 83 be more than 83? How can 37% of 83 be 0.3071? This simple demonstration made it clear that my students knew how to push buttons but they didn't know which buttons to push or in what order.

They didn't understand the basic concepts necessary for calculating simple percentages. Now, mind you, this wasn't some obscure, little-used mathematical process. These students routinely encounter 30% off sales at the mall. They pay 8.8% sales tax when they buy a pack of gum. Many pay double-digit percentage interest on the credit cards they use on a regular basis. As I looked at their answers, I couldn't help but think how easily they could be ripped off by an unscrupulous sales clerk, car dealer, or credit card company. The really unsettling thing, however, was their unflinching confidence in whatever came up on that little screen. They have so fully accepted the infallibility of this device that they really don't feel the need to question the logic of the answer, to figure out if the answer makes sense. If the calculator says so, it must be right.

Kids may be able to solve sophisticated math problems using the calculator, but their understanding of the fundamental underlying concepts is lacking. Recently, a group of 200 prestigious academicians, including the heads of the math departments at Stanford and California Institute of Technology, four Nobel laureates in physics, and two recipients of the Fields Medal, the world's top honor in mathematics, issued a declaration urging the Secretary of Education to withdraw the government's endorsement of math programs that have abandoned traditional teaching methodologies, purposely avoiding lessons with "predetermined numerical results" (that is to say, answers that could be gotten wrong) instead urging young children to "count" using calculators, while replacing textbooks with "manipulative kits" featuring pattern blocks and cubes. These esteemed mathematicians pronounced these curricula "among the worst in existence."[23] Their emphatic message is that returning to the time-tested methods of developing skills that are essential to a basic mathematical foundation is imperative.

If the calculator can help reduce the drudgery of repetitive or time-consuming calculations, that's great, but it doesn't mean that kids don't have to memorize their multiplication tables. Just because the computer can do a spelling and grammar check, that doesn't mean children don't need to learn how to spell and use correct grammar. We need to be very careful how much power we surrender to these machines. They may be able to do amazing things, but, as of this writing, true intelligence can only be found between a pair of human ears.

Despite this, however, I am fascinated and amazed by how much trust most people put in these machines. For example, in my early years of teaching, when teachers calculated grades by hand in an old-fashioned grade book and sent home report cards that were filled out by hand, it was quite common for students and parents to question or challenge the grade. I remember the arduous task of checking the grade book, redoing the calculations, usually to find out that the grade was correct. The problem wasn't the accuracy of the grade; it was the acceptance of the grade by the student or parent. When schools adopted computerized progress reports and grading, an interesting phenomenon occurred. Handed a computerized printout of their grades, students and parents seemed to be far less likely to question or challenge the outcome. Even though this computerized process is vulnerable to multiple human errors, the accuracy of the reports seems to be beyond question. Just as with the calculator, if the computer says it's true, then it must be true. Like the student who blindly accepted the calculator's proclamation that 37% of 83 was 0.3071, both students and teachers seem to put their full faith and trust in that computer.

Technology has taken on an even more insidious role when it comes to young people's use of free time. Rather than interacting with real people, children of all ages are increasingly spending large amounts of time in solitary engagement with machines, robbing them of vital opportunities to learn social, emotional, and cognitive skills. Many of my students have both their own computer and their own television in their bedrooms. Given the natural developmental tendency of teens to distance themselves from their families as they prepare for independence, parents must work especially hard during this period to maintain a connection and regular communication with their children. This goal is subverted by the ready-made escape provided by a fully technology-stocked bedroom, into which a teen can retreat from the demands of human interaction and normal family life. Although it's important for parents and teens alike to have regular breaks from each other, daily family conversations and shared activities are invaluable building blocks for healthy development and nurturing family life. Of particular concern for pre-teens and adolescents is the ease with which "virtual interaction" can replace the more difficult challenge of interacting with real people in person.

Online communication provides a degree of anonymity that can be particularly appealing to an adolescent struggling with his or her own identity. A teen's online persona can be anyone she wants it to be. The shy, mousy haired, underdeveloped, sexually conservative girl can become outgoing, blond, voluptuous, and sexually precocious behind the virtual curtain. The ability to shed one's warts (and what adolescent thinks their appearance or personality are perfect?) and let the alter ego take over can become a compulsion for immature teens. Rather than facing and dealing with the challenges of figuring out who they are and who they want to become as adults, the virtual world gives teens an easy escape. Unfortunately, unlike the teen who escapes through alcohol and drug use, the virtual escape is often provided for, and condoned by their parents.

Teens are not the only ones afflicted by too much technology. Toy manufacturers promote technologically-based toys to meet several compelling needs of today's parents: the desire for earlier and earlier learning toys for their children; the scarcity of time for children and parents to spend together; and the need for toys that will entertain young children while parents are otherwise occupied. A recent commercial touting a "learning buddy" shows a mother and father peeking in their child's bedroom as the preschooler happily plays with a computerized robot who is helping the child learn language, science, and other subjects. How much more valuable would it be for these parents to invest their time actually interacting with and playing with their child, rather than observing the child interacting with a machine? Even the best learning toy, no matter how entertaining, can't replace the multiple benefits of children learning through regular interaction with caring adults.

Here are a few practical warnings about technology and your child. Be careful not to let your child become too dependent on the calculator or other technological crutch. Be at least as distrustful of information spit out of a machine as you would of the same information given to you by a total stranger. Be careful not to let your child develop a relationship with the computer that replaces genuine interactions with her peers. This is particularly dangerous during the early adolescent years, when the anonymity of electronic communication can seem far more appealing than the difficult task of dealing with pimples, body changes, lack of confidence, and all the other issues that must be dealt with during this period. Be careful how you and your child use technology. Just because a high tech way of doing something exists, that doesn't mean it will be faster, more efficient, or more accurate. Be careful not to put too much weight on availability of technology as a measure of the quality of your child's school. Research has repeatedly shown that the most important factors in school success are parental involvement in the child's education and a high quality teacher, with student to computer ratio not even in the running.[24] Be extremely careful of the wide spectrum of information available to your child through technology. Be careful of how computer games and websites can influence your child. Be careful of the time and energy your child directs toward computers and video games. Be careful of the negative personality traits that can result from too much time spent interacting with a machine. Be careful of the physical effects of overuse.

Too Much Information, Too Little Learning

Too much information causes problems for children in two ways: 1) too much information with too little understanding, and 2) too much information too soon.

In a demonstration to impress me, a proud parent began firing questions at his three-year-old son. Who is the president of the U.S.? The child responded, "Clinton." Who is the Governor of Washington State? "Locke," the child replied with confidence. Who is the Mayor of Seattle? "Schell," came the answer. Wow, this kid must be a genius! He knows his political figures better than a large part of the adult population. This kid's I.Q. must be off the charts. Impressed? You shouldn't be. His parents had spent considerable time training their child to respond with the same answers every time they began the "name game." Asking the same questions in the reverse order would have completely befuddled the child. Besides being a cute little trick for a three-year-old, it reveals a great deal about how we view learning, knowledge, and intelligence, and about the assumptions we make about children's understanding.

When we hear a child respond with the correct answer to such questions, we tend to assume that the child *understands* both the question and the answer. If he knows the President is Bill Clinton, then he must know what a President is and what he does. He must know that there is a First Lady, a Vice President, a White House, etc. On the contrary, I have found that kids are often given too much credit for the few facts they can spout off, while they are missing vital layers of basic factual information. For example, you may have noticed that math curriculums today look quite different than the way they looked when you were in school. Pick up an elementary math book and you're likely to see fourth graders "solving" algebraic equations. You assume that if your child is doing algebra in elementary school he certainly must know all the math concepts leading up to this skill. Not true. In an effort to convince parents and the community that their schools are always improving, always on the cutting edge, schools often shortcut the basic skills and push students to higher levels, regardless of their mastery of the requisite skills and concepts. Those grade school students might be able to find x in an algebra problem, but many of them haven't mastered the multiplication tables. Many can't add or subtract simple fractions. Believe me, I see evidence of this on a daily basis in my math classes. One seventeen-year-old high school junior in my geometry class didn't understand the concept of one-third. She didn't know what the three under the line meant! It took me five minutes and numerous examples (e.g. if you cut a pizza into three pieces, each piece is one-third) to get her to understand this third grade concept. Yet, this girl had passed an algebra class the previous year! Mind you, this example is not from a poor, urban public school system. On the contrary, my school district, which serves a predominantly upper middle class, suburban population, is considered one of the best in the state. If you think this is an isolated case, please feel free to ask the math teachers at your local school for their stories. Just make sure you're not in a hurry; I guarantee they will have plenty.

At least every year there is an article in the newspaper about the sorry state of American students' knowledge of basic facts—state capitols, important people or dates in history, etc. The general public responds by berating the school system and reminiscing about the good old days when schools actually taught students what they needed to know. I always get a chuckle at that last part—what they needed to know. Based on my discussions with adults, that generally means things like memorization of important facts, reading actual books (as opposed to watching the video of Romeo and Juliet), answering lots of questions (in full sentences), doing what you are told, completing homework assignments—focusing on the basics. Today's education experts will tell you that the information age has changed everything and kids no longer need to know isolated facts, as long as they know *where to find* that information. Does that sound right to you? It's not necessary for the child to learn to add, subtract, multiply, or divide as long as they know how to use the calculator. Kids don't need to read books as long as they can watch the video. There's no need to know when the Civil War occurred because you can always look it up on the Internet. You don't need to know how to spell as long as you use your computer's spell check. Do you see the problem with this philosophy? If not, I invite you to a high school classroom, where you may well be astounded by the overwhelming lack of the basics that you assume students are being taught.

Certainly the world has changed and education must change with it. Many of the innovations are rooted in sound principles and grounded in indisputable changes in the workplace. Students *do* have to learn to work together in groups; they *do* have to learn to synthesize multiple bodies of information. But these new priorities should not *replace* the acquisition of the essential building blocks of learning. Rather, they should extend and complement those building blocks, allowing students to organize and apply those building blocks in more sophisticated ways.

We learned this lesson the hard way when school districts around the country adopted "whole language," a popular reading instruction fad that rejected the importance of phonics and the other building blocks of reading in favor of exposing children to good literature. In other words, just give children interesting stories and they will somehow magically figure out how to break the immensely complex code that is the English language. Unfortunately, by the time schools realized the folly of this approach, millions of children's reading education had been compromised. The same thing is happening today in other subject areas, where, rather than learning math facts, students learn math concepts. Rather than learning about the people, places and events that shaped history, students learn history or geography through common themes, such as culture, migration or populations. Clearly, with the explosion of new information that threatens to overcome young people in today's world, it is even more critical than ever that we make decisions about what young people need to learn in a strategic and deliberate way, not being whipped from side to side by the whims of educational fad.

Another aspect of "too much information," has to do with giving children information before they are ready for it. You may have heard the old joke about the three year old who asks her mother where she came from. The panicked mother realizes that it's time for the "birds and bees" discussion and proceeds to give her daughter a thirty minute lecture on women's body parts and men's body parts and how, when a man and a woman love each other and are ready to have a baby, the man puts his penis inside the woman's vagina and deposits a seed there. The preschooler calmly sits and listens to this story, at the end of which she comments, "But Mom, where did I come from?" Mom says, "What do you mean where did you come from. I just told you." The exasperated little girl says, "Jessica said she's from Cincinnati and I want to know where I'm from!" Like this mother, parents today often give their children way more information than they are either asking for or are ready for.

My older sister's childhood friend, Becky, a fifteen-year veteran Health teacher, told me the following story about her then three-year-old son, Nathan. One day at daycare her son began listing the anatomical parts of the male and female reproductive systems. "I have a penis and you have a vagina," he told a classmate. "The man puts his penis inside the women's vagina and they make a baby," continued the preschooler. As she recounted this story, Becky was clearly proud of both her son's advanced knowledge as well as her progressiveness as a parent. She made it clear that she wanted to ensure that her son was not embarrassed about his body or his sexuality and she felt that these early discussions were the prelude to honest and open communication with her son and to healthy sexual development. As I listened to this story, I couldn't help wondering if there wasn't some other motivation in play. It was very obvious that Becky derived some very personal satisfaction from this story. When another parent marveled at Becky's ability to discuss such a sensitive topic so openly with her son, Becky beamed with pleasure. It became clear to me that Becky was using her son as a measure of her hip-ness, her liberalness, her openness, and her competency as a health education professional.

A quick look at the value of such early instruction to Becky's son shows a decidedly different picture. First, is it to the son's advantage to be reciting sexual parts and functions to anyone who will listen? Certainly a preschooler knowing these terms and using them in public is somewhat of a novelty and is likely to generate attention. The resulting laughter would likely increase the chances of Nathan repeating his performance. Unfortunately, a three-year-old is incapable of making distinctions about the social appropriateness of certain language, so it's highly likely that he will use this new information in a situation where it is highly inappropriate. He may be reprimanded at preschool for using "potty language." Parents of other children might find indiscriminate use of such language inappropriate for a preschooler and choose to limit their child's exposure to Nathan. Other adults may find his sexual language offensive and make judgments about him and/or his parents. So, what has Nathan gained? Yes, it is important for parents to teach their children about reproduction and sexuality, but it is just as important that parents understand that information needs to be age-appropriate and tailored to prevailing social norms. Yes, it is important for parents to nurture open, honest communication with their children, but that means giving children honest answers to children's age-appropriate questions, not initiating discussions about topics that are beyond the child's maturity and level of understanding.

There is great value in letting children have a childhood. Bombardment of information—too much, too soon, too often—is overwhelming and a waste of effort and resources. Young children are routinely exposed to experiences designed to teach, enrich, or otherwise benefit them. I have seen squirming, fidgeting, distracted, or sleeping children dragged by well-intentioned parents to traditional Russian ballets, lavish musicals, symphonies, operas, concerts, and celebrity lectures. Do young children really benefit from these events or is it the needs of adults being served here? Are these valuable learning experiences, opportunities for parent-child bonding? Or are they simply one more round in the parental one-upmanship game? How many of these children would be better served by two hours spent just playing with their parents?

Too Much Stress

Many of today's parents put too much pressure on their kids to perform. The effects of this external pressure will eventually be manifested in any of a myriad of physical and emotional problems, ranging from stomachaches and headaches to alcohol and drug abuse, depression or bulimia. Today's kids are faced with performance pressure at earlier and earlier ages. Parents of preschoolers are pushing their children to perform at levels that will ensure their acceptance in the right elementary school, which is, of course, prerequisite to acceptance to the best high school and, ultimately, the prestigious college. Once in school, the emphasis on grades can be overwhelming. Advanced classes and enrichment activities are considered critical to later success. Even very young children's schedules are exhausting, with every minute planned and structured. The world is moving faster, unfathomable amounts of information are available at our fingertips, technology is evolving daily, and your child feels the pressure to somehow do the impossible, keep up. Standards are rising along with performance expectations. Welcome to your child's world. You place your kid on the fast track toward the best university or the demanding pathway to professional sports with little regard to the overwhelming stress this places on your child's development.

In addition to the pressure to be the perfect child, today's children are constantly bombarded with the issues and fears of an increasingly frightening world. Exposure to round the clock media coverage of disasters, war, and violence overburdens the immature psychological capabilities of young people. In the sixties, psychologists studying the negative effects of the threat of nuclear war on grade school kids found that exposure to these kinds of complex, ever-present threats undermined children's feelings of safety. Today's children face the threats of terrorism, AIDS, school shootings, and violence in their families and neighborhoods. Although the actual potential for any one of these dangers to impact the life of a given child is relatively small, children's perceptions of the world are strongly influenced both by what they see in the media, as well as the generalized fears communicated to them by their anxious parents. Add in the normal stresses of growing up—peer acceptance, body image, divorce or death in the family, body changes, sexuality, friends, and school—and it's not hard to see why a faculty member of one Ivy League University recently observed that incoming freshman have startlingly high rates of mental illness. It shouldn't surprise us that depression is the leading mental illness for children today, with children as young as five or six showing suicidal tendencies.[25]

For the last several years I have surveyed my health classes to try to understand the impact of this phenomenon on students' lives. I ask them to identify a man-made device that creates significant stress in their lives. Three things are consistently mentioned, with the top honor going to the automobile. They complain of the stress due to traffic, stupid drivers, and the expense of maintaining their own car. Many students are caught in a cycle of needing to have a car to get to work, but then having to use their wages to pay for their car.

The second most consistently mentioned device is the clock, an interesting way of conveying that they don't have enough time in the day to do all that is expected of them.

Finally, the third stress inducer is the computer. Having lived all of their lives with this technology and having witnessed the ever-increasing speed at which both hardware and software become obsolete, they feel they will always be running a losing race to keep up with the changes. Just when they feel they have mastered the current technology, something newer comes along, and they feel constant pressure to keep pace. Society pushes them forward and the kids try their best to keep up with our expectations.

The increasing complexity of today's world certainly contributes to children's stress. As a parent you may feel helpless to control this aspect of your child's life. However, you do have the power to control the unnecessary and unproductive stress that you add to your child's life through unrealistic demands and expectations. In far too many families, no longer is it enough to be the top student. Children increasingly feel pressured to also be the best athlete, the best musician, and the all around perfect child. If this describes your family, you need to ask yourself some hard questions. Why is it so important to you that your child be the best? Are your child's needs being served or are your needs being served? What are the potential negative consequences of this constant pressure in your child's life compared to your perceived gains?

Childhood should be a wonderful time. Mine was, filled with carefree feelings, boundless fun, developing lifelong relationships with friends, spontaneous games played for hours, responsibilities at a minimum, and imagination gone wild. That's the way I remember growing up. I can't imagine not wanting that for my own kids. Parents today are in such a hurry to have their kids grow up that they are cheating their kids out of a very precious and developmentally important experience. Child development experts have long known that play is children's work. It develops important cognitive, social, and emotional skills. Children learn to cope with their emotions through childhood activities. Childhood is not wasted, unstructured time. It is nature's way of preparing a well-rounded individual. Parents today seem to be constantly trying to push the fast-forward button on children's development. They need to be in the advanced classes at school; algebra needs to be taught years before you learned it; playtime is replaced with lessons; daydreaming diminishes with every additional class scheduled for that week; regular teams aren't good enough, only the select teams are acceptable for the child on the fast track to success; childish silliness is replaced with adult behaviors; and normal gender specific play discouraged for more politically correct pursuits. Your kids don't need to grow up so fast. Let them enjoy the unique joys of childhood. Instead of pushing your kids to adulthood, you should be actively promoting childlike fun for as long as possible. But in order for that to happen you need to allow childhood to take its natural course.

A recent study of affluent, suburban middle school students confirmed the negative effects of too much stress. Columbia University researchers found an unusually high incidence of depressive symptoms in girls and a high occurrence of substance abuse in both boys and girls in sixth and seventh graders in an affluent community in the Northeast. The researchers attribute these problems to "excessive pressure to excel, not only at academics but extracurricular activities." They also cite being isolated from adults and lack of adult supervision in the hours immediately after school as being significant factors.[26]

In your push for perfection, are you emphasizing the right things? Despite this country's current obsession with test scores and academic standards, current research shows that emotional and social competencies are at least as important for success in the adult world.[27] Do the standards and expectations you hold for your child balance academic achievement with the increasingly important skills of getting along with others, communicating effectively with all kinds of people, reading and interpreting others' emotions and body language, understanding and managing group dynamics, and leadership? Maybe the pressure and stress is misplaced. Maybe the emphasis is being focused on the wrong qualities.

Spend some time evaluating your child's life. Is every minute of her time scheduled? Has she shown any of the symptoms of excessive stress, such as headaches, digestive problems, sleep problems, eating disorders, reoccurring respiratory illness or inflammation of the ear, exacerbation of major ailments (asthma, infections, injuries), fatigue, psychosocial problems, depression, substance abuse, or attempted suicide? If any of these symptoms exist, your child may be over stressed.

Too Many Choices

One of the greatest sources of stress for young people is the ever-increasing number of choices they have in every aspect of their lives. Hundreds of cable channels, an endless selection of movies, enough video game choices to keep kids occupied for days, all kinds of music from multiple sources, and the Internet can fill in the blanks where the others leave off. As if the typical mall didn't provide enough shopping choices, you can now buy just about anything online. Even the school cafeteria now offers a choice of full meal, a la carte, salad bar, or grill. Even drinking water has become an agonizing decision, with countless choices available.

Have you ever stood in front of the toilet paper section at the grocery store and pondered why there are so many choices? You're buying a product whose sole purpose is to, well, you know, and you have to wade through a multitude of choices. Do you get single or double ply? What size bundle? four, six, twelve, or the jumbo twenty-four pack? Maybe you should just buy singles? Colored, flower print, white, extra strength, extra soft, or extra absorbent? And, of course, my personal favorite, the oxymoron of the toilet paper world, scented or not? All of these are seemingly insignificant choices, but choices that you nevertheless have to make. Am I the only one that thinks there are way too many meaningless choices? Personally, I just buy the cheapest.

While this overabundance of choices is anxiety producing for many adults, it can be downright debilitating for children. Although many parents want to empower their child by providing choices or use choices to teach them decision-making skills, as always, too much of a good thing often goes bad. Last summer I watched this play out in my local Baskin-Robbins ice cream shop, where a father and preschooler had stopped for ice cream on their way home from the park. As I sat eating my double-decker cone, I observed with interest the reaction of the toddler to this treat. Clearly excited when he entered the shop, the child asked his father to pick him up so he could better assess his choices, as he had been told he could have whatever he wanted. As he eagerly scanned the bins, he would point to a flavor and ask his dad, "What's that?" to which his father would reply with the name of the flavor. The patient father walked back and forth three or four times, often repeating the flavors of interest to the child, who, on each pass, picked one or two flavors that he wanted. However, each time he repeated the scan of the bins, the child changed his mind. After the third pass, I noticed that the child was becoming somewhat agitated and seemed to be experiencing this treat less as an exciting adventure and more as an overwhelming dilemma. Well, of course it was an overwhelming dilemma! How can a four-year-old possibly keep the names and attributes of thirty-one different kinds of ice cream in his head! As I watched this scenario unfold, I knew it would end with a crying child. Sure enough, the father's patience began wearing thin, particularly as other customers came and went with their ice cream and he began pressuring the child to "just pick what you want." By then the child was so confused and stressed that he just burst into tears. His father ended up ordering a chocolate cone and carrying the wailing child out to the car. What began as a pleasant father-son experience turned into a disaster.

Young children need limited choices. As they get older, they can handle a few more. However, even teenagers (and adults) need to be protected from the constant stress of too many choices, especially when those choices involve decisions that have little meaning or value to the child (like the toilet paper!).

Limiting the spectrum of choices for your child will do two things. First it allows your child to be freed from the extra burdens associated with copious insignificant choices. Secondly, your child is being given the opportunity to concentrate on the more critical aspects of life—learning in school, concentrated effort on activities, awareness of family relationships, and a focus on her future. Isn't it more worthwhile for your child to expend her energy on those important choices rather than wasting it on trivial matters?

Too Much Coddling

An interesting paradox seems to exist in many of today's families. While children are subjected to greater demands for high performance in a wide array of areas, these same children are being robbed of the experiences that will best equip them to face these increased demands. Children are expected to perform in more and more adult ways, yet in many significant ways they are the most overprotected generation of children in our history. I don't believe it's a coincidence that today's young adults seem reluctant to grow up. A colleague's recent story about his son illustrates this phenomenon. After several summers interning with a large software company, this twenty-three year old graduate of an elite private school and a prestigious University, was offered a rare opportunity to work at this company full time. How do you think this young man responded to this opportunity? "Dad, I can't go to work there. If I do, I'll probably work there for ten or fifteen years. That will mean I'm a grownup and I'm not ready to be a grownup!" Is it possible that these young people realize at some level that their over-achieving, privileged childhoods have not adequately prepared them for the challenges of adulthood? Or perhaps they are determined to extend their adolescence indefinitely because they were never really allowed the freedom to just be a kid.

From the minute they are born, children are capable of taking their first steps on the long road to self-sufficiency. A fussing infant who is allowed a few minutes to try to soothe herself before the parent comes to the rescue is learning an important skill and developing confidence in her ability to influence her environment. Those early experiences at self-regulating form the foundation for her ability to manage her emotions later in life.

When I was in grade school, I remember a teacher telling us about a species of bird whose hatchlings must struggle to break through their shell on their own in order to survive. If humans interfere with this process and help the hatchling break through the shell, the bird's chances for survival are reduced. The initial struggle of breaking through its shell helps prepare the young bird for its struggle for survival in the outside world. Humans need to take note of nature's lesson and learn to allow their children to experience the struggles that will prepare them for the outside world. When you do your child's homework, run to school to defend inappropriate behavior, intimidate teachers for grade changes, badger the coach for more playing time, or fabricate excuses for why your child didn't get the job done, you are denying your child the opportunity to learn how to be a strong, surviving individual. If you are the primary problem solver for your child, how and when does he learn to solve his own problems? Although you undoubtedly do so out of love for your child, coddling is a very *unloving* behavior, because it will create an adult who is ill-prepared for the daily challenges of life and without the internal resources to survive a major crisis.

When I think back to my early days as a new parent I can't help but chuckle. Every decision seemed to come with such great potential consequences. We worried about what toys he should play with, what kind of baby food he should eat first, whether he was getting too much or not enough sleep. In fact, human infants require adult nurturing and protection for longer than any other species. However, as with all other species, the ultimate goal of childhood is independent adulthood. Unfortunately, many of today's parents seem to have forgotten that goal. Rather than gradually allowing children to experience a series of increasingly demanding challenges and frustrations that build their resilience, confidence and competence, parents create an artificial existence for their children in which struggle and frustration are eliminated, problems are routinely solved by adults, and children's needs and wants are met on demand. Somewhere along the line, parents seem to have forgotten to notice that their infant was becoming a toddler, that their toddler was becoming a preschooler, their preschooler a young child, their young child an adolescent, and their adolescent a young adult. They seem to have forgotten that the skills needed for healthy adulthood don't just magically appear when a child turns 21.

As a result, parents seem to constantly flip-flop between too much protection and too much freedom. In one family I know there are stringent restrictions on television viewing because the parents don't believe it is educational enough. The school-age children in this family can only watch certain channels and are limited to one hour a day of television. Unfortunately these well-intentioned parents have no such guidelines for use of the computer. Of course, they have employed appropriate controls to ensure that their children aren't accessing dangerous websites or chat rooms, but beyond that, anything goes. Each child has a computer in his bedroom, all loaded with plenty of educational software, and the kids spend countless solitary hours mesmerized by this electronic pacifier. Naturally, all of this time spent plugged in is time not spent being physically active, learning social skills by interacting with other children or adults, or developing creativity through normal play.

One area where parental overprotection seems to be particularly blatant is in shielding children from the negative behaviors of other children or adults, for fear that exposing children to objectionable behavior may cause them to mimic that behavior. This assumption is patently untrue. In order for children to differentiate between right and wrong, between good and bad behavior, they need to be exposed to examples of both and shown the difference between the two. When my oldest son was about three years old, my wife asked me to talk to my older brother about refraining from smoking when he was around our son. I certainly wasn't pleased with my brother's habit, but I also saw this as an opportunity to educate my son on the evils of smoking. At a holiday gathering at my brother's house, he casually lit a cigarette and sat down on the couch to smoke. Seeing this, my son climbed up on my lap and quietly observed this unfamiliar behavior before asking a series of questions.

"What is he doing?"

"He's smoking a cigarette," I whispered in his ear.

"What's a cigarette?"

"Your uncle is burning tobacco and breathing in the smoke. See how he sucks the one end," I replied.

"Why?"

"Because it's a habit he started years ago and now he can't stop. Smoking is very harmful to your body and your uncle is hurting his body inside. I hope you never smoke because I want you to be healthy."

My son then stared at his Uncle for a few more minutes, quite puzzled. My son was fortunate to see this lesson through to its end two years later when my brother quit smoking. Careful to ensure that my son was nearby and listening, I asked my brother why he quit and how he felt after stopping. An avid and talented athlete like my son, he responded that he had realized that he couldn't even manage to play a full quarter of basketball without having to stop and catch his breath. He realized that smoking was keeping him from doing things he really loved to do. He emphatically stated that he felt a million times better since he had quit, and, in fact, he had recently played a full game of basketball with a group of much younger men and had played almost as well as he had in college! Later my son told me he was sure glad Uncle John could play basketball again and he also was happy that his Uncle wasn't, "hurting his insides any more." I concluded this mini-lesson for my son by congratulating my brother for his hard work in breaking this difficult habit.

Many parents I know view these types of experiences differently. They think it's better to shield their children from people doing things of which the parents disapprove. My question to these parents is, "How do you expect kids to understand and avoid the pitfalls of the world they will eventually enter if you protect them from seeing that world?" These experiences are windows of opportunities to teach everlasting lessons or values. Take advantage of these maximum opportunity moments. I assure you they will be much more powerful than the lecture you might give your child to, "just say no." These types of natural learning experiences help your child learn the relationship between an unhealthy behavior (such as smoking) and undesirable consequences (can't play basketball). Don't be afraid to let your child experience his neighborhood or community. Rather than hurrying your child across the street to avoid exposure to the homeless man sleeping in the park, take advantage of your child's natural curiosity to talk about circumstances that can lead to homelessness—mental health problems, substance abuse, etc. If your child is exposed to profane, derogatory or other inappropriate language, explain your expectations about that type of language and teach your child what the consequences of such use might be. When a disaster or crisis occurs, use it as an opportunity to teach your child how to cope with difficulties or loss, how to manage painful or distressing emotions, and how to keep herself safe. Accept the fact that bad things will happen and use them to your advantage.

Overprotecting your child sends a clear message to the child that you don't believe she is capable of handling this on her own. Regardless of their age, all children want to feel competent and powerful. When parents or teachers fail to gradually and systematically expose children to the realities of life in today's world, they rob children of those feelings of competence and power. It informs children that you don't really have enough confidence in their abilities.

Examples of parents overprotecting their kids are everywhere. In Everett, Washington, a state representative called the Superintendent of Schools on behalf of two sets of parents to pressure the school into changing a student's schedule so the child could have a particular teacher.[28] The parents of a teenager who had been dumped by her boyfriend immediately rushed her to a therapist to help her cope with this "crisis." The mother of a seven-year-old who was not invited to a classmate's birthday party complained so much to the teacher that the teacher initiated a rule that students must invite all of their classmates if they're going to have a party. Even tragedies occurring on the opposite side of the globe are considered so traumatic for students that they need adult help in coping. Whenever difficult emotions are involved, our typical first response is to rush in an army of adult helpers to soothe young people's pain and solve their problems for them.

When I taught junior high, I was often involved in dealing with emotional outbursts, which usually began with a girl entering my room crying. Ninety-nine percent of the scenarios involved one of three things—grades, boyfriend problems, or girlfriend arguments. In fact, I usually began the exploration process by asking the blubbering adolescent (who was crying so intensely that she was unable to speak, so she answered my questions with a series of nods) from which category her anguish stemmed. This helped me quickly diagnose the severity of the problem. In my three decades dealing with teenagers I have learned that very few of these "crises" really demand the kind of immediate intervention that the student seems to believe is required.

Generally, they are simply dealing with the natural process of learning about themselves and their relationships with other people. They experience the pain and emotional torment that accompanies such an episode and subsequently learn how to cope with the despair. They survive the ordeal and take a step closer to maturity.

I have experienced hundreds of these episodes and have found one approach that seems to work the best. In my early years I dutifully tried the techniques I had learned in college. I would listen empathetically, attempt to put the child in touch with her feelings, then identify the first step towards a solution, etc., etc., etc. Over time, I began to wonder why I had gotten into teaching when it seemed like so much of my time was spent counseling. After a few unsuccessful years using this strategy, I discovered that problems never really got solved. In most cases, the distraught student was often milking this emotional crisis for the attention it garnered—parents were worried, teachers backed off, counselors were there to listen, and friends came running to give support.

Frustrated with the ineffectiveness of this approach, I decided to try a different twist. One morning a student came up to my desk, blubbering friend in tow, requesting that she be allowed to go outside and console her distraught friend. I figured this was a good chance to try out my new strategy. I looked at the girl who was crying and said in a very honest and firm voice, "I have full confidence in your ability to deal with this problem on your own." The girl, who minutes earlier had been crying uncontrollably, looked at me and immediately stopped blubbering. The facial expression and demeanor of both girls immediately changed and they returned to their respective seats ready to begin the day's lesson. I was so shocked that I couldn't stop thinking about the situation. I realized that the previous approach (the one they had taught me in education school), not only failed to solve the problem, it actually exacerbated it. The student was never allowed or given permission to engineer her own solution. The overreaction and coddling by the grownups in her life convinced her that her problem was indeed a crisis that she could not possibly solve without the aid of the bigger, stronger, smarter adults.

Of course, there are some issues that *do* require adult intervention and support, but too often adults step in when the child is perfectly capable of solving her own problem. A teenager's response to this adult coddling is similar to the reaction I used to see in my sons when they were toddlers. When they would fall down, they would look at my wife or me to see what our reaction would be. If we rushed over to them and made a fuss, they would start crying. If, however, we ignored them or calmly said, "You're fine," they would get up and go about their play. You might be thinking that this sounds a bit callous or unfeeling. I believe that refusing to allow them to experience the heartaches and struggles of life is to not really care for them. A parent who allows a child to learn the hard lessons of life is a more deeply loving parent. Just as the fragile hatchlings must struggle, so must your child struggle if you want her to grow up to be a strong, confident, self-reliant adult.

In my upper middle class school district, rescuing children from the consequences of their behavior runs rampant. I learned this lesson early in my career when my wife and I were chaperoning the end of the year ninth grade dance at my school. This formal dance was the culmination of the year for the graduating ninth graders. As you might imagine from my earlier description of Prom night in my school district, this junior version was just as elaborate and just as big a deal to kids and parents alike. My wife was assigned to supervise the girls' restroom, keeping an eye on comings and goings and just making her presence known. About halfway through the evening, she walked into the restroom and found two girls conducting a drug transaction; one girl was handing another a pill in exchange for money. She immediately took the pill, the money, and the two offenders to the Vice Principal and explained the situation. The Vice Principal promptly called the girls' parents to tell them their daughters had been caught with illegal drugs on school grounds and explained the details, including the fact that they had been caught red-handed by a chaperone. He explained that possessing and/or dealing drugs on school property generally warranted police involvement. However, because the two girls involved were good students who had not been in trouble at school before, he had decided to let the parents handle the situation and not involve the police. When he requested that the parents come pick the girls up immediately, he was astounded to be met with a totally unanticipated reaction. Both girls' parents protested that their daughters would never do such a thing and the school couldn't ruin their big evening by sending them home. After all, the girls had been looking forward to this for months! Sending them home would embarrass them in front of their dates and their friends! When he got over the shock of this irresponsible parental reaction, the Vice Principal calmly told the parents that they had a choice. They could choose to have their daughters suffer the embarrassment of being sent home with their parents, or they could choose to have them suffer the embarrassment of leaving the dance in a police car and spending their "big night" at juvenile hall. The angry parents chose to pick up their daughters but it was made abundantly clear that their anger was at the unfair treatment their precious princesses had received, not at the dangerous and illegal behavior in which their daughters had engaged. Imagine the powerful lesson those young girls could have learned had their parents allowed the natural consequences of their behavior to occur. Unfortunately, what they learned instead is that nothing is ever their fault and that their parents will do whatever is necessary to protect them from bad feelings or difficult circumstances.

A couple of years ago I had a student assistant who came to school one day very excited. He had just received his driver's license. For his sixteenth birthday, his parents had bought him a very nice, but used, Porsche, which he had driven to school that day. The very next day he informed me that on the way home he had gotten a speeding ticket. The following day he hit the curb and lost control, totaling the car. Since he didn't have a car to drive, he hitched a ride to school with a good friend who had also just received his license. On the way to school the next morning, they got in an accident, totaling the friend's car as well as the car that they had hit. In order to protect his son's insurance record, the friend's father purchased the totaled car from the victim for its full pre-accident value. No more than two days later, each of the boys showed up at school driving nicer cars than the majority of the teaching staff. What do you think those boys learned from being continually rescued from the consequences of their behavior? Do you think they learned to be responsible?

If we want children to be able to face life's challenges with resilience and confidence in their ability to overcome difficulties, we must allow them to struggle with tough situations. We must allow them to experience the consequences of their actions and learn from their mistakes. For many overprotective parents, the first step is to simply refrain from rescuing their child from the natural consequences of her actions. When tempted to rescue, parents should ask themselves, "What's the worst that could happen if I allow my child to experience the natural consequences?" and "Is the lesson learned worth the temporary discomfort my child will experience?"

Remember the end you have in mind for your child. Your child *will* grow up to be an adult and he will live the majority of his life without you to protect him from the big, bad world. Will he have the confidence and self-reliance required to meet life's inevitable challenges? You can be assured that your child will, at some point in his life, have to face difficult situations that you can't fix. A girlfriend will dump him. He'll fail a test or a class. He'll be cut from the team or lose the big game. He will have to face the death of a pet, or a friend or a grandparent. Eventually he will lose you. Your job as a parent is to spend the first eighteen years of his life gradually preparing him to face life's challenges on his own.

Too Much Media

The media has been blamed for many of society's ills over the last half century, but from the perspective of its influence on young people, the most significant problem is not the *content,* but the amount of time it takes away from other activities. The average American child spends thirty-eight hours a week consuming media, the largest amount of time being spent watching TV, with almost three hours a day spent glued to the screen. When you include weekend viewing, some children spend as much time watching television as their parents do working. Two out of three children eight years or older have a TV set in their bedroom and one out of ten have computers with Internet access in their bedrooms. In many families, the TV is on during meals, increasing the isolation and separation of family members. Only 5% of parents routinely watch television with their children, meaning that the vast majority of television time is also unsupervised time.[29] For previous generations of children, church, home, and school were considered primary influences on young people's development. Today, the power of media must be recognized and addressed.

The media makes a convenient scapegoat for kids' undesirable behavior. We've all seen these examples—a violent attack by a teenager attributed to repeated exposure to a violent movie, a child who attempts suicide after listening to a specific song, a student who runs away from home to meet a lover met in an online chat room. Certainly media has an effect on young people, but the degree of influence varies tremendously for individual children. Exposure to negative influences in the media shouldn't be pinpointed as the single, or even most important, contributor to antisocial behavior. Rather than looking at those young people who are exposed to antisocial media and asking why they act out, perhaps we should be looking at the vast majority of kids who are exposed to the same media and ask why those kids *don't* commit delinquent or violent acts.

Blaming some nameless, faceless entity for all of society's problems is a popular form of scapegoating in this country. I am constantly amazed at how often stories of "kids gone berserk" result in public outcry and calls for silver bullet solutions to problems with deep and complex origins. Does anyone really believe that a teenager who is doing well in school, has plenty of friends, and enjoys a good home life is going to decide to gun down teachers and classmates because he watched a violent video or listened to hard rap? Yet, we continue to ignore the deeper, more entrenched problems while focusing time and attention on those easy targets that make us feel like we've addressed the problem.

So we require rating systems for videos, CDs, video games, even television programs. We call for software to block inappropriate websites. We equip televisions with V-chips. These strategies are all designed to return control to parents. Wait a minute. I thought parents already *had* control. Why do parents need a microchip to exert their parental authority? Why do parents need a ratings panel to tell them that a television program is inappropriate for their nine-year-old? As so often happens, these solutions often exacerbate the problem because they fail to address the root causes of negative behavior. They attempt to use external *controls* to influence children's behavior instead of teaching skills, rearranging the environment to promote the desired behavior or applying direct parental influence on children's choices.

Let's take the example of a young teenager visiting inappropriate websites. Mom walks into Junior's room one day and finds him looking at a pornographic website. Her solution is to install monitoring software that blocks his access to certain websites and tracks where he is going on the Internet. It never occurs to her that her first step should be to *get the computer out of the kid's room and stop allowing him to spend so much time online*! You can bet that, if the computer is in the family room, where the parents are sitting reading the paper or watching television, Junior is going to be far less likely to surf for porn. It never occurs to her to sit down and talk with him about why she finds those sites offensive, dangerous, or inappropriate for him. So, what does Junior learn from this solution? He doesn't learn to make good choices. He doesn't learn anything about his parents' beliefs about pornography. He probably either learns to: 1) go to a friend's house and use an unmonitored computer, or 2) surf the net to find tips for bypassing the control software.

Like most good parenting practices, dealing with the influences of media requires parental time and energy. If you want to know what television programs your child is watching, watch with her. If you want to determine whether or not certain music is appropriate, talk to your children about the CDs they want to purchase. (Hint: It doesn't take a "ratings panel" to determine that a CD with songs titled, "I Wanna F... You" (Violator) or "Cocaine Dreams" (50 Cent) or "Got Yourself a Gun" (NAS) may not meet your approval.)

Above all, don't focus your attention on media influences to the exclusion of those factors that have a much more significant impact on your child's development. It's simple; the more time a child spends watching videos, listening to a walkman, watching television, surfing the Internet, or playing video games, the less time he is spending with parents or others who might be positive influences. Your time and positive influence will have far greater influence than the occasional violent movie or video game.

As our sons were growing up, my wife and I talked about these issues at length. Should we limit their music selections? What about videos? Is it G-rated until age 13? We made several key decisions early on. First, we have never had more than one television in our house, which was always in the family room. So we usually watched TV and videos together as a family. The computer has also always been in a common area. Our kids have never had Nintendo, Sega, X-Box or other video game players, although they do play them when they're at friends' houses. We have always used common sense to guide our choices of what is appropriate, with an emphasis on teaching them to make good choices on their own. Both of our sons like Rap music, although they are equally happy to listen to Motown, to which they have been exposed since they were infants. They watched me dance to the beats and move to the Motown groove. In fact, the pre-game warm-up music for my son's varsity basketball team was a Temptations' classic hit.

So are we worried about the profanity and vulgarity in much of the Rap music our kids listen to? No, because my sons don't use profanity in our presence because that's always been the rule in our home. My wife and I don't swear in front of them, they don't swear in front of us. When they were in their early teens and first began to show an interest in this music, my wife talked to each of them about the language in some of the songs they listened to that bothered her. She explained that it wasn't the profanity that bothered her, because she knew that they knew better than to use that language. However, it disturbed her that some of the songs used language that was violent or degrading to women and she found that extremely offensive. She did not, however, forbid them to listen to that music; she just shared her opinions, beliefs, and concerns, with the understanding that she trusted them to make good decisions. The unspoken agreement, therefore, was that they could listen to their music with headphones on, but it could not be played where anyone else would hear it. Even as young adults, when they drive her car they are careful to make sure they remove their CDs from the CD player before they return the car.

Other parents wonder what limitations they should place on videos or television programs. The ratings given movies or television programs are artificial judgments assigned by strangers who know nothing of your beliefs or values. Rather than relying on these strangers, parents need to take the time to choose age appropriate movies and watch them with their kids. If you are active in the selection process and use this as an opportunity to teach your child important lessons about your beliefs and values, the issue of inappropriate movies becomes a non-issue.

My wife and I never made a big deal out of what films our sons could watch. When my oldest son was about seven I decided to run a little test. I had stopped on the way home to get a video. I purposely chose one that had received excellent reviews but was R-rated. Without informing my son that we had a video, I sat down and started watching the movie. After a few minutes, he came into the room, looking for something to do. I said nothing and he sat down and watched for about ten minutes, during which there was some brief nudity and a few vulgar words used. I didn't react to these things, except for a slightly over-dramatized look of disgust when he glanced at me after hearing the third cuss word. After about ten minutes, he got up and left, declaring that, "this movie is boring." From that point on, we rarely limited their viewing because they limited it themselves. The few areas that we found inappropriate for them, especially when they were younger, were horror and violence against women, which wasn't really a problem, because we rarely watched those kinds of movies ourselves.

Overall, we weren't overly concerned about the influence of media on our kids' values and behavior, because we felt confident that our influence was far greater. We trusted that our early investments in teaching them right from wrong and what behavior was okay and not okay would pay off, which they have. The side effects of overindulgence in media, such as obesity, depression, poor school performance, sleep problems, violence, hypersensitivity to issues of fear (natural disasters, earthquakes, nuclear war, airplane crashes, the evil stranger, etc.), just are not issues in our home because the amount of media our kids were allowed to consume was balanced.

Another important aspect of media's influence on kids is the degree to which your media consumption behavior serves as a model for your child. The degree of influence media will have on your child is in direct relationship to how much influence media has on you. If you are a sophisticated and critical consumer of media, your kids will learn how to make good choices, as well. If you are mesmerized by the media's spell, then your child will likely be equally afflicted. My sons don't always like the same movies I do or have the same taste in music, but what they do have is a keen sense of what media is all about. They understand the role of profit and advertising in media. They watch programs with a critical eye, evaluating the material, and not always accepting what is being presented as fact. They understand the difference between reality and sitcoms. They spend moderate amounts of time consuming media and moderate amounts of effort judging what they will consume. A little bit of silly TV mixed with a little informative programming makes for a good balance. Listening to some edgy music tempered by the classics promotes well roundedness. Formal Internet research for school papers along with a little frivolous surfing exposes the powerful potential of the Internet. A good action movie coupled with an Oscar-winning film broadens their view of the world. As in so much of parenting, balance is the key. If accompanied with a little common sense, you can ensure that media will not play a starring role in your child's development.

As the old saying goes, "Too much of anything can be bad." The areas of "too much" that we've discussed in this section all add up to conditions that hinder healthy development for children: too much stimulation, too much to do, with not enough thought given to what is really beneficial. Attention spans in the last three decades have decreased significantly. All you need to do is watch MTV videos for a few minutes and you will get a taste of your child's attention span. Constant changes in image (approximately every two seconds), bright colors and spectacular scenes, painfully loud volume, and ever more spectacular special effects, are all designed to capture and hold the attention of your child. The bar for maintaining attention has been raised to a level that cannot be duplicated in real life, as teachers fighting to keep the attention of their students for sixty minutes know all too well. The pace of young people's lives has been escalated to a point where it shouldn't surprise us that so many are checking out. Indeed, we should be amazed that so many are still holding on.

Perhaps nothing so clearly captures the world in which our children are growing up than the latest addition to America's cultural lexicon—24/7. Is 24/7 really good for kids? We have sacrificed the leisurely, natural unfolding of children's talents, skills, and interests for a high-pressure, fast-paced, stressful, structured existence. The mental connections the brain once formed through thought and imagination are now being replaced by an array of technologies. The TV set placates the mind instead of outside play stimulating thought and exercise; the DVD player and on-demand programming ensure that young people have access to an endless array of video choices at any time of the day or night. Video games continually push the limits of excitability, desensitizing young minds to reality. Computers think for the child, so basic skills are considered superfluous. Adults schedule activities for their children, feverishly fending off the whining, "I'm bored." Parents organize leagues and teams, robbing children of the chance to learn to lead. And society is progressively eliminating life's obstacles so kids don't learn to solve their own problems. Instead of scheduling the next enrichment opportunity, maybe it would be in your child's best interests to schedule an hour of unscheduled time. Kids who live in a 24/7 world desperately lack the opportunity to relax. Rather than directing your energies toward *increasing* their opportunities, choices, and activities, perhaps you should take responsibility for counteracting the effects of a world that already offers too much.

If you are wondering about the effects of "too much" on your child, ask yourself the following questions:

Do you frequently (more than once a week) purchase gifts for your child?

Do you find the value of those gifts progressively increasing in value?

Does your child demonstrate a preoccupation with material things by frequently asking for money, expecting financial rewards for every effort, believing that money can solve most problems, preferring friends who have material wealth, complaining about not having what others have, or displaying selfish or egocentric tendencies?

Do you feel expenditures for private school, camps, or lessons are a financial burden?
Do you feel overloaded with your child's activities and lessons?

Do your kids consistently complain about having to go on another cultural or enriching event?

Does your child show any of the physical symptoms of stress, such as eating disorders, overuse injuries, headaches, stomachaches, depression?

Does your child demonstrate obsessive behavior with any of the media sources?

Has your child taken on a trophy-like quality (you judge yourself by your child's accomplishments)?

Does your child spend large blocks of time away from the family (camps, nannies, daycare, boarding schools)?

Do you find yourself rationalizing your child's behavior or shortcomings? (The instructor's teaching style isn't compatible with your child's learning style difference, the daycare provider just doesn't understand how "gifted" your child is, other parents just aren't comfortable with how "active" your child is)

Have you changed your own social life as a result of your child's behavior? (Not going out to dinner, not getting together with certain friends who don't appreciate your child)

Do you have inflexible standards or demanding expectations for your child (read a book a week, rigid conditioning programs, new enriching event once a week)?

Do you love your child, but find yourself often not *liking* him?

If you find yourself relating to a few of these questions, you are sowing the seeds of a child who will likely eventually suffer from "too much." If you agreed with more than half of these questions, you desperately need to change your ways before these symptoms irreparably damage your child's future.

We've spent considerable time on the elements of "too much" in families, now let's turn our attention to the issue of "too much" in schools.

TOO MUCH IN SCHOOLS

Have I gone totally nuts? How can schools have too much? Don't we read daily about the lack of resources and the progressively deteriorating educational facilities throughout the country? Lack of books, outdated texts, inadequate science labs, archaic math programs, unsafe equipment, crumbling classrooms, malfunctioning heating systems, overworked staff, and underpaid teachers, hardly signs of a system that is suffering from too much. But, just as money can't buy love, financial resources are not the only determinant of the quality of an educational system. Although few states have a system to fund schools adequately, that is not my focus in this section. Instead, I would like to address issues unrelated to financial solvency or funding inequities. I would like to direct attention to another group of forces that compromise your school system on a daily basis.

TOO MUCH "PASSING THE BUCK"

The children served by this country's schools enter their classrooms with increasingly diverse and multifaceted needs. The school systems that serve these children are large, complex, multi-layered bureaucracies. Even in so-called decentralized school systems, where decision-making and control are pushed down to the school building level, fragmentation and lack of coordination are more the norm than the exception. School boards and district administrators who coordinate the entire district's needs are often detached from the realities of today's classrooms. Overwhelmed and preoccupied by other issues, their priorities may focus more on reacting to crises than on proactive planning for the educational welfare of students. Balancing budgets, protecting district image, competition for more students (which translates into more money), political issues within the community, satisfying state and federal regulations, and the ever-present search for more money are priorities that tend to devour the time and attention of these individuals. As a result, their decisions are often based not on the needs of students but on criteria far removed from the classroom. When decisions are made that will directly influence the ability of the teacher to run an effective class, accountability for that decision is rarely established. If the decision is a complete failure, there is rarely an evaluation process to activate its reversal.

To add insult to injury, most district administrators are reluctant to defer decisions about instructional issues to those who are most influenced by those decisions because of fear that it will weaken their authority or compromise their egos. Therefore, even if teachers are willing to accept responsibility for instructional or disciplinary decisions, administrators rarely relinquish that control. As a result, countless decisions are made that directly impact the functioning of the classroom, yet when those decisions produce negative results, the frenzied finger pointing starts and the buck stops nowhere, because ultimate blame is bounced from person to person in the bureaucratic labyrinth like a pinball in a pinball machine. The buck needs to stop someplace. That's the price of leadership.

A clear demonstration of this lack of accountability took place in the district in which I teach just a few years ago. Having a comfortable revenue source from its affluent taxpayer base, the district was able to carry a sizable cash reserve. Over the course of a few years, the superintendent of this district repeatedly made poor fiscal choices, severely reducing the cash reserve. Ignoring the repeated warnings of the district's financial staff, the superintendent continued to spend haphazardly. This blatant lack of fiscal accountability ultimately resulted in a multimillion-dollar decrease in cash reserves, a sizeable sum for this small suburban district. To offset the deficit, significant cuts were necessitated in many areas. Everyone involved with the school district paid a price for the incompetence of this one individual.

When we learned of this gross mismanagement of district funds, we naturally assumed that the Superintendent would be held accountable for her behavior. Certainly a blunder of this magnitude couldn't be ignored. But we had misjudged the situation, failing to remember that we weren't talking about a healthy, functioning system, but a system that is weak, spineless, and void of accountability. Not only did the Superintendent keep her job, the school board nominated her for Superintendent of the Year. A few months after the release of the information about her financial mismanagement, she was chosen the State's Superintendent of the Year and went on to be honored as one of the top four

Superintendents in the Nation. Sound unbelievable? It *should* be unbelievable. Such behavior should never be tolerated in a system supported by hard-earned taxpayer dollars. Yet, this is just one of many examples of a system that allows unbelievable, irrational behavior to survive, and flourish.

Why does education always seem to be floundering? Is educating children really such a complicated, difficult process that tens of thousands of school systems around the country can't seem to get it right? No, although educating children in today's world may be more complicated than in previous generations, it's still not that hard. The problem lies with a system that is set up to obscure accountability; a system that promotes buck passing; a system in which no one is willing to put his or her neck on the line and accept responsibility for what happens. In the last decade, school systems have taken to comparing themselves to the business world, with Superintendents as CEOs of their school districts. Unfortunately, I find it hard to believe that any business would survive for long with the kind of freedom from accountability that exists in most school systems. The recent spate of corporate scandals has shown that, not only is such financial mismanagement likely to result in losing one's job, it may result in criminal action. Are these irresponsible chief executives being nominated for Executive of the Year?

Leadership is about making knowledgeable decisions and taking responsibility for them. A school district leader must be in close contact with those who do the "work" of schools, meaning they must be constantly interacting with the teachers who spend their days educating students. Education takes place in that thirty-by-thirty foot classroom, not in the district central office, the boardroom, the textbook company, or the university education department. If research consistently shows that the best way to increase student success is through good teachers, shouldn't that simple, indisputable fact be the guiding force in our decisions about education?

A friend of mine works for a large publishing company. His company conducted research that showed that the most important factor in their customers' decisions about whether or not to buy their product was the quality of the account executive (salesperson) with whom they had contact. As a result, the company went through a major reorganization to focus the majority of their resources on ensuring that those sales people were well-trained, well-compensated, and well-supported. They redirected resources from things that their research indicated weren't contributing to increased sales and profits to resources that directly impacted their sales staff. They recruited the best of the best and worked hard to keep them that way. The strategy paid off and the company has consistently outperformed its competitors.

So why do school systems find it so hard to adopt these logical processes? And why aren't the millions of taxpayers who support these school systems demanding that they change? Again the answer is simple. No one is willing to publicly challenge the dysfunctional system. No one is willing to commit to doing the tough and long-term work required to effectively educate students. No one is willing to force discussion of issues that are politically charged or historically taboo. No one is willing to say that things have gone too far and some things haven't gone far enough. No one is willing to be a spokesperson for the child and the teacher. No one is willing to stand up and tell the American public that schools can't solve all of society's problems. No one is willing to take on the fact that attracting and retaining world class teachers will require revamping teacher compensation to be more competitive with other fields vying for the same top scholars. No one is willing to demand that school funding mechanisms be radically restructured to provide for the kind of long-term, reliable, comprehensive funding required. Sure, we have "Education Governors" and "Education Presidents," but none of those politicians are willing to compromise votes by suggesting that the public schools that American citizens overwhelming say they want will require new taxes. What is the common thread running through all of these statements? Leadership. School systems are large, complex bureaucracies. Bureaucracies are made up of people and human systems need leadership and accountability to produce results.

I once tested this passing-the-buck process in the context of one of the never-ending, always changing state programs designed to supplement woefully inadequate state funding of public schools. Individual schools were given a one-time lump sum of money (a tiny sum, of course) to be spent as the school saw fit. The state had issued guidelines for use of the money, but they were vague and left considerable room for interpretation. The idea was that school staff would get together and decide how best to use this new money. At my school, a committee was formed (schools *love* decision by committee) to develop initial recommendations to be shared with the rest of the staff. I volunteered to be on the committee. I had an idea for use of these funds that would address one of the most pressing problems in our school—student discipline. I was fairly certain that my proposal didn't fit within the guidelines, but I thought the idea was valuable enough to give it a try. When I shared my idea with the Principal, she dismissed it, saying that it didn't fall within the guidelines. When I asked her to specify exactly where in the guidelines she had found the documentation to support her rejection, she couldn't do so and told me to call the Superintendent. I decided to see how far I would have to go to actually find someone who would take responsibility and say no. So I called the Superintendent and explained my idea. He wasn't enthusiastic about it but wouldn't say it was outside of the guidelines. He referred me to the person in the district responsible for the allocation of the state funds. She didn't like the idea either but wouldn't say no. She told me to call the state office that was administering the program. The head administrator there also didn't like the idea but couldn't bring himself to actually say no. This wasn't a high-stakes, high profile situation! It wasn't a large sum of money. Yet, three high-level administrators were incapable of taking responsibility for this simple decision. The buck never seems to stop anywhere.

Too Much Jumping on the Bandwagon

One result of a system in which accountability lies with no one is that classroom teachers are constantly being forced to expend energy adjusting to new programs or complying with new mandates. This constant change is exhausting and frustrating. Like some kind of cyclical mating ritual, schools become infatuated with a trendy educational philosophy every few years and promote it with an all-consuming enthusiasm. Whether it's cooperative learning, integrated thematic learning, or the seven intelligences, school systems swallow the newfound concept and force-feed it to everyone in the system. Large sums of money are spent dispersing the latest, greatest fad. Mandatory seminars consume time and money. Teachers are marched through the new indoctrination system, armed with new knowledge and the promise that this is the one true thing that will solve all the problems they face in their classrooms. It may be days, it may be weeks, it may be years, but at some point they inevitably discover that this latest panacea also fails to address the real obstacles debilitating the classroom on a daily basis. It doesn't take too long for new teachers to realize that this is just another game that needs to be played.

These new fads are wolves in sheep's clothing. The public likes these trendy things because it gives the appearance that schools are being improved. Schools like this public approval because it makes them feel progressive and productive. But in the final analysis, "nothin' changes but the changes." I can truly say that in my entire teaching career I have not attended one, single in-service training that motivated me to incorporate any of the new techniques or information into my teaching. On the contrary, some of these workshops have actually cemented my commitment to concepts that directly opposed the current fad.

In his book, "Confucius Lives Next Door," author T.R. Reid compares American school systems to those in Asia, particularly in Japan.[30] One of the key differences he identified is that, in Asia, excellence in teaching is seen as a function of continuous repetition, practice, and honing of an instructional approach. In other words, Asian cultures consider the quality of the teacher (experience, expertise, and excellence) to be far more significant to student success than the content of the curriculum. In contrast, American educational curricular fads come and go so quickly that no teacher really has the opportunity to develop expertise and excellence with a given program or curriculum before it is zapped to make room for the latest new silver bullet. In this context, even highly skilled and experienced teachers are always rookies, because they are continually starting from scratch with a new program. This focus on curricula as the be-all, end-all of academic success is shortsighted and inconsistent with the research on the most significant factors in student achievement. Study after study has found that a high quality teacher is far more important than the type of curriculum used.[31] Yet the American educational system pours hundreds of millions of dollars and vast amounts of time and energy into keeping the curriculum development companies in business, while both the quantity and quality of teachers willing to brave America's public school classrooms continues to decline.

So, how does it hurt schools to try something new once in a while? Isn't innovation a good thing? The real problem lies in the huge waste of time and energy sucked up by each new program that comes down the pike. I think most teachers, myself included, would be more than willing to put in this extra time and energy if the changes *actually produced the desired results*. Unfortunately, I've seen scores of such innovations come and go and not a single one has produced the changes it promised.

Another negative side effect of this constant bandwagon-hopping is that it often divides the faculty philosophically. On any faculty, there are those teachers who will dive into the latest trend, either because they naively continue to believe that these Band Aid solutions will work or because they want to be a good team player. On the other side are those teachers who oppose the change, either actively or passively, because what they do works, because they have already tried this latest "innovation" in its previous guise and found it to be ineffective, or sometimes just because they are tired of the constant change and want a chance to try something long enough to actually get good at it. Because of schools' predilection for constant change, this means that teachers are always choosing sides in the latest battle; a climate that is unlikely to foster the kind of collegial environment that would really support effective education. Ultimately the kids will always be the ones to suffer.

Educating a child is not a difficult thing, certainly not as difficult as the current educational landscape, littered with failed school systems, failed schools, and failed students, would have one believe. There is a broad and deep body of knowledge that stretches back to the days of Socrates on how to effectively teach children. Although new brain research has helped us better understand *how* children learn, this new information simply provides confirmation to support the effective practices that good teachers have always used. The field of education, particularly those who inhabit University Schools of Education and District Administrative Offices, like to think each new idea is a fresh discovery. The truth is that every new educational fad is really a recycled idea presented in a new package. Veteran teachers will tell you nothing is new.

When I first started teaching in 1977, "blocking" classes was a well-established practice. English and History classes were routinely combined into longer class periods so the subjects had crossover elements and teachers could reinforce writing and reading skills. This practice was later discarded after new research demonstrated students learned better in subject-specific classes, which allegedly increased concentration and focus. Two decades later, blocking is back. Now research says that combining the classes promotes continuity in learning. Repackaged and re-labeled as team teaching, interdisciplinary teaching, or cross-curricular teaching, blocking is back in the educational limelight. Given a facelift and reinforced by a new set of researchers, blocking is still the same stuff it was twenty years ago.

Too Much Waste

The first thing wasted in the educational world is time. Most teachers spend inordinate amounts of time creating things that have already been developed—unit plans, tests, projects, quizzes, worksheets, anything that you need is already developed. Whatever teachers are looking for probably already exists in their own buildings. If not, these things certainly exist somewhere within the district. As a last resort, the Internet is filled with sites devoted to helping teachers present the best curriculum imaginable. Over the course of my teaching career, in which I have countless times been asked to teach a class for which I had no formal training, I have found that there are often so many materials available that the real chore is choosing the best ones. This leads me to the Golden Rule I share with my interns, college students doing their practice teaching with me in preparation for certification. The first thing I tell them is, "Don't work any harder than you need to." I also tell them to steal as much as they can, from whomever they can. Ask for ideas and examples of what others have done and found effective. Communicate with other schools to find out what they do and what has worked best for them. Collect information from those who are about to retire. Check out the Internet and modify the material to fit your teaching style and curricular needs. Then, go home on time.

One of the reasons so much time is wasted in school systems is that most educational decisions start with individuals who are far removed from students—researchers, central office administrators, policymakers, even politicians—all claiming to know what's best for students. The people most distanced from the classroom are the very ones who attempt to catalyze dramatic educational change. Some of these individuals have the best of intentions, but they are so disconnected from the reality of today's classrooms that their ideas are doomed to fail. Researchers, for example, may demonstrate great success with a particular innovation under tightly controlled experimental conditions, but those experimental conditions are rarely or never found in the real world. Policymakers and politicians, on the other hand, have a tendency to believe that passing a law (mandating high-stakes testing or requiring anti-bullying policies in schools) will somehow magically effect changes, even when those mandates are not accompanied by the resources required to address the fundamental systemic issues underlying these problems. Central office administrators, of course, need to promote constant change in order to justify their jobs.

So, we jump on the next bandwagon, wasting time and resources that could be better used to address the long-term systemic changes that are the only legitimate solution to the problems facing public schools. The current standards-based philosophy is the latest panacea, sucking up billions of dollars in school districts and states around the country. Increasing standards for student achievement sounds like a great idea; the higher the standards, the smarter the kid. It seems simple until you begin to ask some critical questions. In 1993, the State of Washington embarked on an ambitious education reform agenda that included defining the curricular standards that should be expected from a well-educated student in our state. Progress toward those standards is measured by the Washington Assessment of Student Learning (WASL) test, given annually to fourth, seventh and tenth graders. The culmination of this standards-based assessment process is a high-stakes test given to tenth graders, who must pass the test in order to receive the state-mandated Certificate of Mastery. Students in the earlier grades who don't pass the WASL will not be allowed to matriculate to the next grade. High school students who do not receive their Certificate of Mastery won't graduate. So far, the

State of Washington has spent over $50 million designing the tests, training staff, revamping curricula to better prepare students for the kind of questions measured on the test, and piloting the whole process.[32] Early pilot testing has produced discouraging results. In my upper middle class, suburban school district, which is always at the top of the state in test scores, just under half of the students are failing. The larger urban districts are experiencing failure rates closer to 71.9%, with the state average running 70% of students failing to meet standard in all four subjects.[33] Even with continued teacher training and curriculum redesign, how much can we realistically expect to be able to reduce these dismal failure rates?

When I was first exposed to this reform agenda, like many of my colleagues I had a number of questions about the wisdom of such an approach, as well as the feasibility and logistics. In an attempt to understand this massive undertaking to which we had been committed, I began trying to get answers to the following questions. All of these questions have been asked of Principals, Superintendents, and the Superintendent of Public Instruction multiple times without any satisfactory answers.

1. If one out of five kids cannot pass on to the next grade, what will you do with those kids who fail the test?

2. Will the schools set up remedial classes at all levels (4th, 7th, 10th) to re-teach the basic academic skills?

3. If so, who will teach those classes and where will the additional money come from to house and instruct this special population?

4. What happens to those students who repeatedly fail? Will there be teenagers attending elementary schools?

5. Will there be special considerations given to any student who has special needs?

6. Will special need kids have to meet the same standards as mainstream students?

7. Will parents accept their child not progressing to the next grade because of a failing WASL test?

8. Will high schools really keep students from graduating if they have passed all the required classes but have not passed the WASL?

9.Will a Certificate of Mastery really be of value and carry respectful weight in the real world?

10. Are universities and colleges on board with this new way of

assessing students and are they adjusting their acceptance procedures to this new system?

11. Are there schools that have already tried this process and found it to produce better results?

12. Are there going to be provisions for those students with limited English proficiency?

13. For those students who do pass the WASL in tenth grade, how will the school keep the rest of their high school experience meaningful?

For many teachers, myself included, these questions seemed critical and should have been adequately addressed before committing to such an expensive and disruptive process. In fact, one of the most striking things to me as I have watched this process unfold is how little concern there appears to be that these glaring holes exist in a system into which we are pouring phenomenal amounts of money and time.

However, ten years later, we are beginning to discover some of the answers to these questions.

1. If one out of five kids cannot pass on to the next grade, what will you do with those kids who fail the test?

According to results collected in pilot testing, failure rates average 70%, not even close to the one out of five failure rate that spurred teachers to ask this question. Schools are not equipped to deal with the burden of well over half of students not moving on to the next grade.

2. Will the schools set up remedial classes at all levels (4th, 7th, 10th) to re-teach the basic academic skills?

Although everyone supports the idea of remedial classes for students who fail the test, there is no plan.

3. If so, who will teach those classes and where will the additional money come from to house and instruct this special population?

No one has a clue where the additional money or personnel will come from. (As we go to press the Washington public education system is in a severe budget crisis.)

4. What happens to those students who repeatedly fail? Will there be teenagers attending elementary schools?

According to the "get tough" attitude of the program, this is a possibility. But don't worry, school systems aren't exactly known for holding firm to bottom lines.

5. Will there be special considerations given to any student who has special needs? *There will be considerations given for those students who have special needs. What considerations, no one knows. And, no one has yet defined what qualifies as special needs in terms of the WASL.*

6. Will special needs kids have to meet the same standards as mainstream students?

All public school students must take the WASL, including special education students. Accommodations can be made (readers, scribes, extra time, etc.) but these students must meet the same standards as mainstream students. Only 5% of special needs students can be exempt, which translates into about 2 or 3 students per school.

7. Will parents accept their child not progressing to the next grade because of a failing WASL test?

Having spent the last 27 years dealing with parents who routinely challenge teachers who give their child a B instead of the A that the parent and student want (regardless of what the student earned), I have no doubt that the first lawsuit challenging this new process will be filed within weeks of the first student denied graduation because of failure to achieve the Certificate of Mastery.

8. Will high schools really keep students from graduating if they have passed all the required classes but have not passed the WASL?

No. As I write this chapter, the Superintendent of Public Instruction for Washington State announced that she is proposing to give students more ways to pass the state's high-stakes test by changing the passing system and using alternative assessments for those students who fail repeatedly. According to the Superintendent, the bottom line is skills. There are a lot of ways to assess those skills. How true! Maybe things like regular classroom assessments and grades given by teachers trained to assess student progress—things that we were already doing before we decided we needed high-stakes testing to assess students' mastery. In fact, the Superintendent suggested that students be given four chances to pass the WASL, then, if they don't pass, they should be assessed using an alternative tool, such as an essay to be graded by teachers! *Notice that the focus is not on providing additional resources to ensure that all students have the skills required to pass the test, rather it is on finding ways to ensure that no students fail. Does this truly serve the interests of students or does it serve the interests of those promoting the high-stakes testing process? Virtually all states that have adopted high-stakes testing have been forced to significantly lower or compromise those standards because they are unwilling to accept the inevitable failure rates.*

9.Will a Certificate of Mastery really be of value and carry respectful weight in the real world?

Why would it be? Why would a potential employer place more value on a Certificate of Mastery than on a student's grades or a high school diploma?

10. Are universities and colleges on board with this new way of assessing students and are they adjusting their acceptance procedures to this new system?

Some colleges and universities are reluctantly bowing to pressure to include the Certificate of Mastery in their acceptance process. However, grade point averages and S.A.T. scores have proven to work well for them. If they are going to rely on standardized tests, they will certainly stick with those well-established nationally-normed tests with which they are familiar.

11. Are there going to be provisions for those students with limited English proficiency?

There will be accommodations made, but to what degree no one knows. It is likely that they will join the growing pool of students for whom the "standards" are not really standards at all, but an arbitrary level at which they can pass.

12. For those students who do pass the WASL in tenth grade, how will the school keep the rest of their high school experience meaningful?

No one knows what high schools will do to keep these students actively engaged in school once they have satisfied the requirements for their Certificate of Mastery. Presumably this will be less of a problem for college-bound students who must fulfill additional requirements for university entrance, but it is likely to adversely impact those students who are at highest risk for dropping out.

So, to summarize, the State of Washington (like most other states around the country) has engaged in a process that has cost millions of dollars and countless hours of staff time. That process was designed to improve academic performance for all students by raising the bar, identifying quantifiable standards that we expect all students to achieve and then administering a regular test that would assess the attainment of those standards. Such a system would allow the public (parents, employers, the community at large) to regain their confidence in the "product" being produced by public school systems. In other words, a student who had achieved a Certificate of Mastery would have the equivalent of the Good Housekeeping Seal of Approval, assuring the public that the student had mastered a certain body of knowledge and skills and had demonstrated that mastery in an indisputable way. A sizeable chunk of the resources expended in this process were to develop and test the assessment instruments. Presumably these new tests were needed because the old assessment methods (teacher assessments, grades, standardized tests, etc.) were judged inadequate. However, just as with other assessment methods, some students did very well on these high-stakes tests, others did average, and some failed. Unfortunately, this particular system was set up under the very questionable assumption that *all* students could pass. When reality intruded and the powers that be realized that such an ambitious goal was unattainable, the scurrying began—the test was changed, more and more students were exempted from the standards, and, finally, standards were lowered. And what happens when a student can't even pass the lowered standards? The test is thrown out the window and students are assessed the old-fashioned way, using an essay graded by a teacher. Now, am I crazy or was this all a very expensive exercise in futility? A system that begins with the assumption that a teacher's assessment is fundamentally unreliable, proceeds to spend millions of dollars to bypass that flawed assessment, then comes full circle to a fall-back position that relies on the teacher's assessment. That's progress!

The final blow in this farce? The Washington State Superintendent of Public Instruction's call for alternative assessments for students who fail the WASL comes with a significant price tag (that's in addition to the millions that have already been spent on this fiasco). An alternative test that will require teacher training and allowing students four chances to pass the WASL was repeatedly deemed too expensive in the past.[34]

Unfortunately, as a result of the federal No Child Left Behind policy, all states that receive federal funding must now go through this absurd process. More time, effort, and money wasted, yet just as many students left behind.

Did anyone really think that changing the test would somehow equalize student achievement? Did anyone really believe that if we just raise the bar for student achievement, that, miraculously all students will be able to jump over it? In track and field, the bar is not raised until *after* the athlete has first cleared the bar. One noted education researcher who has studied the standards-based reform movement aptly says that we are producing too many students who are learning to limbo under the bar.

So why would school systems embark on such a doomed endeavor? Much of the blame lies with the bureaucracy that runs school systems. Central office administrators and State education administrators constantly need to reinvent their jobs. Ongoing reform efforts ensure job security. A constantly changing system requires countless administrators to facilitate and monitor that change process. Creating a complicated paper chase within the system guarantees employment.

The second reason school systems engage in this endless pursuit of change for change's sake is purely a matter of public relations. If the schools are constantly adopting the latest, greatest new thing, the public feels as though their schools are cutting edge and forward thinking. The never-ending change fools the public into thinking that things are getting better, even when evidence is to the contrary. It's almost as though schools are performing a massive sleight of hand designed to distract the public from the stark reality of public school education—some students do well regardless of how they are taught, some students are distinctly average, and some percentage of the student population will always fail, as long as there are students whose daily lives include significant barriers to learning, such as poverty, family or neighborhood violence, poor parenting, etc. that must be addressed by the broader society, not through higher standards, different tests, or even improved curriculum. Yet schools continue to search for, and the public continues to endorse, the silver bullet that will solve all of society's problems in one easy, fell swoop. Whether it's whole language, project-based learning, integrated, thematic units, or standards-based testing, we can count on schools to jump on the next bandwagon.

The waste of time, effort, and money in schools will continue as long as the established decision-making structure is allowed to exist. Classroom teachers are keenly aware of what is needed to produce greater achievement for their students. Our opinions are rarely solicited, and, if they are, they are never actually considered and acted on. Businesses around the country have learned from the Japanese the importance of pushing decision-making down to the front-line worker who is closest to the product or customer. So, the chairman of Ford Motor Company trusts an assembly line worker to advise him on how best to reduce defects on the line, but the educational establishment wouldn't dream of asking teachers how to increase academic achievement and then acting on that input. As Winston Churchill once said, "The Americans will always do the right thing… after they've exhausted all the alternatives." Public schools exemplify this insanity. The answers are known but we choose to ignore them. Just ask any veteran teacher.

Too Much Interference

Imagine you are an electrician hired to update the wiring in an older home. After assessing the current situation you sit down with the homeowners and explain your plan for completing the job. You clearly outline the process that will be followed in the re-wiring, a routine procedure that you have performed thousands of times. As you explain the procedure, the homeowner becomes agitated and begins to question your plan for completing the work, the materials and process you will be using, and finally, your skill as an electrician. Not content with challenging your professional competency, the homeowner proceeds to question your motives and integrity. After considerable verbal abuse, he demands to see your supervisor and continues his assault on your professional ability and personal integrity. This discussion with your supervisor results in your being reprimanded and a letter of concern being placed in your personnel file.

This scenario is hard to believe for a variety of reasons. Your actions were motivated by a desire to complete the requested work in a professional manner. The job is straightforward and the process not difficult. You are highly trained and have performed this type of update countless times with great success. You consider yourself a skilled tradesman and have always behaved in an ethical and professional manner with your clients. You are the expert, having gone through rigorous training and apprenticeship, and assume you were hired for that expertise. You have a spotless record, both professionally and personally.

It's hard to imagine a scenario like this happening in other fields, yet similar situations occur in schools every day. It is not at all uncommon for teachers to be questioned on their teaching methods or discipline techniques. It is not uncommon for administrators to have to politely endure the hysterical ramblings of a parent who believes their child was treated unfairly. It is not uncommon for the school district to field phone calls from citizens or community groups who are furious at something they have allowed or not allowed to happen at a school-sponsored event. The sheer volume of challenging and negative communication that bombards school staff is staggering. Take the time to converse with any person in the school system at any level. You will hear story after story of berating, defaming, attacking, provoking, upsetting, abusive, challenging, and threatening behavior from the public. It happens too often to too many. So how did this happen? When did everybody and their brother become experts on educating children? When did we lose the backing and respect from parents who trusted the school's leadership in educating and disciplining students?

Although I remember seeing the change coming, it was a slow and subtle shift. Seeing parents on campus changed from a rarity to a daily occurrence. I recall walking through the library one day with a sage teacher who had a reputation as being somewhat cynical. As we passed a group of mothers planning a school event, he turned to me and said, "There will be a price to pay for having them here." At the time I passed it off as a manifestation of his dry humor, but he was right. It was the beginning of a pattern of parental interference that plagues schools today.

In an attempt to foster a partnership between schools and parents, in my judgment, schools have lost. Parental interference is smothering and prevents us from doing our best with students. The difference between the example of the electrician above and the similar but all too real situation in schools today is that you probably trust your electrician. You see that person as having knowledge and skill that you value and appreciate. You believe that his skill and knowledge of electrical systems is greater than yours and you, therefore, would be hesitant to question his judgment. You see him as the expert. Do you see teachers this way?

Few people do, which is why so many parents feel they have the right to interfere. Parents see themselves as the unquestionable expert on their own child. They have read the parenting books, gone to the workshops, talked to the right people and done the right things. They know what their kid is like and what he is capable of doing. Now, don't get me wrong. Parents often *do* know their children very well. They often *do* have valuable insight into their children's education. However, it's easy for parents to forget that, despite the fact that their little Johnny learns best when he's allowed to explore the environment on his own schedule and draw his own conclusions, such an approach may not always be possible when the teacher is trying to meet the needs of thirty other children. They may not realize that even though Johnny may be a perfect angel at home, his behavior may be completely different at school, which is a very different environment than home.

The lack of respect afforded teaching as a profession in this country makes many parents think they are more qualified to teach their child than their child's teacher. Primary teachers often complain about having to undo the damage done by well-intentioned parents who try to teach their young child to read. Although most teachers welcome and encourage parental support for their children's education, that involvement is most effective when the parent plays the supporting role, not trying to usurp the teacher's role. Attending teacher conferences and school events; providing a time, place and tools for homework and checking to make sure it gets done; reading to children and listening to them read; taking them to the library; showing an interest in what they are learning; and making sure children are healthy and rested are all important ways parents can support their child's education. But too many parents let their involvement take a much more intrusive path. Many elementary teachers greatly appreciate the extra set of hands provided by parent volunteers, at least until they run across the parent who thinks that their volunteering entitles them to tell the teacher how best to teach their child or how to discipline students.

The extremes of this parental interference are captured regularly in the news. Let's return to the previous example of the Everett, Washington, elementary school principal who received a phone call from a state legislator's assistant trying to talk the principal into reconsidering a student's assignment to a particular teacher's classroom. It seems that the child's parents were not pleased with the random assignment process used by the school, which resulted in their child not being place in the favorite fourth grade teacher's classroom, so they solicited the help of their local legislator. Healthy parental concern often takes a dangerous turn toward obsessive micro management.

The flood of interference that continues to castrate educators seems to be growing exponentially. There are statements signed by doctors or psychiatrists describing a child's unique condition that demands accommodation by the school and adjustments by all staff members. Lawyers defend the rights of a student, regardless of that student's disregard for his responsibilities as a student. Local advocacy groups demand equal time for their own special interest in the curriculum. Religious groups push the envelope with their own agenda. Affluent parents manipulate the system with financial contributions. The active PTSA parent expects special treatment as payback for her time and effort. There is a never-ending parade of parents who are more than willing to tell you how to do a better job at teaching students. To those people I say, "Walk in my shoes. For a day, a week, a month, a year; then let's see what you have to say."

When did all these people become education experts? And why do schools continue to ask for their input and allow them to have so much influence? I thought the reason I attended college and earned a teaching certificate was to be the expert in the classroom. I am the one who is in that classroom every day observing behavior and facilitating learning. I am the one who has worked with thousands of students and can set each child's needs and progress in the context of other students his or her age. I may not be as invested in your child's future, but I am deeply invested in his complete education.

Teachers do not get into teaching so they can pick on kids or feel powerful. We don't wake up in the morning wondering whom our target for that day will be. Conversely, teachers enter the profession because they enjoy kids and believe education is paramount. So let us do our job. Interference impedes our ability to deeply influence kids who need to learn an important lesson or need to hear the truth spoken about their behavior. If you want to support your child's education, support your child's teacher. Don't go running to the school complaining about every little thing your child doesn't like about school. Much like the kid who learns to play one parent against the other, students learn to play parents against the school. When parents consistently side with their child against the teacher, students learn to disrespect their teachers and they learn to manipulate the adults in their lives to get what they want. I routinely find that when I present parents with the facts in an objective and non-defensive way, they usually recognize their child's attempts to manipulate. For example, when I find students cheating on a test, I call the parents, who usually respond, "My child would never cheat. You must be mistaken." I then ask the parents to come in for a conference, at which time I place their child's paper and the paper of the student from whom they cheated side by side in front of the parents and ask them to compare the two papers and tell me if they think their child cheated or not. Presented with this evidence, most realize that, yes, their child *did* cheat and yes, their child *did* lie to them about cheating.

If schools are to regain their ability to be a truly powerful influence on young people's lives, they must reclaim themselves. Administrators need to take charge, make the tough decisions and accept the accompanying responsibility. Teachers need to assert their power and be the experts they have been trained to be. And parents need to trust the abilities and judgments of these professionals. Rather than being jerked from one extreme to another by the fear of public opinion, loss of funding, or lawsuits, schools must begin making decisions based on what is really best for *all* the students in their care. Steps should be taken to minimize outside influences that threaten the school's ability to do what needs to be done. Parental bullying, threats, and frivolous lawsuits must be stopped. When you get the urge to rush to school to tell your child's teacher or principal how to do their job, think about how you would feel if they showed up at your workplace and told you how to do yours.

Perhaps the most powerful source of interference comes from within students themselves. Students who are preoccupied with personal issues and challenges are unable to focus their attention and efforts on schoolwork. My sister, a thirty-year teaching veteran, says that we are given defective materials that we are expected to turn into a perfect product. Although she means no disrespect to students, the point she is making is that more and more kids are coming into the classroom with problems and challenges that make teaching and learning difficult. Whether their mind wanders because of divorcing parents, lack of sleep, depression, homelessness, substance abuse, or too much pressure to achieve, the classrooms of today are filled with kids whose attention is poorly focused. This situation presents our biggest challenge and the one we are most afraid to tackle.

Although most of these situations are very real conditions in kids' lives, the problem lies in the way we have conditioned ourselves, and students, to react to these problems. My approach to this situation is considered by many to be radical, unfeeling, even cruel. It defies many accepted schools of thought, is a difficult position to sell and an even harder commitment to maintain. What I can tell you from my own experience is that the students who have gone through this unorthodox process all end up thanking me. Many continue to keep in touch.

My unconventional approach was actually inspired by a story my father told me about his childhood. One night over dinner as I was telling my father about my then two-year-old son's swimming lessons at the local YMCA, my father said, "Well, the way I learned to swim was a little different than that." One day when he was eight years old, torrential rains began to flood his small village in China. His mother, who was across the road at another family member's house, screamed to him to climb to the highest part of the house, as high as possible, to escape the raging waters. My nimble and athletic father did what he was told and climbed up onto the roof. The wind was blowing and the water steadily continued to rise. As the waters lapped at the rooftop, he realized that, if he were going to survive, he would have to jump into the water and swim to higher ground. Without as much as a single lesson, not having ever stepped foot in a YMCA, he jumped into the moving water and headed for higher land. That's how my father learned to swim. He did it because he had to.

His story reminded me how different my students' lives are from the world in which my father grew up. Everything they do is broken down into small pieces and carefully parceled out to ease the blow of a new experience. The adults in their lives spend so much time trying to protect them from failure, pain, or discomfort, that, when those efforts aren't successful, young people are left feeling hopeless and helpless. Even to mention the dark side of life seems to imply unbearable burdens that young people could not possibly survive. On hearing my father's story, I began to question this approach. Maybe, rather than dwelling on difficulties and allowing young people to get sucked into despair, perhaps it would be better to confront the issue, acknowledge that, yes, bad things do happen, but then move on. Maybe the best approach is to tell the student that everyone has problems and obstacles to overcome and that those problems can't be an excuse for not doing what he is supposed to be doing. Maybe what we need to do is present this as a challenge to conquer and then convey our wholehearted confidence that the young person can rise to the challenge. Maybe we should present it as a problem that can be overcome with effort and determination. Maybe we need to point out how they have control over this burden and they have a choice over how much they will allow it to affect them. Maybe the best thing to do is to tell them to buck up and stop being such a baby, to grow up and realize that life isn't always happy and pleasant.

After having honed this technique over several decades and used it with countless students, I have become convinced of its effectiveness. Students invariably see it as a vote of confidence. I am telling them that they have the power to overcome difficulties. The unspoken message is that I believe they are strong enough to withstand the challenge. The current politically correct approach seems to stop at having them express their feelings about the problem or crisis. Actually, it doesn't *stop* at having them express their feelings, it just seems to be a never-ending litany of expressed feeling, with no end to the *feelings* and no *beginning* to actually solving the problem. I wonder if this continued rehashing of their problem doesn't have a backlash effect on kids. In other words, if we keep talking about how terrible a child's problem is and how bad they feel about it, we convince them that it is, in fact, a horrible thing, and that, yes, they should be distraught about it.

Too Much Interruption

Studies repeatedly document the importance of two critical aspects of educational effectiveness: 1) the quality of the teacher; and 2) time on task, which means the amount of time teachers and students are actually engaged in teaching and learning. Over the last fifty years, the quantity of material to be covered during an academic year has increased exponentially, while the number of instructional hours has remained the same, if not decreased. Whereas the subject matters taught in your elementary school may have included arithmetic, science, art, social studies, language arts, and physical education, today's elementary curriculum covers those subjects *plus* computers, multi cultural education, environmental education, AIDS prevention, violence prevention, drug prevention, bullying prevention, etc., etc. Despite this very fundamental problem of too much to be taught in too little time, I am constantly amazed at the amount of time my students and I are dragged off task by the educational system. Faculty meetings, department head meetings, committee meetings, technology meetings, parent conferences, student support team meetings, building meetings, union meetings, financial or budget meetings, meetings with community groups, P.T.S.A. meetings, are all vying for teachers' time and energy. I know that worthless meetings aren't unique to school systems, but, in a profession with so little time to accomplish so much, it seems particularly irresponsible to sacrifice valuable teaching or preparation time for meetings that accomplish nothing other than to give people a chance to hear themselves speak.

One of the greatest disruptions to a teacher's day is the deluge of paperwork. I'm not referring to the paperwork that is inherent to the job, such as grading papers, recording grades, or developing lessons. The interference I'm talking about is the redundant and pointless paper shuffling that interrupts teaching and devours energy. Let's start at my mailbox before the day begins. Unlike Charlie Brown, who is devastated to find his mailbox empty, I never start my day without a deluge of paper. Bulletins, notices, announcements, schedules for upcoming events, special messages from an array of school clubs, sports information, student changes, requests for homework from a long-term absentee, and the endless cascade of catalogs advertising things that I need but can't afford to purchase. As the day progresses, student forms need my signature, special needs students need grade updates and comments, counselors require discipline information. There are forms for having worksheets copied, forms for field trips, forms for absences, forms for poor work, forms for good work, forms for more forms, all pelting me throughout the day. Why are so many trees sacrificed for so little gain? Because someone's job depends on the paper chase. If they don't pump out regular volumes of paperwork, they might be forced back into the classroom!

State law dictates that schools must practice fire drills once a month. When you add in disaster drills, earthquake drills, and the latest addition, lock-down drills (instituted after the Columbine shootings), the drilling is so frequent that students often take a flippant attitude toward these events. The constant interruption of intercom announcements, communiqués from the office, phone messages to students, things being delivered, requests to report, all play a role in the disruption of concentration and thought. Then there are the scheduled interruptions: mandatory assemblies to observe national holidays, cultural assemblies to celebrate diversity, recognition assemblies to build self-esteem, sports assemblies to show support for athletics, and pep assemblies to boost school spirit. As worthwhile as some of these activities may be, they are still interruptions to the teaching and learning day. When you add to this the growing list of students who leave class for field trips, sickness, student government, choir, band, etc. you begin to understand how today's classrooms are in a constant state of flux—establishing focus, interruption, regaining focus, interruption, refocus, ad infinitum.

Several years ago I had a unique opportunity to observe the amount of unnecessary interruption that takes place during the school day. Due to an unexpected influx of new students, a portable had to be added to our campus. I volunteered to teach in the portable, which was good-sized and presented an adequate teaching station. What I didn't know when I volunteered was that the portable had not been properly wired for anything except basic electricity. I had no intercom connection, no phone line, no computer outlets; not even a functioning fire alarm, none of which caused me undue concern. I nicknamed the portable "Outer Wong-olia," put up a sign to that effect and it quickly became an established school joke. I spent two extremely peaceful years in that portable cut off from the mainstream of school communications. During that entire time, I didn't miss one meeting, there were no crises that couldn't be handled, my grades were never late, my students and I functioned perfectly well, despite the fact that I was isolated and removed from the constant flow of information that is deemed so important. Another side effect of this isolation was that I wasn't nearly as stressed or frazzled at the end of the day. With interruptions minimized, student focus was maximized. Clearly, these constant interruptions are detrimental to teachers and students alike.

Too Much Responsibility

Unlike many teachers, I actually don't mind attending the annual school Open House. In fact, quite often, by the time the evening is over, I feel pretty good about myself and about what I have accomplished with my students. The parents are usually very complimentary and are genuinely interested in their kids' progress and the curriculum. However, one year I learned an interesting lesson about the unrealistic expectations and responsibilities placed on the shoulders of teachers and schools. This particular night was an informal Open House, which meant there was no set schedule and the parents could wander the campus, stopping in to chat with teachers or other staff. As I fielded the usual types of questions from the steady flow of parents, one father stopped me in my tracks. Without so much as a preliminary opener about the class or his child's progress, he began to explain to me how teachers were responsible for world hunger. He carefully outlined his theory, presenting an interesting, albeit absurd, argument that clearly found teachers guilty of offenses that, in his mind, lead to world starvation. As ludicrous as his claims were, I did find myself thinking about this discussion on the drive home. It struck me as illuminating that this man truly thought that schools had the power to create or eradicate world hunger. How absurd that a group of underpaid, overworked teachers, who were responsible for preparing students academically for the world they would enter upon leaving school, could possibly be the cause of, or the solution to, world hunger! Yet, when I returned to school the following day, I was struck with the realization that the junior high health curriculum that I was then assigned to teach was designed to solve many of society's most entrenched problems. My health class existed to cure the ailments of a suffering nation. I was charged with building strong self-images, rebuilding damaged self-esteem, stopping self-destructive behavior, curbing obsessive habits, decreasing addictions, promoting healthy lifestyles, stopping teenage pregnancy, increasing abstinence, establishing normal sexuality, and generally making each and every student a thriving, healthy, sound individual.

That evening I picked up the newspaper and began reading an article about what schools should be doing to solve the problem of guns in schools. Finished with the paper, I turned on the TV and began watching a news magazine show featuring stories of what schools were doing to stop racism. How did it come to this? When did the weight of the world descend on the shoulders of teachers?

Educating a child is no longer about reading, writing, and calculating. Somehow the responsibility of solving all the problems of society has come to rest with the school system. Society seems to believe that, because children spend so much time in schools, schools should be the place where all social problems are solved. Schools are routinely blamed for problems over which they have no control and for which they bear no responsibility. I could understand this designation of schools as the one-stop shopping for solutions to all society's problems if they were given the resources and power to tackle them. But how can the public expect schools to solve any problems when they are chronically under-funded for even their core academic mission and their staff has been stripped of influence and respect? Schools have the responsibility to educate students. Responsibility for producing civilized, tolerant, responsible human beings must be shared by parents and the other social institutions in the community. Schools have their work cut out for them simply educating children for the increasingly complex world they will enter as adults. Even to fulfill that core mission requires support from others. It takes parents who emphasize education and support their child's endeavors. It takes a stable living environment, where the child's basic needs are met and their intellectual development stimulated. It takes a school system that is focused and committed to excellence. It takes administrators who are confident and inspiring leaders. It takes teachers who are more than just competent, but outstanding. It takes a school environment that is safe and a facility that is sound. It takes a community that strengthens the school with its trust and resources. It takes a state to fully fund this important investment and a federal government to make education a priority.

It is impossible for the schools to solve all the ills of a society. The school's focus should be on the education of children. Imagine what could be accomplished if schools were given the time and resources to focus on that singular goal and the rest of society took back their responsibility for the other aspects of children's healthy development. As long as schools continue to be held responsible for curing all of our society's problems, they will continue to flounder in an ocean of impossible expectations and all of us will pay the price.

CHAPTER 8: NOT LIKE MIKE

One aspect of our culture of excess that is so pervasive and damaging that it deserves its own chapter, is parents' unrealistic assessments of their children's capabilities.

Ask a nine-year-old boy what he wants to be when he grows up and his answer is likely to be, "I want to be a professional basketball player." Ask a nine-year-old girl what she wants to be and her answer is likely to be, "I want to be Britney Spears." The hopeful, though thoroughly unrealistic dreams, of these innocent children are inspiring and refreshing. Unfortunately, these young dreamers often live with parents whose hopes are equally fanciful. We all want the best for our kids. We want them to be the most popular kid in class, a straight-A student, the star athlete, the best musician, the lead in the school play. We want them to receive awards, trophies, and accolades. We want them to attend the best university, be loved and admired by everyone they meet, and generally be the best kid to ever walk the surface of the earth. Unfortunately, that's not going to happen.

I know what you're thinking. What a negative attitude. How can this guy suggest that I should limit my expectations for my child? He clearly doesn't know *my* child. Acknowledging that there are limitations on any child is not acceptable in today's "everyone is a winner" climate. After all, this is America, the land of equal opportunity. But "opportunity" is the operative word here. We *can* provide equal opportunities to all children, but each child brings a set of talents, skills, and abilities to those opportunities. Different children will experience differential success with those opportunities. Even though we'd like to believe that every child can be the next Michael Jordan or the next Stephen Hawking or the next Britney Spears if he or she chooses to be, the reality is that the odds of your child or my child reaching this level are astronomical. Let's take Mike.

Michael Jordan is the best basketball player of all time. His shooting, ball handling, jumping, and mobility are unmatched. His presence on a team can be the difference between an average season and a championship. His commitment to winning is all-consuming. His determination to be the best is legendary. He gives 110% in every game, under any conditions. He is the ultimate competitor. And nine-year-old boys across the country want to be just like him. But what we aren't telling these young boys is that Michael Jordan is a freak of nature. First and foremost, genetics separates the good from the great, the great from the exceptional, and the exceptional from the freaks. Do you think Jordan would be who he is today if he were only five foot nine? Even given his genetically endowed 6'7" height, think of the contribution his hand-eye coordination or sheer speed contribute to his superiority over other exceptional athletes. What about his genetically circumscribed muscle composition, fast twitch vs. slow twitch muscle? Jordan can maintain a body fat percentage under 10% year round. Most of us would kill to be 10% body fat just for a few summer months. Ninety-nine percent of our kids are eliminated from the professional athlete fantasy from birth, purely due to genetic limitations. Added to his genetic superiority, Jordan's level of determination and competitive spirit is rare. Contrary to the stereotype of the dumb jock, exceptional professional athletes must have the intelligence and understanding of human behavior required to consistently intimidate their opponents. Great athletes also must have the poise and composure to withstand the demands of constant competition as well as the pressure that accompanies stardom. Jordan had to cope with fame, wealth, adulation and constant public scrutiny at a very young age, in addition to the incredible pressure to consistently perform at spectacular levels on the court. Is Michael Jordan simply a good basketball player? I think not. He stands alone. He is the extreme exception to the rule. He is unique. He is a freak of nature. And yet, how many parents across America think their child is the next Michael Jordan?

Although I use Michael Jordan as an example of this phenomenon, the same holds true for academic, musical, theatrical, business, or other superstars. Whether your dream is for your child to be the next Stephen Hawking, the next Yo-Yo Ma, the next Oprah Winfrey, or the next Bill Gates, the odds are equally overwhelming.

I have been exposed to literally thousands of students. That's not including kids I have coached or have been involved with in other activities. That's a pretty good sample of kids. I can truthfully say that, of those thousands of kids, very few have been truly exceptional. Sure I have seen outstanding athletes, and gifted mathematicians, and talented artists and musicians, but the vast majority of kids are quite average. As a parent you hope for the best, pushing and prodding for greater achievements. But, like it or not, it's highly unlikely that all your pushing and prodding will transcend the fact that your child is, like most others, just average. Your dream of your child becoming a doctor may not be realistic if he is having trouble passing high school geometry. Visions of watching your daughter dance Swan Lake as the prima ballerina for the New York City Ballet might be improbable if her body fat index at age sixteen is 30 and she has short, stocky legs.

Acknowledging our children's limits is not a negative act. On the contrary, it can be very liberating to understand the natural selection process that is at work in society. Having realistic expectations for our children can protect us from the frenzied, ultimately unproductive pursuit of impossible dreams. It allows us to relish and delight in our children's successes, for their own sake, not as a stepping stone to later glory. I know this is not what many of you want to hear. You want to be told that your child can be anything he wants to be (or that you want him to be). But, after all, you're a grown up, and, as harmless as it may be for your child to harbor dreams of superstardom, when you fail to view your child through loving, but honest eyes, the long-term outcome can be devastating.

My two sons are very athletic. They have been involved in a multitude of athletic activities, including soccer, baseball, golf, basketball, bowling, swimming, water-skiing, wake-boarding, and circus sports, and have experienced moderate to exceptional success. Beginning in early elementary school, they competed in juggling and unicycling competitions. By the time they were in their early teens, they were teaching these skills to others.

I played basketball in high school and my wife was an accomplished gymnast. Our children's grandparents were all talented athletes, excelling in everything from horse jumping to golf to pole vaulting. My sons draw from a deep pool of athletic genes. I have helped them take advantage of this genetic head start by coaching them in many of the sports they've played. Although my sons were usually among the top players on their respective teams, I have always been careful to temper my expectations with realism. Just because my son was the starting pitcher on his 12-year-old All-Star team, I knew that didn't mean he was going to be a professional baseball player. Being the leading scorer on his junior high basketball team didn't mean I should start planning on his becoming a Seattle Sonic.

Sitting with my father-in-law, watching my older son play baseball, I remember this proud grandpa confidently proclaiming, "He's going to play big college ball!" Although I knew he was viewing my son through the idealistic eyes of a grandfather, this unrealistic assessment of my son's potential made me examine my own beliefs about my sons' abilities. After all, in reality, what were the odds that my son *could* play big college baseball? On his 12-year-old Little League team, where there were no cuts and everybody played, his chances of playing were quite good. By the time he reached his early teens and was playing on All-Star teams that drew from the best players in the area, he was competing for that starting pitcher position with five to ten other pitchers who had been equally exceptional on their own teams. His high school baseball team drew from an even larger pool of talented players. However, even though he excelled at that level, his school was one school in a league with ten other schools, most of which had equally talented pitchers on their rosters. Even had he been the best pitcher in his league, that league was one of dozens of leagues in the region, which was one of many regions in the state. High school programs can go for years without a single athlete receiving any kind of college scholarship. Of all the best pitchers in all the high schools around the country, only a handful will be recruited by top college teams. Making it to the professional level then becomes a million to one shot. The same holds true for other professions. Only a handful of people become the CEOs of Fortune 500 companies, become movie stars, or discover the cure for a major disease.

Although this may seem like a depressing view that somehow puts unnecessary limits on your child's potential, I would argue just the opposite. As a parent, a coach, or a proud grandparent, when you view a child's true potential through a more realistic lens, you can more clearly focus on the real benefits of participating in sports or other activities. The tendency to push too hard for unrealistic results disappears. The overemphasis on winning can be redirected toward personal improvement, sportsmanship and teamwork. The inevitable pressures that develop between an over-invested parent and his or her child lessen. Rest assured, as an athlete and a coach, I am not diminishing the important lessons of competition, of learning how to win and how to lose. But the value of these lessons is not in their ability to prepare a child to compete in professional sports. For 99.9% of young athletes, the benefit of participation in competitive sports is measured by the amount of personal growth that is achieved, the valuable lessons learned. It may be learning to lead or learning when to step down. It may be the recognition that hard work pays great dividends. It may be in the experience of meeting new people. It could be in the confidence gained by meeting new challenges. It could be any of a thousand things that have the potential to inspire a goal or add to an important chapter in that young person's life. The important thing to remember is that, when you focus your energies, and your child's energies, on the highly improbable end goal of becoming the one and only greatest "whatever," you run the risk of diverting him from the valuable life lessons that could be learned on the journey.

No matter what activity your child is involved in, a focus solely on winning or being the best will inevitably backfire, undermining your child's motivation and progress and damaging the relationship between you and your child. You know the signs: the barely controlled parental frustration after a lost game or poor performance, the strained silence punctuated only by a play by play of "helpful" feedback; the poorly masked disappointment when the child fails to live up to the unattainable expectations so clearly communicated by his hopeful parent. You've seen children whose earlier enthusiasm and passion for an activity have gradually been crushed by the unrelenting demands of rigorous practice. Children quickly recognize the pattern—when I win, my parent is happy and I am loved; when I lose my parent is angry and turns away. We all understand what motivates this kind of parental behavior. We all want our kids to be successful. None of us likes to see our child lose. Unfortunately, too often we forget that our kids are just kids. We try to drag them prematurely into the serious, winner-take-all world of grown-ups.

I know this process all too well because I experienced it in my own childhood. My father demanded exceptional performance and 100%

effort in any and all endeavors. Like most parents, his heart was in the right place but his actions were sometimes counterproductive. The harder I tried and the better I performed, the greater his expectations of me became. In an effort to make each and every moment an opportunity to improve some aspect of me, he systematically sucked the fun out of activities that I had previously enjoyed. I vividly recall a family vacation to Disneyland as a seven-year-old, full of excitement and anticipation. The Matterhorn was the big attraction at that time and even the long wait in line for the ride did nothing to dampen my enthusiasm for this long-awaited adventure. My older brother and sister were paired in one car and my Dad and I in the other. As I sat in front of him as we slowly chugged our way to the top, bursting with excitement for the ride of my life, my Dad began to lecture me on how to negotiate the turns with my body. As we descended through the first turn, I felt two strong hands guiding my shoulders left or right, as the corner demanded. This continued throughout the entire ride. I recall getting off the ride thinking, "That wasn't fun at all. Why couldn't he just let me enjoy the experience?" My father simply didn't realize that every moment doesn't have to be a teaching tool or an opportunity for improvement. Sometimes there is great value in just enjoying the moment.

Baby Boomer parents' obsession with over-achievement has fostered a parental climate that is systematically sucking the joy from childhood. I often hear about the schedules of elementary and middle school students that would quickly bring healthy adults to their knees. My high school students routinely complain about not having enough hours in the day to do all that they are scheduled to do. The result is they choose to forego sleep. Pre-teens and teenagers often try to survive on four or five hours a night. Although we can all remember the occasional all-nighter during our teen years, few of us had the kind of schedule that demanded that sacrifice on a regular basis. A simple look at the physiology of the developing adolescent should cause us concern over this pattern of sleep deprivation. Their rapid growth and the enormous physical and emotional changes their bodies are undergoing mean they require *more* sleep than they did when they were younger, not less. The constant sleep deprivation experienced by so many over-scheduled young people impacts their health, their learning, and their emotional stability. The stress-related ailments that currently plague so many adults are gradually filtering down into children at younger and younger ages. Why would so many parents risk their children's health and well-being? Why are so many parents willing to steal their own son or daughter's childhood? Because they are convinced that their child will be the next great athlete, or scholar, or musician, or artist. And they are certain that the race for greatness starts early and is won by the person who races the fastest and the hardest. They are confident that the sacrifice will pay off.

Think about your own childhood. What did your days look like? How did you spend your free time-after school, on weekends, during summer vacations? I recall lazy, unstructured days; filled with whatever activities my friends and I could dream up. Was that time wasted? Would it have been better spent in tightly scheduled "productive" activities? I don't think so. It's important to remember that growing up is hard work—physically, mentally, and emotionally. Children need plenty of unstructured time to rest, recharge and struggle through the challenges of moving from childhood to adulthood. They need time to think about who they are and who they want to be.

When parents push too hard and are over-involved in their child's activities, the effect is often exactly the opposite of what the parent wants. One thing I know for certain about kids who are truly exceptional and who go on to pursue excellence later in their lives is that those children truly enjoy what they are doing. Their drive to excel comes from deep within them, not from their parents. Yes, you can motivate, inspire, bribe, persuade, cajole, or trick your child for a period of time, but ultimately the motivation to pursue excellence will come from the child's own passion for the activity.

I saw this phenomenon play out with my oldest son. He had enjoyed all kinds of sports throughout his childhood. During his freshmen and sophomore years in high school he played on the golf team in the fall, the basketball team in the winter, and the baseball team in the spring. Although he did well at all of these activities and generally enjoyed the competition, his true passion soon emerged. During his junior year he lost interest in baseball and became obsessed with golf. He got a job at a golf club, where he would work his shift, then go out and play as many holes as he could get in before dark. When he got home, he would go out in our backyard, where he had a golf net set up, and practice hitting balls for several more hours. We never had to remind him to practice; conversely, our challenge was to keep him from overdoing. On his days off he would play 18, 27, 36, or his personal record of 45 holes in a day. His passion for the game is obvious and it is clearly what drives him to perfect his game. It didn't come from my pushing him to be the next Tiger Woods. It didn't come from my sending him to golf camps when he was seven. If I did anything to contribute, it was to allow him to explore all kinds of sports, without external pressure to be the best, so that he would have the opportunity to discover his own passion.

I encourage you to take a good hard look at your motivation for pushing your child to excel. Is what you're doing really in your child's best interest? Are your expectations realistic? Is your over-involvement and excessive pressure to excel worth what is being sacrificed in your child's life? Your child is not you. She has her own physical make-up, temperament, intellectual capabilities and her own goals in life. Her natural talents, skills, and interests may be very different from yours. She is not you and her job is not to become what you always wished you had become.

Are you satisfying some personal need through your child? Are you attempting to fulfill a long-abandoned dream for yourself through your child? Do you feel the need to control someone else's life? Are you searching for lost youth? Are you reclaiming lost opportunity from your own childhood? Are you using your child as a measuring device for your own success? Are you using your child as a showpiece or trophy? Any of these and more could be at the core of the excessive pushing and over-achieving behavior that may be driving your child to illness, depression, rebellion, or nonperformance. Most curative procedures begin with an honest look in the mirror. Don't be upset, there's good news. If you are part of the problem, then you can be part of the solution.

Each of us has dreams for our child, a picture in our head of what we want that child to become. We may want a miniature version of ourselves; we may want the artist, or athlete, or intellectual that we never became. One of the greatest, but most important challenges of parenting is to surrender those dreams and fully accept and embrace our child as a unique individual. All children are different. They have varying natural skills, talents, and interests. Even within the same family, siblings have surprisingly different capabilities. One may show early evidence of physical coordination while another demonstrates an affinity for words and reads and spells at an exceptionally young age. Others may show early talent in art or a flare for performance. Every child has some natural talent, some area in which he clearly excels. The challenge for parents is to help uncover and develop that talent by providing plenty of opportunities for their child to try out different activities in non-threatening, low-pressure ways. You can discover your child's talents by watching him in all different kinds of situations, by listening to the hidden subtext of conversations about the activities in which he is involved; by letting his passion and talent unfold rather than carefully scripting his life and thereby narrowing his options. Really pay attention to what she enjoys; what she is motivated to do on her own, without adult intervention; what she loses herself in and can do for hours on end.

Whether your child's natural talent is kinesthetic, musical, linguistic, artistic, mathematical, or interpersonal, you need to cultivate these talents, regardless of your own preferences. This can be difficult for the intellectual parent whose child's talent leans to the artistic. It can be difficult for the athletic parent whose child prefers chess to basketball. It can be difficult for the majority of us who are average athletes, scholars, musicians, etc. but who hoped that our child would break the mold and rise to the top of the field. Instead of hoping for, or expecting, your child to be the best at something, put your energies into helping your child discover his passion— something that he can be successful at, and, more importantly, something that he loves doing.

Too often parents let their preconceived expectations obscure the realities of their child's actual talents. If you *really* want your child to be the next Michael Jordan, you may be looking so hard for signs of physical giftedness that you miss your child's true talent for solving complex problems, or leadership, or seeing things from others' viewpoint. Your challenge is to identify and promote your child's innate talents, not to mislead her about her own abilities or force her to play out the smoldering, unresolved issues of your own past. Can you face the fact that your child is likely to be very average in most ways? Are you willing to allow your child to live his own life without the burden of trying to live the life you always wanted but didn't achieve? Are you prepared to support your child as she discovers her own place in the world, rather than pushing her down the pathway you want her to go?

It's true that, as renowned pediatrician T. Berry Brazelton said, "Every child needs someone who is crazy about him."[35] But the love, support and enthusiasm you give your child must be tempered with reality. The consequences of ignoring the reality of your child's true capabilities can be far-reaching and devastating. It may seem harmless to daydream about your child being a movie star or inventing the cure for cancer, but when your daydreams turn into unrealistic expectations communicated to your child, you are headed for trouble. Demanding the performance of an academic genius from a child of average intelligence sets your child up for failure. If your child senses that you really want him to be a star athlete, but his natural abilities allow him to be simply a good athlete, he will constantly feel as though he doesn't measure up and is disappointing you. Children want to please their parents and live up to their expectations. When those expectations are too high, the child feels like a failure. Even though you may think you are communicating confidence in your child and helping to build his self-esteem when you tell him that he is the best pitcher or the smartest kid in his class, he will inevitably learn that your assessment isn't true and one of two things will result—he will believe he failed you or he will realize that you are lying to him and begin to question everything you say.

Entitlement

The current parenting and educational philosophy of viewing every child as special and gifted has negative consequences in schools and families. One example in schools is grade inflation. You may recall a time in your own schooling when a "C" was considered average and an "A" was reserved for those students who performed at exceptional levels. In the high school where I teach "A's" are considered routine. In fact, 45% of all grades given each year at my school are "A's." Are today's students that much more intelligent? Are they studying harder and putting much more time and effort into their schoolwork? Of course they're not. Teachers have been systematically coerced, blackmailed, or forced into lowering expectations and giving higher grades. Students *expect* an "A" just for showing up. Their parents have told them all their lives that they are the smartest kid in their class and they have come to believe it. Rather than connecting good grades with hard work and aptitude, students have been led to believe that they *deserve* high grades because they are special.

One particular student stands out for me as the epitome of this attitude. A senior in my algebra trigonometry class, this girl had struggled for the entire year. She rarely asked for help and often didn't turn in her homework. As a result, she was earning a "C" in my class. Her grade was not a mystery and should not have come as a surprise. She had received "C's" and "D's" on her tests and had received regular progress reports and quarter grades throughout the year. However, like many of my students, she expected to go to a prestigious university, with high admission standards. The "C" she was getting in my class would threaten her chance of getting into the college of her choice. When she got her grade, she came running into my classroom, agitated and indignant, and shouted, "You gave me a C!" I calmly responded that, yes, she had earned a "C." I pulled out my grade book and showed her the points she had earned and how that number of points clearly translated into a "C" grade. When I refused to react, she changed tactics and told me that, by giving her a "C," I was going to keep her from going to the college she wanted to attend. This young lady clearly believed that *wanting* a good grade and believing she *deserved* a good grade should be the deciding factors in how I graded her. This girl was 18 years old! She wasn't born believing that she deserved something for nothing. Although she was convinced that *I* had failed her, in fact, many other adults in her life had contributed to this erroneous belief that her success was unrelated to ability and effort. Those adults failed her.

Thinking back on your own schooling, how many classes do you remember in which you could earn extra credit or bonus points? I can think of just a few in my entire academic career. In today's classroom, bonus points are routine and expected. In fact if a teacher doesn't use them, students accuse the teacher of being unfair. Rather than being an honest and accurate assessment of a student's progress and feedback designed to improve their performance, grades have become a game at which students expect everyone to be a winner. I have had parents question my compassion for not having an extra credit program. After falling short of the grade they believe they deserve, students often try to badger me for additional extra credit; whatever it takes to get the "A."

Another consequence of this entitlement mentality is that young people develop very twisted ways of measuring their own status. My students live in a very affluent community, where it is common for young people to measure themselves using a materialistic scale. Fancy cars, designer clothes, waterfront mansions, and exotic vacations are all yardsticks used to determine status and promote prestige among this group of kids. The problem is that the kid's status and position in the group is determined by external factors that require no effort or ability on her part. Her status comes from the power, accomplishments, and financial position of her parents. When young people's position in their peer group is determined by the accomplishments of their parents, what do you suppose will happen when they leave their parents' home and are inevitably measured by their own accomplishments and achievements? How can they possibly measure up to the lifestyle and expectation that they have enjoyed under their parents' wing?

Complicating this situation is the fact that sociologists and economists predict that the current generation of young people may be the first in recent history to have difficulty exceeding their parents' standard of living. So, when these young people, who have grown up using their parents' money and possessions as indicators of their own worth and believing that they are entitled to whatever they desire, leave their parents' nest and strike out on their own, they expect to have everything their parents have immediately—the nice home, the fancy cars, the yearly vacations. But not only will they not get those things immediately, it's unlikely they will ever reach their parents' level of affluence.

Special Schools

Another example of parents' belief that their child is so exceptional and gifted that they require special accommodations is the growing popularity of private schools. The very notion of public school reeks of ordinariness, the greatest fear of these parents. In their minds, public schools cater to the masses—the middle of the road, ordinary, average kids. If that's the case, then public school certainly can't be the best place for their exceptional, talented, gifted child.

Of course, few parents of private school students would admit that their choice of a private school education for their child was a result of their belief that their child was too special to be educated with the masses. Rather, they would tout the superior test scores or percentage of students going on to four-year colleges, or higher standards and better discipline. This notion that private schools hold some secret key to education is absurd. The truth is that, unlike public schools, private schools can choose their students, and they tend to choose students whose parents are better educated, more affluent, and more committed to their child's academic success than many public school students. If private school students don't measure up academically, socially, or behaviorally, they can be kicked out. Public schools have no choice but to take the private school "rejects." Public schools are required to educate every child, regardless of the child's aptitude, abilities, motivation or behavior and regardless of the parents' financial status, commitment to education or support for their child. Of course public schools' statistics won't be comparable to private schools. Private schools begin with a select group and end with an even more select group, resulting in a homogeneous experience that can have deleterious effects on several areas of a child's growth and development.

Where public schools can outshine private schools is in their ability to expose students to the realities of life in a diverse world. Many of the greatest lessons learned in public schools are not found in the formal curriculum, but in the opportunity to interact with other students whose lives are vastly different in countless ways. Several of my oldest son's elementary school classmates were refugees from Southeast Asia. I don't think he'll ever forget the story told by a first grade classmate about his family's escape from Cambodia by crawling through the jungle on their bellies for ten days. In my sons' public school classrooms, they encountered kids whose families were financially well off, as well as kids who lived with thirteen other family members in a two-bedroom apartment. Their classmates came from all different cultures, spoke a variety of languages, and came from many types of families.

All of these differences provided valuable opportunities for my children to learn about people. My sons have gone to school with

National Merit Scholars, classical pianists, and Eagle Scouts. They have also gone to school with bullies, gang members, teen mothers, drug users, and car thieves. They have learned how to read both groups and how to earn their respect. Learning to deal with the "bad" kid is just as important as learning to deal with the "good" kid. That bad kid may have some enlightening things to say about life and how his circumstances have affected him. My sons have learned how to avoid or negotiate potentially dangerous situations and they have witnessed the often-painful consequences suffered by peers who have not learned these lessons. They have learned that there is pain, unfairness, and suffering in the world; that not every child lives in a nice home with two loving parents who earn a decent living and can provide most of life's necessities for their children. They have learned that, despite speaking a different language, having different customs and beliefs, living in different family situations, or any of the other myriad differences they have encountered with their public school peers, people are pretty much people. Their exposure to the full economic, cultural, and racial diversity of our community has prepared them to function effectively in that world as adults.

Let me be the first to say that my own kids are astoundingly average. They get slightly above average grades (probably due to grade inflation), have average academic skills, and they hover right around the norm in their standardized test scores. They have average artistic talents and very little musical capabilities. They are below average readers, with little desire to read. Their athletic abilities are above average, and their greatest gift is a very high E.Q. (emotional quotient). They are below the norm in a few areas and above in a few others, but, overall, very average. Public school has been the best choice for them, as it is for most students.

If you are one of those parents who believe that your child needs a special school, you may need to check the chicken meter. Are you afraid to have your child exposed to others who are different? Are you afraid she will see things that are not always pleasant? Are you afraid there could be negative influences preying on your kid? Are you unsure of your child's ability to cope with the demands of a heterogeneous environment? Or are you chicken to admit that your child is really just very average and would do fine in an average school?

As teachers and parents, our greatest responsibility is to help children grow up to be competent, independent, responsible, self-confident adults. When we are too chicken to tell children the truth about their own abilities, we are withholding important information from them that could help them achieve their full potential. When we distort their talents and award undeserved accolades, we set them up to hear the truth later on, most likely from someone who cares about them far less than we do. As we discussed earlier in this book, the key to self-esteem is that it must be earned. Children must expend effort, feel challenged, gain experience, and see successful outcomes in order for their actions to produce authentic feelings of self-worth.

Keep in mind that your child is, like most people in the world, good at some things, not so good at other things, and average at a lot of things. Your child has his own individual temperament and a unique set of talents, interests, and abilities that will influence his response to every situation. You cannot ignore those essential individual characteristics and mold him into the fantasy person that you may want him to be. Trying to do so will almost certainly backfire, causing stress, depression, lack of motivation, or rebellion. It will also threaten your relationship with your child, because he will either spend his whole life unsuccessfully trying to be what you want him to be, or give up and resent you for not accepting him for the individual that he is. What you can do is help him discover his passion and nurture and support that passion. You can have the guts to hold up a mirror that accurately reflects back to him both his strengths and his weaknesses. You can encourage and expect your child to put in the effort required to be successful, and not fall victim to the entitlement trap.

Relax. Parenting can be an enjoyable experience if you just accept a few simple truths. Bad things will happen to your child; expect it. Self-esteem is earned, not given. Failure is a great teacher. Unearned success is counterproductive and devaluing to your child. The value of life is in the journey. You are not in control of all that happens, but you are in charge. Be a parent not a friend. Life shouldn't always be serious. Let kids enjoy their childhood; life is not a race. And finally, they are not like Mike.

CHAPTER 9: DISCIPLINE

Of all the aspects of raising a child or managing a classroom, discipline seems to be the one area that creates the most anxiety and presents the most challenge. Throughout the years, when parents or other teachers have approached me for advice, the crisis inevitably revolved around some behavior that threatens the smooth functioning of the family or classroom. Whether it's dealing with mildly rebellious behavior or a teen whose actions have landed him in jail, the common thread is the adults' inability to appropriately handle this area of dealing with children. The behavior of children and teens seems to leave many adults perplexed at best, overwhelmed at worst.

Surveys of both parents and teachers consistently report discipline as the number one concern. How is it that the most well-educated group of adults in our nation's history can't seem to figure out how to manage the behavior of children? I can't tell you how often I have witnessed grown men and women, some of whom command the respect and compliance of scores of people in their professional lives, cowering under the thumb of a preschooler or toddler. Parents of two-year-olds routinely whine, "But I can't make him go to bed." Parents of school-aged children bemoan the fact that their child will only eat three foods, won't pick up his toys, or constantly picks on his younger sibling. And, by the time that child becomes an adolescent, with years of parental manipulation under his belt, these chicken parents have often simply given up on their ability to influence their child.

In the classroom, the ever-present disruption of poorly behaved students compromises the learning environment for everyone. The amount of time and energy wasted dealing with these students is staggering. The toll on the physical and mental health of teachers is overwhelming. The fifty percent of new teachers who leave the profession within the first five years aren't driven off by the difficulty of the subject matter, or the condition of their buildings, or even the pitiful compensation many receive. Most are worn down by the constant stress of trying to maintain a sense of order and discipline in their classrooms, often in spite of a school and community culture that undermines that very goal. This pervasive lack of standards for behavior permeates the entire school environment, with teachers, administrators and coaches increasingly buying into lowered expectations for students' civility, responsibility, and commitment.

Have you ever wondered who's really in charge in your school or your family? Do you really feel that you have the kind of authority and respect that was given parents and teachers when you were growing up? Unfortunately, adults seem to be tired; they have surrendered their power to tyrannical children.

With so many adults failing at their disciplinary responsibilities, one might conclude that disciplining a child is a difficult or complicated process. Do we need more studies on what works in managing children's behavior? No! On the contrary, managing young people is really a very simple task that is no different for today's generation than it was for their parents and grandparents. The foundations of effective discipline are well-established and have been thoroughly researched. We know what works to produce positive behavior change. We have ample documentation of what it takes to socialize children from birth to healthy, responsible adulthood. The same child management techniques that work in families also work in schools. So what's the problem? The problem is that most parents and teachers *choose* not to do what works.

At the heart of the discipline problem is the very word itself. For most of us, the word "discipline" has a negative connotation, conjuring up images of screaming parents or teachers with paddles. It might help us to re-frame our view of discipline if we understand the real meaning of the word. Discipline comes from the same Latin root as disciple, meaning, "to learn." If we think about discipline as helping children learn, we begin to see more clearly the critical role of discipline in raising responsible, productive, independent adults. In other words, just as children must learn how to walk and talk, just as they must learn how to decipher the code that comprises the English language, just as they must learn to add and subtract and multiply, they must also learn how to manage their emotions, interact with other people, follow rules, and the other basic skills of civilized behavior. To avoid teaching children these important skills is just as irresponsible as not teaching them the academic skills they will need to survive in the world. Thinking about discipline as teaching also helps turn what is often a *reactive* process into a *proactive* process.

If you regularly find yourself feeling anxious, frustrated, angry, or hopeless about your child's behavior, chances are you are operating in a reactive mode, responding to discipline situations as they happen, without any kind of coherent plan or strategy in place. This puts both you and your child in chronic crisis mode. Without a plan, you end up dealing with many issues after the fact that could have been prevented instead. Without a plan, your response to a discipline issue is often inconsistent and unpredictable, both of which make it more difficult for your child to learn how to behave appropriately. Without a plan, you tend to focus more on punishment for inappropriate behavior than on teaching and recognizing appropriate behavior. So how do you develop a plan for managing your child's behavior?

As with every other aspect of parenting, the Five Steps provide the road map for successful discipline. Let's take a look at discipline through the lens of: 1) the Big Five; 2) What's the Lesson? 3) Taking Charge; 4) Balance the Approach; and 5) See if it's Working.

The Big Five

The foundation of the Big Five is that you have a set of big picture goals that describe the kind of adult you want your child to become. Those goals are the end you have in mind. Regardless of your specific Big Five, it's a pretty safe bet that all parents want their children to grow up to be adults who can manage their own lives competently. After all, if you didn't want that, you'd be raising a child, not an adult. So, as with everything else, discipline begins with your Big Five. Your overall discipline strategy is designed to gradually develop the characteristics described by your Big Five. If one of your Big Five is being responsible for their actions, then you need to look at all discipline situations through the lens of "How will this make my child more responsible?"

What's the Lesson?

The best disciplinarians, whether parents or teachers, are those who do the up-front work required to make it as easy as possible for children to behave appropriately. Decades of research have repeatedly shown that children thrive in environments where three conditions exist: guidelines, monitoring, and consequences. These three conditions are the foundation of effective family management as well as effective classroom management. They provide the blueprint for the lessons you want your child to learn about managing his own behavior.

Guidelines. The process is amazingly simple. First, children need to know what is expected of them. That means they need to know what kind of behavior is and isn't acceptable in their families or in their schools. Those guidelines need to be clearly and consistently communicated to young people. By clear, I mean that the child knows exactly what behavior is expected. So, "I want you to be polite" is subject to considerable interpretation, whereas, "I expect you to say 'please' when you ask for something and 'thank you' when someone gives you something or does something for you," tells the child exactly what behavior you expect.

Just as important as clarity in giving guidelines is ensuring that the expectations we have for children are consistent from day to day, and, to the extent possible, across different areas of children's lives. So, ideally, a child should experience similar expectations at daycare as he does at home. He should expect the same rules from Mom as he hears from Dad, even if Mom and Dad live in different houses. And, the rules should be the same regardless of the mood you're in at a particular time of day.

Again, think about how children learn other skills, such as riding a bike, or spelling a word. They learn through repetition and practice. Imagine how difficult it would be to learn how to spell if the rules of spelling changed at adults' whim. Imagine how much harder it would be to learn to ride a bike if each time you rode you had to use a different bicycle. Children need that same consistency in learning to follow guidelines and expectations.

So why do guidelines and expectations seem to be such a problem for so many parents and teachers? First, setting guidelines and expectations implies that you are the adult and that you have special knowledge and maturity that children don't have. As I have said before, many Baby Boomers shy away from that grownup role. They prefer to think of themselves as the kind of parent or teacher who gives kids freedom to be themselves. They associate absolute rules and expectations with their parents' authoritarian, dictatorial approach to parenting. Many parents feel uncomfortable with non-negotiable guidelines for their children, especially for older children and teens. They don't want to take a stand. This is particularly true when guidelines involve behaviors such as drinking, drug use, or sexual behavior. I've had numerous parents ask me, "How can I tell my teenager not to drink alcohol when he sees me drinking?" They're afraid of appearing hypocritical so their solution is to avoid taking a stand on underage drinking. The answer to this one is so easy that I find it hard to believe it stumps so many intelligent parents. *Drinking alcohol is illegal for minors!* Your child is a minor and you are not. The guideline is that you expect your child not to do illegal things. You needn't get into discussions with your child about *your* drinking behavior. The discussion is about your child's behavior, and illegal activities aren't okay in your family. I know what you're thinking, "But what if my teenager asks me whether or not I drank when I was her age?" Again, a simple answer, "Whether or not I drank when I was a teenager was my parents' problem to worry about. Whether or not *you* do illegal things is *my* problem to worry about and your problem to take responsibility for."

The second thing that causes problems with guidelines and expectations is that there are often multiple adults who interact with a given child on a regular basis and this can make consistency of expectations more challenging. For many children, they interact with Mom in the mornings and evenings, the teacher (or multiple teachers) during the school day, the childcare provider after school, and Dad on the weekends. It's great if all these adults are working together to communicate consistent expectations to the child. But that's seldom the case. More often, Mom expects Dad to lay down the law, the childcare provider expects the parents to teach their child the rules of civilized behavior, and the teacher is too overwhelmed trying to teach thirty other children how to pass the standardized test at the end of the year. So, the child learns that every expectation is negotiable with someone.

Clear and consistent expectations show children the sides of the road within which they must learn to maneuver. Have you ever seen the bumpers that can be used by beginning bowlers? These padded tubes sit on each side of the lane and keep the ball from going into the gutter until the bowler becomes proficient enough to keep the ball in the lane without the aid of the bumpers. Without these bumpers, bowling can be a pretty frustrating sport, especially for children or beginners. Without the support of the bumpers, they routinely end up in the gutter and can quickly become discouraged. Guidelines operate similarly for children. They help the child stay on track until she has developed the skills and maturity to manage her own behavior. Without adults who have the wisdom and fortitude to set and enforce clear guidelines, children have to learn appropriate behavior through trial and error, a process that can be confusing, frustrating and unproductive.

So, how do you know what guidelines to set for your child? Like everything else you do as a parent, guidelines start with your Big Five. If you have identified your Big Five, then you can ask yourself the question, "What guidelines and expectations would help my child reach our Big Five?" Your guidelines should be appropriate for your child's age and abilities. For example, if one of your Big Five is to be responsible for your own actions, then a guideline for your seven-year-old might be that she is responsible for picking up her toys before she goes to bed. For a sixteen-year-old, a guideline might be that, when she drives the family car, she is responsible for returning the car as she found it, meaning with a full tank of gas and no garbage left in it. You will need to regularly revisit your guidelines and check to make sure they still work for your child as she gets older. Taking the time to really think through your guidelines and expectations and then making sure your child knows what those guidelines are helps head off an astonishing number of problems before they even get started.

Monitoring. Once we give children guidelines, someone needs to be paying attention to whether or not they are following those guidelines. Think about your own behavior when it comes to following expectations or rules. There are all kinds of expectations for us as adults in American society. We are expected to follow the laws governing our city, state, and nation. We are expected to show up for work every day on time. We are expected to pay our taxes. Most adults follow these expectations. But how many of us do so because we know someone is watching? One only needs to watch the behavior of drivers when they notice a police car at the side of the road to know that most of those drivers were speeding *until* they realized they were being monitored, at which point they slowed down to the speed limit. Even as mature adults, most of us require some monitoring to ensure that we follow society's rules. Children, who are still learning how to manage their own behavior and control their emotions and impulses, require even more monitoring as they develop their own capacity for self-discipline. So, what gets in the way of monitoring in today's world? Today's fast-paced lifestyle is the chief culprit. Working parents who spend the better part of the day away from their children must rely on someone else—teachers, daycare providers, older siblings, the child himself—to monitor the guidelines they set for their child. Imagine a 13-year-old who cares for himself after school until his parents get home from work. His parents have very clear guidelines about what they expect from him during that time: he has to finish his homework before he plays; he is allowed only one hour of television or video games; he can't have any friends over; and, of course, he is not allowed to use the Internet to access inappropriate websites. But how can his parents be sure he is following these guidelines? A tough task; however, lack of monitoring isn't just a problem for latchkey kids. Even when parents are home, too often the adults are in one room, watching TV or on the computer, while the kids are in their bedrooms with their own television, video games, and computer, doing who knows what.

Another problem is that some parents seem to need permission to monitor their children. They don't want to be too nosy. They want their child to have her own "space." They don't want to nag. Again, this attitude harkens back to the Baby Boomers' tendency to give their own children what they wanted when they were children. And didn't we all want our parents to just leave us alone when we were teenagers? However, just because we wanted something when we were kids doesn't mean we should have gotten it or that it's good for our own kids. There was undoubtedly a very good reason our own parents made the decisions they made; they knew what was good for us because they were the adults and we were the kids.

Will your children welcome your monitoring? Of course they won't. Think about some of the typical expectations and guidelines parents might have for their school-age child: do your homework before you go out to play; clean up your toys after you're done with them; resolve sibling disputes without violence. Do you think these are things your child will want to do out of the goodness of his heart? He's thrilled when he can get away with violating these guidelines because nobody is paying attention to whether or not they're being followed. Remember, your job as a parent is *not* to ensure that your child is always happy; your job is to guide him toward productive, responsible, independent adulthood. When we think about discipline as teaching, monitoring is the way that parents observe how their children are doing in learning to manage their own behavior. Monitoring whether or not your child follows guidelines and expectations is hard work. It takes time and commitment. It may take sacrifice on your part. Just saying, "Here are the family expectations," and walking away hoping that the child will miraculously step up to the plate and follow them is wishful thinking.

Consequences. Okay, you've set clear guidelines and expectations for behavior, you're monitoring whether or not your child follows those guidelines, now it's time for the third step in the effective discipline process—consequences. Consequences provide the motivation for children to follow guidelines. It's important to remember that consequences don't always have to be negative. The value of monitoring is that you can catch your child being good as well as identifying when undesirable behavior needs to be changed. This allows you to balance positive recognition for following the guidelines with appropriate negative consequences when guidelines are violated. Using positive consequences when kids follow guidelines also helps you avoid the false praise syndrome that I discussed earlier, where kids get recognition for everything they do, regardless of the outcome or the effort they put into it. This helps kids learn that they don't get recognition, rewards and praise just for existing in the world.

Here are a few cautions about positive consequences. In an effort to be the good guy we have a tendency to overreact to behavior change.

Our standards can become compromised as we reach for any sign of positive change to reward. The desired behavioral goal won't be reached if you don't acknowledge the positive change. But you will create a new problem if you tend to over reward for change that is in a positive direction but that really doesn't fulfill the expectation. Deciding how much change to expect before recognizing positive behavior is a judgment call best made by the parent or teacher who knows the child well. The decision will depend on the age of the child and the issue that you are working on. Some children need intermittent reinforcement as they gradually move toward a new behavior. Others should be expected to fully comply before they get the positive consequence.

I have a number of students each quarter who have trouble getting to class on time. After two or three tardies, they experience the consequence set out by our attendance policy—detention. Often, when they arrive on time the next day, they will ask me what they get for coming to class on time that day. Needless to say, I quickly disabuse them of the perception that making it to class on time one day is a significant achievement that deserves a reward.

Rewarding too quickly can also sabotage the desired outcome. The struggle to succeed is just as important as reaching the desired goal. Allow the child to experience the hard road to success. It will mean more to them in the end.

Positive consequences can take many forms. Children can be rewarded with stickers, small treats, a special dinner, money, a special privilege, or a favorite outing. The possibilities are endless. One potential problem with these extrinsic rewards is that they can lose their value over time and the ante is upped to an impossible level. I have students who have been paid for "A's" since they were in elementary school. I'm sure that in first grade they probably received a quarter, possibly fifty cents for each "A." However, as juniors and seniors in high school, some of these kids are making a small fortune for a good report card! When material rewards are used too frequently, the reward often seems to become the focus, not the positive behavior for which the reward was given. That doesn't mean that material rewards should never be used, it simply means that they should be used sparingly and judiciously.

Use intangible rewards, such as time and attention, to recognize positive behavior whenever possible. A smile, hug, pat on the back, or thank you goes a long way. Time spent doing whatever the child wants to do is invaluable. The most widely used acknowledgment in my home has been the family dinner. When my children accomplished something especially significant, the whole family went out to dinner at the restaurant chosen by the child being honored. For less spectacular achievements, the child would get to choose his favorite meal for dinner that night.

This is the fun part of parenting, getting to play the role of good guy. Take pleasure in the role but be prudent in your decisions and approach. Be aware of how your rewards are influencing your child and ultimately helping achieve your desired goal. If a positive consequence is not reinforcing the desired behavior, then you need to rethink your approach. If the reward itself begins to complicate the situation then an alternative reinforcement should be used. Keep your vision of your child as an adult as a beacon to guide you moment by moment.

In our "discipline as teaching" model, consequences teach children a very important natural law that will affect everything they do in life— behavior has consequences. If I do X, then Y will happen. Unfortunately, positive consequences exclusively won't be enough to teach your child all the lessons she needs to learn to achieve the Big Five goals you have for her as an adult. Sometimes her behavior will require negative consequences in order to teach those valuable lessons. The sooner your child learns that her behavior has consequences, the less likely it is that she will have to learn this immutable fact of life the hard way as an adult. In adult life, if you don't pay your taxes, you will be fined or jailed. If you don't show up for work, you will lose wages and eventually be fired. If you don't pay your mortgage, your house will be taken away.

This is an incredibly important lesson that too few children are learning because their parents are routinely rescuing them from experiencing the natural consequences of their behavior. Consequences are an extremely powerful and effective tool for shaping children's behavior. But the hardest thing for parents is often just allowing those consequences to happen; letting their children feel the disappointment, frustration, struggle or pain of learning this important lesson.

There are several important things to consider about consequences. First, the best consequences are those that don't require intervention from an adult; they happen naturally as a result of the child's actions, as long as the adult can avoid rescuing the child. These types of consequences have several advantages. First, they are natural and predictable. If you don't eat the dinner that we've prepared for you, you will be hungry. If you hit your brother, he will hit you back. If you don't put your dirty clothes in the hamper, they won't get washed. Over time, children allowed to experience the natural consequences of their behavior begin to learn that it is *their behavior* that causes the consequences, not the judgment of some adult. In my classroom I can tell the difference between students who have learned this important lesson and those who haven't. When faced with a poor grade, the former realize that they *earned* the poor grade while the latter believe *I gave them* the poor grade. Although this may seem to be a subtle difference, it has a profound impact on how each student approaches solving the poor grade problem. The first student may study harder, be sure to turn in her homework or come in for extra help. The second student is likely to try everything possible to change *my behavior* (get me to change the grade) by whining, crying, complaining, threatening parental intervention, etc., but doesn't ever consider changing her own behavior.

The second important thing about consequences is that they need to be effective in changing behavior. Remember, consequences are a teaching tool, not punishment for the sake of punishment. If a particular consequence is not effective in teaching the behavior you want to teach, then it's not a good consequence to use. For example, one consequence of not putting your dirty clothes in the hamper is that they won't be washed. For some children, this would be an effective consequence because they would eventually run out of clean clothes to wear. For others, wearing dirty clothes is not a problem at all, so that consequence would probably not be effective in teaching them to put their clothes in the hamper. Sometimes the natural consequence isn't effective because it's too unpredictable. For example, if you leave your new bike outside, it *may* get stolen. However, if it doesn't get stolen, the child doesn't learn to take care of her things. In other situations, the natural consequence is too dangerous or severe to be allowed to happen. For example, the natural consequences of a toddler playing with a sharp knife, or a preschooler running across the street, or a teenager's drinking and driving, or unprotected sex, or hanging around with peers who are involved in criminal behavior, are too severe and life-threatening to be allowed to happen as a lesson to kids. When natural consequences aren't a good option for any of these reasons, you need to select another consequence that is logically related to the behavior, appropriate for the child's age, and effective.

In the "discipline as teaching" model, it's also important to remember that, once the lesson is over, life can return to normal. This means that while you are imposing a negative consequence, your demeanor may be firm and perhaps even cold. You want the child to understand the seriousness of her transgression. However, once the punishment has been handed down and the child has served her time, you put the situation behind you and go back to your normal relationship. This may take longer for your child than for you. As the adult, even when there has been significant conflict, it is up to you to assure the child that you can go back to your previous way of being together. Depending on the degree of conflict involved, she may still remain angry with you. As she is working through her emotions, make sure that you leave the door open for reestablishing positive communications. In my experience, once the child realizes that his tantrums, sulking, etc. are not going to make you back down, he can move on to more productive behavior. The timing of this reconciliation will differ with the temperament of the child and the seriousness of the confrontation. It's important that you are available and attuned to the child's tentative efforts to reconnect because his attempts may not be obvious. The gesture may take the form of asking for your help with something they generally do on their own, such as homework, a chore, advice on clothes. He may walk near you, sit closer to you, volunteer to help, or do something without prodding. You need to be astute enough to recognize this offering and respond appropriately.

In order for this natural process to take place, you must be available. Learning to handle this kind of conflict is a maturation process for kids. They are learning how to take a risk and initiate positive actions. That means you must be physically available for that moment when they gather up the courage to make the offer of reconnecting. Be more visible around the house. Instead of isolating yourself in your office, do your work on the kitchen table or somewhere within easy access. Make it easy for your child to make the gesture by just being around. In raising my own sons I made sure that if I had to discipline them for something one day, I deliberately initiated a positive contact with them the next day. If I have a confrontation with a student one class period I make a point to have some type of neutral conversation with her within a few days. This lets children know that they can be punished, disciplined, or criticized and still be okay. People make mistakes, learn from them, and we move on. We choose how we react and I am showing them one healthy way to deal with difficulty.

Sometimes the best strategy is to open up communication yourself. The child may be unsure of the seriousness of this confrontation, particularly if this is a new way of behaving for you. They may be worried that this sudden change in your discipline behavior means you don't love her anymore. This is a great opportunity to teach children that the world won't come to an end if people disagree or have a conflict. They need to know that these conflicts are normal and that the uncomfortable feelings that go with them are also normal. Make it easier for them by initiating conversations about everyday things so they can see that, just because you are in conflict over one issue, it doesn't mean you have stopped talking to them, seeing them, caring for them or loving them.

Sounds simple, right? This process can be very simple and effective, especially when it is started early in a child's life. In fact, using guidelines, monitoring, and consequences is an excellent way to proactively teach children how to manage their own behavior. The real pay-off of this "discipline as teaching" process is that it gradually transfers the responsibility for discipline from you to the child as she learns how to manage her own behavior. This is, of course, the ultimate goal of discipline, whether in families or in schools. The goal is not for the adult to effectively control the child's behavior; it is for the child to eventually learn how to control his own behavior.

If you are a parent or teacher who has spent years trying to control children's behavior, you know that it is an exhausting and ultimately futile exercise. If the child is dependent on you to exercise control, the minute you turn your back the control is gone and the child is left with no internal skills for managing himself. However, if a systematic process for teaching the child to manage his own behavior is used consistently throughout a child's formative years (birth to age sixteen or so), you will find yourself doing considerably less disciplining by the time the child is a teenager. Contrast this with the situation in which most parents find themselves; their child's adolescence is a living hell because they are faced with trying to maintain control over a young person whose every instinct is to break free from that control. Unfortunately, rather than phasing themselves out of the role of disciplinarian when their child reaches adolescence, many parents seem to finally wake up, realize that their child is out of control and frantically try to become the disciplinarians that they should have been thirteen years earlier.

Discipline as teaching works. However, as logical and simple as this process sounds, chicken parents and chicken teachers still have trouble using it because it requires them to confront some very basic fears and misconceptions. If you are a parent of a school-aged or teenage child and you haven't been using this process for the early years of your child's life, you may have some remedial work to do. If you are a teacher, you have to work with your students as they come to you; you have no control over how they were parented or taught for all those years before they entered your classroom. Effectively disciplining young people often requires that you face your own fears and take a difficult stand. The following steps will help guide you through this process. The process is simple and its effectiveness is well-established; summoning the internal strength to execute the process is where the challenge arises. So, let's take a closer look at how you can move from chicken to in charge.

Take Charge

The reason most parents and teachers fail to discipline children is that they are paralyzed by fear. We're afraid our kids will hate us; we're afraid we'll have to make sacrifices to follow through on the consequences we've imposed; we're afraid of turning into the dictatorial, authoritarian parents or teachers we vowed never to become; we're afraid to take the responsibility and make the decisions. We have swallowed the positive approach because it is easier and makes us feel better. We avoid confronting unacceptable behavior because we don't want to appear mean or uncaring. We give kids second, third, tenth chances so that we can be seen as fair. We progressively expect less so that everyone can be a winner. We pay more attention to kids' *feelings* than we do to their *behavior*. We avoid taking a stand because someone might challenge that position. We are more concerned about having kids like us than we are about the results we hope to achieve—children who become healthy, productive, responsible adults.

When we keep our focus on that end goal, it is easier to face the fears that prevent us from doing our parenting or teaching job effectively. Taking a stand has always been difficult. Taking an unpopular stand takes real guts. True accounts of individuals who do what it takes to produce the desired results for kids have been celebrated in film over the decades. The classic sixties film *To Sir, With Love* told the story of a high school teacher in a disadvantaged part of London, whose consistent demand for high expectations in academics and behavior eventually won the hearts and minds of his students. In the seventies, *Stand and Deliver* introduced us to Jaime Escalante, who fought against all odds to establish a math program that increased the performance of inner city students in Los Angeles to exceptional levels. We continue to hear about schools that consistently produce superior outcomes despite serving a student population at very high risk for failure. What do all these stories have in common? They all describe an individual who stood up, faced his fears and did what was necessary to get the job done. The pivotal moment for the teacher in *To Sir, with Love* was his realization that his students were not kids; they were young adults who wanted desperately to be treated as young adults. So he made a reasonable bargain with them, he would treat them as adults and they would behave as adults. He didn't treat them like adults just because they *wanted* to be treated like adults. He didn't treat them like adults because he thought it would make them *feel* better. He took responsibility for teaching them that behavior has consequences. When you act like an adult, people treat you like an adult. Mr. Escalante was successful because he established and enforced high expectations for both his students' academic performance as well as for their behavior. Both of these exceptional teachers were successful because they kept their eyes on the prize—they wanted to see their students thrive and excel despite overwhelming odds. They confronted their own personal fears to embark on a journey fraught with peril. They stood firm in their vision of success, established a plan, endured the skeptics and challengers, fought the battles one by one, and eventually earned the respect and love of many students, colleagues, and others in their communities.

Take a moment and think about the kind of disciplinarian you are right now and the kind of disciplinarian you need to be in order to reach the vision you have for the adult you want your child to become. Do you find yourself rationalizing your child's out-of-control behavior as just a typical developmental phase that will resolve itself in time? Do you seem to fight the same battles with your child over and over again? Do you find yourself looking forward to the time your child is away or asleep and dreading the time you have to spend with her? Are you secretly hoping that your child's school will be able to change your child's behavior? Maybe you are counting on your child's coach or daycare provider to get this child in line. One thing is for certain, if you are unwilling to take responsibility for teaching your child appropriate behavior, sooner or later he will run up against someone who *does* hold the line, who won't listen to excuses, who refuses to look the other way. It may be a school administrator, it may be your teen's employer, or it may be the police. Unfortunately, unlike a parent, these individuals don't necessarily have your child's long-term best interests at heart so they will be less likely to use discipline as a way to teach your child valuable lessons. They may simply punish your child.

Ultimately, of course, it is none of these other people's job to teach your child how to behave. That's your job. There is no magical solution to your child's unruly ways. Procrastination won't make the problem go away; it is likely to exacerbate it. If denial is keeping you from recognizing the truth about your child's behavior, you need to pull your head out of the sand. It is your job to guide and discipline your child. You head the list of people who have the power and responsibility for changing your child's behavior. Whether you like it or not, you are the leader in your family and you need to act like one. Don't let fear be the guiding emotion for your actions. Stop waiting, wishing, and blaming—and start parenting.

Limits

You've heard it before and it's really very true—kids *want* limits. Having no one else to help manage their behavior is scary for kids. It's too much responsibility for a child who is still learning self-control and self-discipline. Although you may want to think that you are allowing your child freedom by failing to set limits, you are really putting incredible stress on him, because it forces him to do your job *and* his job. He is forced to expend considerable energy making choices that should be made for him by a responsible adult who is looking out for his well-being. Once again, if you think that your child is going to thank you for setting limits, or willingly comply with those limits, you're dreaming. Just because it's the right thing to do doesn't mean it's the easy thing to do. Children *do* test limits; it's their job to challenge the convictions of the adults shaping their world. These challenges help them determine your level of commitment. In fact, constant testing and conflict is often a sign that the child is challenging you to take a stand. The more you refuse to take a stand, the more the child escalates his behavior until he forces your hand. He will continue to push as long as you continue to retreat.

If a boundary is always shifting, the child concludes that it must not be something you value very highly. If it's not important enough for you to stand up for, then he assumes that it's not important enough for him to follow. As the challenges escalate and the bottom lines dissolve, parents become more frustrated and kids more unmanageable. All the experts who have convinced you that your goal as a parent should be to only have happy, positive interactions with your kids were wrong. They have misled you and endangered your child's healthy development. Failing to be the adult in your family is *not* loving behavior. Refusing to do your job just because it's uncomfortable or difficult is *not* caring. Don't confuse being *nice* with being *loving*. How loving is it to stand back and watch your child risk his future through experimentation with alcohol because you're afraid to confront his behavior? How loving is it to allow your child to behave in ways that make other adults loathe to be around her, simply because you're afraid your child will say he hates you? A loving, caring parent does *what is necessary* to ensure that their children grow up to be healthy, productive, responsible adults. Sometimes those things are pleasant, positive interactions; sometimes they are not.

Your kids are begging you to stand up and give them limitations. They demand your attention through their constant challenging. Ultimately they will see this entire struggle as proof that they are worth your efforts. As I've said many times before, kids aren't stupid. They realize that anyone can be positive and pleasant to them. It's not really any sweat off an adult's back to praise a kid or tell her how special she is. That's the easy stuff and kids know it. But it takes real commitment to tackle the harder, more unpleasant task of teaching kids how to manage their own behavior and to stick with it even when the child pulls out all the stops.

The first time you stand up to your child you may find your fear intensifies. Don't run away. Instead embrace it. When you bring the enemy closer you will be able to use it to your advantage. Recognize the influence it may have over your decisions and actions. The more practice you get confronting your fears, the less control they will have over you. The more control you have over your own emotions, the more good you will be to all those who count on you for strength, advice, nurturing, and guidance. Being strong and in charge is a choice.

Think about one of your child's undesirable behaviors. Choose the one behavior that, if changed, would make the biggest difference in your family. It may be a common problem like back-talking, failure to do chores, tantrums, fighting with a sibling, or it may be something more serious, such as drinking, skipping school, or staying out all night. Focus on one problem area at a time. Don't try to work on a whole laundry list of behaviors simultaneously. Once you have successfully tackled one issue, you can take on another. Remember, that by taking a stand now and addressing the problem once and for all, you will avoid having this behavior continue to poison your family environment in the future. The big payoff to taking a stand on discipline issues is that, once you change the behavior that is causing so much grief in your family, you will actually have the time and desire to spend pleasurable time with your child. That's when real connections and influence can begin.

Resistance

Expect the child to resist. One of the difficult things about discipline is that it usually involves either: 1) getting a child to do something he doesn't want to do; or 2) getting him to stop doing something you don't want him to do. Few children want to turn off the TV and go to bed; most would rather not pick up their toys or put their dirty socks in the hamper. So, if you're expecting your child to smile and passively comply with your expectation, you're certain to be disappointed. Your discipline has a goal, a lesson that you want your child to learn. Understand that the battle has just begun with your line drawn firmly in the sand. You will surely be challenged. Your child will exhaust every means of manipulation she has. She will pull out all the stops to weaken your resolve and test the strength of your commitment. The contest will continue until your child is satisfied that you cannot be swayed. The secret to withstanding this onslaught is to remain calm and composed. You want to convey strength, maturity and confidence. This approach will minimize the conflict and maximize your civility. If your child fails to cooperate, repeat the request in a firm but controlled manner. Do not get sucked into arguments about your request or resort to lectures. Remember that a soft, firm voice will get your child's attention more effectively than a shrill, demanding, scolding or nagging voice. If you have trouble remaining calm as your child cycles through her bag of tricks, simply repeat your request and then leave the room.

Habits

It's helpful to remember that your child's way of responding to discipline is a habit that he has learned over a period of time. Your child's investment in being uncooperative plays a big part in his endurance. He reacts the way he does because he *gets something out of it*. Chances are that his tantrums, sulking, whining, threats, etc. have worked in the past to get you to back down, so you are going to have to convince him that standing firm is your new modus operandi. How do you convince him? He will become convinced when he sees your new behavior repeated over and over again.

Like any other habit, your child's inappropriate response must be unlearned and replaced with the response you want to see. The amount of time required to unlearn these old habits differs from child to child and from behavior to behavior. Some behaviors can be changed in days; others may take years. Some children are more persistent than others and will take longer to give up their old behavior.

Remembering that discipline is about teaching helps you keep from approaching discipline as a battle. You aren't focused on winning or losing; you're focused on ensuring that your child learns a valuable lesson. Your child, however, is likely to approach the situation as a battle and she may be a very seasoned and skilled warrior. If she's beyond infancy, she has probably learned well which of your buttons to push. She knows your weaknesses and, like any clever combatant, will use them to try to overpower you. Remember: you are in charge; you are the adult; you have your child's best interests in mind and are doing what is necessary to ensure that she learns the lessons required to become the adult you want her to be.

One of the most difficult things to do in this process is to remain calm and objective. If you let your emotions guide your behavior or take the situation personally, you will fail to achieve your goal and probably compound the problem. Effective discipline isn't about power; it is about change. When you let yourself become personally invested in the situation, when you allow the child to drag you into a power struggle, you aren't addressing the issue and you won't be successful in changing the child's behavior.

I became a more effective teacher and parent when I stopped caring so much. I know that sounds awful, but before you slam the book to the ground in disgust, let me explain. First of all, I believe that all children need and deserve caring from the adults in their lives. However, I take issue with the way caring has come to be defined in today's society. What I see from too many parents and teachers is behavior that masquerades as caring, but which really serves the needs of the adults, not the children. When adults make a discipline decision based on power, they are meeting their own need, not the child's. When adults give in to a child just so the child will like them, they are meeting their own need, not the child's. When adults fail to set limits on a child's behavior because they are afraid of the disapproval of other adults, they are meeting their own need, not the child's. When adults refuse to confront inappropriate behavior because they can't handle the discomfort of the child's unhappiness, anger, or other negative feelings, they are meeting their own needs, not the child's. If adults are not helping children develop the attitudes and skills they will need to become a mature, functioning adult, then their actions are not caring.

Is it more caring to step in and fight a battle for your child or to sit back and have your child wrestle with the situation, develop his own skills and confidence, and come to a successful outcome on his own? Is it more caring to artificially confer success for an undeserved effort or is it more deeply caring to support his continued efforts toward real success by allowing him to face the realities of hard work and focus? Is it more caring to protect your child from bad feelings and unpleasant situations or is it more deeply caring to let him learn how to gradually deal with these realities so that he is prepared for the real world when he enters it?

So, when I say I stopped caring so much, I mean that I stopped caring less about things that had nothing to do with the end goals I had in mind for my sons or my students. Rather than worrying about whether they liked my class, I began concentrating on whether my students were learning what they were supposed to learn. Rather than focusing on trying to control my sons' feelings about a given situation, I began focusing on what they were or could be learning from those situations. I also stopped worrying so much about solving the problem immediately and began to attend to long-term solutions.

When your child sees you handling discipline challenges in an objective, calm and controlled fashion, you are also modeling an important life skill. As he continues to observe balanced and civilized behavior from you in difficult situations, he will gradually internalize that behavior in his own interactions with others. As a parent you teach your child many skills; controlling yourself with dignity and civility in intense situations is just one of them. It will begin a ripple effect that will continue to pay dividends for generations.

Balance the Approach

Life has taught me one important general rule: The best approach is always the balanced approach. With hard work there must be enthusiastic play, with seriousness there must be passionate fun, with focused effort there must be spontaneous frivolity, with guidelines there must be freedom, and with discipline there must be acceptance. The natural world is rife with examples of the fundamental principle of balance.

A balanced approach is critical to disciplining children. Research shows that both overly strict and overly permissive parenting styles are linked to problems such as drug abuse, early sexual activity and delinquency. By contrast, the most effective management strategy is a balanced style that experts call "authoritative." Throughout the discipline process, balance should be an integral part of your decision-making.

When it comes to the important decisions, focusing on your Big Five can help you achieve the appropriate balance. One of the first skills you had to learn as a new driver was to keep the car going in a straight line. Like most new drivers, you probably overcorrected and over-steered, jerking from side to side as you struggled to keep the car moving forward in a straight line. Fortunately, when you're learning to drive, there are a number of visual clues that help you gradually learn to negotiate this complex new skill: the white lines designating the lanes, the shoulders marking the outside edge of the road, etc. These boundaries give you a visual sense of the parameters in which you have to navigate. Sure, within those parameters, you still probably did some weaving from side to side, but, with practice you gradually learned the appropriate level of steering required to stay on track. Once that skill was solidified, you could graduate to curved roads, different speeds and more complex driving situations.

The clear and consistent guidelines and expectations you have for your children function in the same way. They provide the "sides of the road" within which your child learns how to manage his own behavior in a safe and protected environment. The structure you establish in your home creates a comfort level for everyone involved. Children know what to expect. They know what they need to do to thrive in their home environment. Children know the difference between parents and kids and they know that each of you has a unique and important role to play. They aren't burdened with adult worries because that is your role in the family. This gives them the freedom to concentrate and focus their energies on the important things they need to do to mature toward adulthood. When children aren't being forced to use their energy testing ever-changing or nonexistent boundaries, they are free to concentrate on developing their bodies, minds and emotions. This important balance between allowing appropriate freedom within secure boundaries is a critical factor in healthy development.

As you set guidelines, are you balancing the child's need for parameters and boundaries with her need to make age-appropriate decisions on her own? One hint: Whenever the outcome of the decision doesn't matter, let the child make the choice. Giving up control over all those unimportant decisions serves two purposes: 1) it frees you to concentrate on the important decisions, and 2) it gives your child plenty of practice making decisions in a safe context where the outcome isn't critical. For example, when our sons were young and we first moved them to their new downstairs bedrooms, we used a creative method for avoiding fights over bedtime. They had to be in bed at a certain time and they had to sleep downstairs. However, they could sleep anywhere they wanted downstairs. Both of the boys had sleeping bags and they were usually so busy figuring out where they wanted to sleep that night, they didn't have time to argue about staying up later. Some nights they slept on the floor of the playroom, other nights they slept in one of their bedrooms, with one child on the bed and the other on the floor. The bottom line was that we didn't really care *where* they slept. What we cared about was that they went to bed on time and did so without an argument.

Remember, your goal is to prepare your child to gradually make decisions on her own. Is she ready to make this particular decision? Does she have the knowledge and skills to make the decision on her own? What would be the consequences if she made a poor decision?

Another important aspect of balancing your discipline approach has to do with consequences. Children need a balance of positive consequences for following expectations and guidelines and negative consequences when guidelines are violated. Unfortunately, many adults are perfectly willing to play the role of good guy dispensing positive consequences but quickly lose their enthusiasm when it comes time to impose a negative consequence. Although it's great to catch kids being good and reward them with positive consequences, there are times when negative consequences are the only appropriate choice. Kids understand and appreciate the balance. Just as they easily sniff out false praise, kids know when they've violated the rules and guidelines and they expect to experience a negative consequence.

On the other hand, some parents go overboard on the negative consequences, which is equally damaging. Failing to recognize and appreciate positive behavior while doggedly catching every inappropriate behavior can leave kids feeling hopeless, unloved, and unmotivated. Years ago, I watched an interview with Bing Crosby's son, shortly after his father's death. In recounting his childhood, the son described his father as a strict, perhaps even abusive, disciplinarian. The statement that most captured my attention reflected the imbalance that this man had experienced as a child. He said that he could have endured all the physical punishment and emotional manipulation the elder Crosby dished out if his father had only been as vehement with his love and attention.

My experience with kids has taught me that what they really care about is fairness. This means that, if they see another student or a sibling receiving a positive consequence for following an expectation, they expect to receive the same recognition. If they violate a guideline, they can accept negative consequences as long as those consequences are perceived as fair.

For parents with a child who never seems to do anything wrong, you need special assistance in this area to achieve the appropriate balance. Children who are consistently following the rules and doing all that is asked of them desperately need relief from the burden of always being good. If you don't balance out the good behavior with a little planned naughtiness your child will eventually become off kilter. Although it's tempting to sit back and count your lucky stars that you have such a perfect child, it truly is your responsibility to step in and purposely take this stable vehicle off-track. Giving your child the opportunity to release and taste a little harmless naughtiness is very healthy. It shows the child that there is more to life then being good and always doing the right thing. Of course, you must be careful and selective as to what you design as your "naughty" experience. The goal is to challenge or cross a behavioral boundary, not to shatter it completely. You are giving them a taste of what it is like to be naughty so they can understand and have experience in this emotional arena. So, what sorts of activities belong in this category? (Keep in mind, we are talking about kids who are seriously obedient individuals day-in and day-out.) Here's where your own judgment is critical. You know your child best and can most accurately gauge how far to push the boundaries. My oldest son was on track to become one of these "perfect children" so I began planning naughty experiences for him at a fairly young age. When my kids were four or five years old and I would spot a hole in one of their socks, I would chase them down, wrestle them to the ground, put my finger in the hole, tickle their feet and eventually tear the sock to shreds. They were initially shocked that I would do something so outrageous. Are Dads supposed to do that? Of course, it didn't take long before they began looking for holes in *my* socks. When they got older, we would go skinny dipping in the lake where we have our summer cabin. We would go out late at night, just to be out when most other people were doing the right thing– sleeping. As adolescents, I would make faces at them in stores or other places just to push the edge a little bit.

Kids get tired of always being good. Sometimes they must bend with the wind or break. I have seen many examples of perfect kids who eventually lose it and go off the deep end. If you have such a child, planned naughtiness allows you to structure relatively harmless activities that allow the child to break out of the perfect mold without having to resort to activities that may, in fact, be harmful. Neither of my sons seemed to have felt the need to rebel in the typical adolescent fashion, and I believe it's because I actually encouraged them to rebel in relatively harmless ways and usually helped them do it.

Classroom teachers can do the same thing. Every year I take my Math classes out to the running track and we do a pacing activity. It usually occurs when the students are in one of those tired-of-being-in-school moods, often in the late spring. I unexpectedly stop doing that day's lesson, ask them to drop whatever they're doing and follow me. They are taken by surprise, wondering what's going on, and clearly intrigued by my unusual behavior. The activity does have a mathematical connection but the real benefit is the fact that the students know that it is really just an excuse to get outside and let off some steam, therefore it has a high "naughtiness" quotient. They also come to realize I needed the moment as much as they did. As we are strolling back to class, inevitably one of my students will turn to me and say, "Mr. Wong, you're weird." Goal accomplished.

I sometimes play music the last five minutes of class, accompanied with a little dance number that always gets them laughing. We play "Name that tune!" with the winners getting to leave early. I sing my favorite oldies. I bring in weird stories from the newspaper that have no relationship to Math. I spend a few minutes most days just talking with the students about whatever happens to have piqued their interest. Sometimes the most valuable educational times I spend during the day are those few minutes just being human. It's great to be good but there is a point where enough is enough.

Another important balance to achieve in discipline is between the short-term and the long-term consequences of a disciplinary approach. Too often we grab for the solution that provides immediate relief, without balancing the long-term consequences of that quick fix solution. If we follow the "discipline as teaching" approach, quick fixes are only useful if they teach the lesson we want to teach and lead to one of our Big Five. One of the most frequent statements made to me by parents during Open House is some variation of, "My kid really disliked you at first but now this is one of his favorite classes." This is by design. I usually have these students for the entire year. I have plenty of time to win them over but only a few days at the beginning of the year to establish routine, rules, and civility. I don't like myself much either during this phase, but it's a mandatory part of achieving my long-term goal, which is a respectful, responsible, civilized relationship between the students and me. Once I have established this foundation, I can reveal some of the more positive aspects of my teaching style and we can build a long-lasting rapport.

See if It's Working

Albert Einstein said, "The definition of insanity is doing the same thing over and over and over and over again, but expecting a different result." I can't tell you how often I see parents or teachers doing the same thing over and over again and expecting a different result. "I've asked you a hundred times to pick up your clothes and put them in the hamper." Well, obviously telling the child isn't working, is it? Or, "I'm sick and tired of having to yell at you people to get your attention so we can start class." Again, yelling isn't working, so why don't you try something different?

The $64,000 question in discipline is, "Did the disciplinary action achieve the desired behavior and will it help me reach the Big Five I have for my child?" If so, the method was successful; if not, the method failed. If your strategy failed, you may have to be a bit of a detective to figure out what part of the process needs changing. Did you not set a clear guideline or expectation? Was the expectation inappropriate for the child's age or abilities? Did you fail to monitor compliance with the guideline? What about consequences? Did you rescue the child from the consequence? Did you fail to give the consequence enough time to work? Was it the wrong consequence? Once you have determined what went wrong, try something different and keep trying different strategies until you get the result you want.

One of the realities that parents and teachers need to keep in mind when working with children is that change takes time. In this fast-paced world we get used to having our needs taken care of instantly. We change channels in a fraction of a second, we get irritated if the fast food takes more than sixty seconds, we want our headache to disappear the second the aspirin hits our stomach, we expect weight to melt away quickly and without effort. In short, we have expectations that are often woefully unrealistic. Changing habits *will* take time. The process of learning a new behavior takes time and establishing that behavior as a routine requires repetition, which takes more time. Different desired outcomes require different time periods to achieve. Changing a student's behavior so that she arrives in class on time may only take a few days. On the other hand, getting an adolescent to understand that he has responsibility for his own learning may take an entire year or more. I have had students, both at the junior high and the high school level, who have achieved great strides over the course of three years. From their sophomore year to their senior year or their seventh grade to their ninth grade year, I often witness significant improvements. Over those three years, small steps are achieved slowly and methodically. You won't find silver bullet, miracle cures in either the parenting or the teaching tool kit. Changing lifelong habits, even for children, is a slow, plodding process that requires commitment and consistency. Be patient. Yes, it will be torturous at times and you will definitely question yourself along the way. Time will be the test.

Remember the question we have encouraged you to ask of yourself throughout this book. What will the child learn from this? If you cave, your child learns that: 1) he can get away with anything if he holds on long enough; and 2) the behavior you are expecting must not be very important or you certainly wouldn't give in so easily. When the child sees that you are going to hold firm in your expectations and that you will go to the limit in reinforcing those expectations, she learns that the expected behavior is of great importance. With time and consistency, that behavior will become part of her personal repertoire.

The Pay-Off

Following these steps establishes the foundation for reaching your long-term vision for your children. Your kids feel comfortable with the routine and you are reaping the benefits of an effectively managed family. Classroom rules and expectations have become internalized and can now take a back seat to the important task of academic learning. You will find that conflict and confrontations are significantly lessened. But possibly the greatest pay-off is your increased rapport with your kids and the fact that you are all just having more fun. By having the guts to take a stand and address discipline issues effectively, you reap untold rewards for years to come. You may sacrifice in the short-term but you establish a lifetime of understanding and clear standards. Once you've successfully taught the discipline lessons your child needs to learn, you can direct your energies toward other goals. When kids feel that adults are looking after their long-term development, when they feel secure in the consistency and predictability of expectations, learning is easier, chores less demanding, emotions are more controlled, anxiety is reduced, performance improves, and relationships are closer. This is truly being in charge. This is conquering your fear.

Using these Five Steps creates a snowball effect; the more cooperation you get from your kids, the more you can enrich their lives, and the more you enrich their lives, the more wonderful everyone's life becomes. The snowball effect also extends beyond your immediate relationship with the child. As your children or students learn self-discipline and self-control, they will take those skills with them into adulthood, making them better employees, better spouses and better parents. I learned the majority of my successful parenting skills from my parents. You too will pass on the gift of constructive parenting to your kids. The snowballing continues to pay dividends for future generations.

Today my two sons are twenty and twenty-three. I basically stopped disciplining both of them at the age of fourteen. By that time they had developed their own ability to control their behavior, to make good decisions and to discipline themselves. Yes, those first fourteen years were hard work. Not all of our experiences together were happy and positive. But the payoff has far exceeded my wildest dreams. Rather than having to *endure* adolescence, as so many parents seem to do, my wife and I enjoyed their company, appreciated their opinions and respected their choices. Rather than having to fight the same battles with a teenager that one fought unsuccessfully with that child as a preschooler, we could focus our energy on supporting them as they prepared to go out into the world on their own.

Children are watching us. They see the messages being sent through adults' actions and behaviors. They understand why parents who smoke have a greater chance of having kids who smoke. They know that it's their parents' job to impose limits on their behavior, to keep them safe and secure. They understand the benefits and pay-offs of hard work and focused effort. They look to you for these strengths. They long for the guidance of a strong parent and need the boundaries set by caring hands. They understand the connection between love and confrontation. They know that it is necessary for someone who loves them to be honest, even if it makes them feel bad. They accept that life will include both success and failure and they know that the latter can be the greater teacher. They realize that adults make mistakes and the best ones are those who have the strength to admit it. They like to present a strong front to you but they hope you can still see the child in them. They want to be held and touched even though they may never ask for it and often appear to be rejecting it. Your child is just that—your child. Make the right decisions today and be the best parent you can be. Take charge of your family and be the source of strength. Prepare your child by your own example for the most important job they will ever have—being a strong, confident, committed parent.

CHAPTER 10: BALANCE

You've undoubtedly heard about the three most important criteria in real estate: location, location, location. When it comes to guiding children from birth to healthy, productive adulthood, the keys are balance, balance, balance. If there is a silver bullet in the world of child rearing, it is balance.

Nature abounds with examples of balance. In the physical structure of atoms, positive and negatively charged ions maintain a perfect equilibrium. Even the smallest of molecules has a balance of electrons, protons, and neutrons, without which chemical substances would be unstable. Nature's ecosystems depend on balance. In the animal kingdom, you are either the predator or the prey. Socrates understood the value of balance when he promoted the integration of mind and body as one. Balance is central to many cultures and religions. For example, in many Asian cultures, the complementary and balancing forces of yin and yang affect all aspects of life. America's founding fathers paid tribute to the importance of balance when they apportioned power to the three branches of government: legislative, judicial and executive.

Viewing child rearing through the lens of balance is a valuable way for parents and teachers to maintain a big picture, long-term focus in their daily interactions with children. When the goal is balance, it only makes sense that with the good, there will be some bad; with pleasure there will be pain; with happiness there will also be sadness; with success comes failure.

Balanced parenting or teaching begins with being a balanced individual who provides a stable and predictable environment for children. This is not to suggest that there is such a thing as a perfect parent or a perfect teacher anymore than there is such a thing as a perfect child. In fact, the beauty of this balanced approach is that it allows us room to be human, to make mistakes. Children recognize and accept this humanity and imperfection in adults. What they crave is fairness. Rather than fretting over creating an ideal world for children, we can concentrate our efforts on ensuring that they are exposed to a balance of experiences.

Although balance is important in all areas of children's lives, there are several areas that deserve special attention in families, and areas that deserve special attention from schools.

Good versus Bad Experiences

Throughout this book I have discussed the importance of balancing these two important and essential aspects of young people's lives. Few parents have trouble providing the good experiences. That's the fun, rewarding, easy part of the job. The unsettling part for parents and educators is the negative element to this balance. When it comes to nurturing children to adulthood, achieving balance requires us to rethink what we have come to accept as normal or good parenting or teaching behavior. We need to stop measuring experiences based on how they will make children *feel* and change our yardstick to what children *learn* from those experiences. If the lesson is valuable and necessary to becoming a productive, responsible adult, then even a painful, frustrating, or unhappy experience isn't bad.

As adults we know that things don't always turn out well. We understand that disappointment, frustration and suffering are part of life. Whether the difficult experiences we have endured are recent events or the scars of long-ago childhood pain, conquering these challenges has strengthened our character and built resiliency. We know that bad things happen to good people and those difficulties are part of the package of human existence. So why do so many adults hide this reality from their kids? Why do they set the impossible goal of having their child's life be pain-free? Why do they shrink from adequately preparing their child to withstand all of life's challenges? Why do they go to such lengths to shelter their kids from normal experiences that have the potential to teach valuable life-long lessons? Why do they protect and pamper their children from the very experiences that build strong character? Why do they let fear dictate their approach to parenting when they know that some of life's best lessons are taught through difficult circumstances?

It is impossible to raise a child to adulthood without bad things happening. Although this may sound obvious, the average parent's behavior reveals that many don't acknowledge this simple concept. When you accept the idea that bad things will happen to your child, it becomes easier to embrace those experiences and view them as maximum opportunity moments, rather than expending valuable energy fighting against the inevitable realities of life.

For example, let's look at how a typical scenario often plays out in today's families. On finding out that their child has been suspended from school, the parents immediately call the administrator. It quickly becomes clear that the parents' goal is to exonerate their child and protect her from suffering the consequences of her behavior. It may start with denial, "My child would never do anything like that." Or, "He's really a good boy. There must be some mistake." The parent immediately seeks out the weakest link in the system, questioning rules or policies, challenging the severity of the child's offense, blaming others (the teacher or the child's peers) for the child's offense, or intimating racial, gender or another type of bias against the child. If satisfaction isn't realized with the teacher and administrator, the parent may continue the challenge up through the district hierarchy.

Now, think about how this scenario would change if the parents were to view this "bad" situation, not as a horrible thing from which their child must be protected, but as an opportunity to teach valuable lessons. They accept the suspension, acknowledging the fact that their child violated some sort of school rule or policy. They use the experience to teach their child about following rules, or respecting authority, or doing the right thing. On the day of suspension, they reinforce the school's position by giving the child a few extra duties, nothing too harsh or lengthy, but an activity to let the child know that being suspended is not a day off from school.

Just such a maximum opportunity moment presented itself in the spring of my son's eighth grade year, when he was suspended from middle school for being in the wrong place at the wrong time with the wrong people. Recognizing that he was at a crucial and impressionable transition point, about to enter high school, I decided that this was an invaluable opportunity to teach him some important, albeit painful, lessons. I began by talking with my son about the situation in which he had been involved, strongly emphasizing the importance of telling me the truth at this point in the process. I informed him that I was going to call the Vice Principal to get the school's version of the story and that, if I suspected my son's explanation was less than truthful, his problems would be compounded. As I spoke to the Vice Principal on the phone, I made eye contact with my son throughout the conversation. The Vice Principal's story matched my son's. I then told my son that the suspension was legitimate and he would not be allowed to attend school the next day. We talked about the reasons why he was involved, alternatives he could have chosen that would have kept him away from trouble, and about the lessons he might learn from this experience. I asked him to do his punishment without complaint and warned him not to use this incident to try to improve his cool factor with his peers. He spent the next day at home serving his punishment, with a number of additional duties designed to occupy his time.

Was this a pleasant experience for my son? Of course it wasn't. Was it a pleasant experience for us as his parents? Quite the contrary; but did he learn valuable lessons? Absolutely. He learned that his parents would support the authority of the school. It's important for you to understand that, in this particular situation, my wife and I both believed that our son was being judged unfairly and that the punishment didn't necessarily fit the crime. However, we also strongly believed that supporting the school was the best position in the long run. We believed that undermining the school's authority in our son's mind was a more damaging consequence than the effects of an overly punitive school response. So, instead of viewing this as an unfair attack on our child, we chose to view it as an opportunity to teach him some important lessons. He learned that it was extremely important to be honest with us. He knew without a doubt that his story had to match the Vice Principal's or, in addition to the consequences imposed by the school, he would face additional punishment for lying. He had the opportunity to tell the truth under great pressure and he rose to the occasion. He learned that just being in the wrong place at the wrong time could get him in trouble. He learned to think twice about the people with whom he chose to associate. He learned that sometimes one must really think through situations and predict what kind of trouble they might produce. These are lessons that wouldn't have been learned through lectures. A window of opportunity opened and we took advantage of it. My son was allowed to express his position and we listened. We accepted his feeling that the punishment was too harsh, without backing down on our support for the school's right to hand down that punishment and his responsibility to take the punishment like a man. He learned an important reality about the world; life isn't always fair.

This experience was an important stepping-stone to maturity for my son. Real life had treated him unfairly and he had to cope with that. Rather than letting this experience undermine my son's respect for the school system, I turned the experience around and used it as a springboard to teach a variety of highly valuable lessons about life. I win, my son wins, the school wins. How much better could it be?

Conversely, think about the message being learned when parents take the opposite approach, immediately leaping to their child's defense and manipulating or challenging the people involved. Parents often take a manipulative and confrontational tactic, playing the defense attorney determined to find any available loophole to rescue their child from the consequences of her behavior. This battle between two groups of adults who are supposed to be working together to set and enforce clear guidelines for her behavior opens up a clear wedge into which the enterprising child often steps, using the conflict to play one against the other. The child learns that the school system is weak and easily manipulated. If her parents have so little respect for the school's authority, why should she feel compelled to accept the rules? It's no wonder that schools are struggling to control their students' behavior.

If we accept the wisdom of allowing an appropriate balance of good and bad experiences in young people's lives, we need to challenge certain well-accepted practices. When I see increasing numbers of students visiting the counselor to get help with emotional crises, I wonder if we are really doing them a favor by training them to run to an adult every time life doesn't go exactly the way they would like it to. Are we teaching them to deal with their own emotional pain or training them to be dependent upon others to solve their problems? Yes, some children do experience significant traumas in their lives for which adult intervention and support is necessary and appropriate. But these true crises seem to be a minuscule percentage of the events that send my students running to the counselors. Instead, we are systematically training kids to expect life to be easy, painless, and endlessly happy.

The more we buffer young people from the normal occurrences that make up a balanced life, the more we delay their maturation. Your daily actions should contribute toward the gradual movement of the child toward independent, productive adulthood. Protecting children from the realities of unhappiness, struggle, frustration, failure and unpleasantness with which they will eventually have to cope as adults will leave them woefully unprepared for adulthood.

Freedom versus Discipline

Creating balance in a child's life begins in the first year of life. The human newborn is dependent on adult caretakers for survival. His earliest feelings of trust in the world around him are developed when adults consistently respond to his needs. When he is hungry, he is fed; when he is wet, he is changed; when he is startled, he is soothed. In the first months of life, the balance between the newborn's needs and the needs of others around him are dramatically tilted in favor of the child. He needs plenty of adult attention and love as he eases his way into the world. However, too many parents are enmeshed in the belief that you can't spoil a baby and fail to realize that their infant has become a toddler who is ready to learn the first important lessons about managing his own behavior; meaning it is time to start disciplining the child, using the "discipline as teaching" approach.

Learning to manage one's own emotions and impulses is the foundation of emotional intelligence, a set of skills and capabilities that have been shown to be better predictors of success in life than IQ.[36] When parents allow their infant to grow into a toddler or preschooler who has never experienced any limits on his behavior and has never been allowed to experience the consequences of his behavior, they are stunting the development of their child's emotional intelligence.

Children learn best through consistency and repetition, particularly when the lesson being learned is a tough one. They need multiple reinforcing messages to fully learn the rules of civilized living. Children, especially teenagers, don't *like* boundaries, however, they *need* boundaries. They need them to function. They need them to differentiate between right and wrong. They need them to restrain their natural tendency to push the limits. They instinctively know they need boundaries and they demonstrate it by demanding them. Pushing the boundaries is a natural and normal reaction. These challenges will vary according to the age and temperament of the child. The "terrible twos" are legendary, as are the explosive teen years, but every stage of development brings its own unique challenges. The road to independence is bumpy, the pathway to self-confidence is often littered with failures, and the door to self-acceptance can have many keys. The cyclical confrontations you have with your child are part of an intricate dance. You are in charge of your response to their steps and rhythm. You guide them through the movements, softening their falls, building their confidence, while always focusing on the end you have in mind.

One day when my oldest son was about three years old we were wrestling in the living room. It was a cold winter day and I had started a fire in the wood stove to help warm the house. For some reason my son became fixated with the stove. He walked close to the stove and reached out to feel the heat. He wasn't close enough to touch the stove so I sat back and observed his behavior. As he felt the heat radiating from the stove he smiled and looked back at me. I said, "Yes, the stove is hot." My son smiled again and slowly nudged closer to the stove. Without moving from my spot I said, "If you touch the stove it will hurt your hand." My son looked back at me with a strange, almost arrogant look and reached for the stove. I repeated, "If you touch the stove it will burn your hand." Understand that I knew the stove was not that hot because I had just started the fire a few minutes earlier, but it definitely was hot enough to hurt the tender skin of a three-year-old. With one last look of defiance my son smirked and touched the stove. He pressed his hand against the heated cast iron for just a second and then his facial expression quickly changed to one of pain. He began to cry and I picked him up and silently took him to the kitchen where we soothed his hand with cold water from the faucet. Within minutes he had stopped crying as the water soothed the pain. He looked at me and I at him without a word spoken. We returned to the living room carpet and resumed our roughhousing.

I have shared this story with other parents and with my students and people often express shock that I would allow something like this to happen. Some have asked how I could be so mean and uncaring as to let my child burn himself on the stove. Others have accused me of irresponsible and abusive behavior. But if you look closely at this maximum opportunity moment you can see how my actions were designed to use a real situation to teach my son an important lesson that, on balance, dwarfs the pain of a small burn. My son was testing me. He was exploring his boundaries. Certainly I could have jumped up and saved him from the peril of the hot stove. But what would he have learned? He would have learned that Dad would always save him from harm, a lesson that I didn't want him to learn, because my vision for him included his becoming a mature, independent adult who could protect himself from harm. Instead, my son learned that I would always tell him the truth. He could then choose his actions, but he would have to pay the consequences. He also learned that the consequences were the lesson; it wasn't compounded by criticism, judgment or lecture. For those of you who are saying, "But he's too young to learn those lessons," think again. Within months of birth, infants train their parents to meet their needs through the type and duration of their crying. They quickly learn what gets results and they repeat those behaviors. Every day I witness toddlers who have learned to manipulate their parents into buying a new toy or getting a treat at the store. Elementary kids can actually explain to you how they manipulate their parents. By the time they hit puberty, they have honed their techniques to such perfection that parents often don't even realize what's hit them. If a three-year-old isn't old enough to be learning the relationship between the choices he makes and the consequences that follow, when do you think he is old enough? Six? Twelve? Twenty? Unfortunately, I see far too many seventeen and eighteen-year-olds in my classroom who haven't learned that valuable lesson yet.

Although it was indeed painful, my son learned a valuable lesson that day that has lasted far longer than the small blister he suffered. He learned to trust me to tell him the truth. He learned that listening to that truth can save him from pain. Over the last twenty years I have told him the truth many times in hopes that he would make the right choice to spare himself pain. I have been amazed at how often he has listened. I chose to balance a moment's discomfort for my son with the opportunity to teach him these valuable lessons.

Support versus Struggle

Another important balance is between the support we provide to young people and letting them struggle on their own. Parents who have a hard time seeing their child frustrated or having difficulty often err on the side of rushing in to give support rather than letting the child struggle through the difficulty and feel the resulting pride that comes with accomplishment. The parent of a preschooler who appears to be getting frustrated trying to put on her own coat swoops in and does it for her. Seeing his teenage son struggling with his chemistry homework, Dad comes to the rescue and helps him. Persistence is an important characteristic for successful adulthood. Some children appear to be born with a more persistent temperament than others. These children protect themselves from overly helpful parents, whether it's the toddler's "me do it" or the teenager's, "I'm NOT a child, you know." Others need to be taught, encouraged and allowed to persist through frustration, struggle or failure. The important balance here is knowing when allowing a child to struggle on her own is becoming counterproductive, giving just enough support to get her back on track, then stepping away and letting her continue on her own.

My younger son has always been a good, creative writer but a slow keyboarder. He also thinks best by talking things through, either to himself or with someone else. Thinking and typing at the same time are very frustrating and distracting for him. So, early on, he and my wife worked out a solution that has proved effective over the years. As he brainstormed his ideas, she typed them for him. Once all of his ideas were down in black and white, he took over and moved things around, made changes, and edited and proofread. This way he gradually improved his keyboarding skills, but not at the expense of freely developing his ideas. By his final years of high school, he rarely asked for her help.

Seriousness versus Frivolity

For many of today's parents, raising children has become a serious, winner-takes-all competition. The "best" kid gets into the "best" schools on the way to the "best" future. Some parents view this competition as such a do or die prospect that they approach it with far too much seriousness. Of course, raising children is serious business; you hold a child's future in your hands. But that seriousness must be balanced with fun and occasional silliness. Sometimes you need to take a break from your serious parent role and join your child in being childish. Home should be where everyone can let down their hair and get goofy.

Over the years, I have actively searched out ways to add the fun factor to our family. When my sons were toddlers, just going along with whatever they were playing was often enough. I'd lie on the floor and they would run and pig pile on me. We would often make up stupid games, silly songs, or stories.

When my sons were about eleven and nine, we were camping with two other families on a lake in the Cascade Mountains. One sunny, hot afternoon we decided to swim across the lake to a spit covered with interesting looking logs. We gathered up the kids, life jackets, and air mattresses and started making our way across. When we got to the other side and tried to stand up in the shallow water, we realized that the ground was extremely muddy. The kids all squealed and didn't want to put their feet in the mud, but having just spent twenty minutes making our way across, I didn't want to have to turn around and swim right back. So, I stood up in the mud, made a big deal about how yucky it was, then reached down and started grabbing handfuls of mud and slathering it all over my body. The kids were, of course, grossed out, but it wasn't long before my older son joined me, anxious to participate in such an unusual activity. Soon, all the kids were rolling in the mud, laughing and having a great time.

I also try to maintain this balance in my classroom. Although many of my colleagues consider me a serious and intense teacher, my students see my silly side on a regular basis. One day recently as I was standing at the board explaining a new concept to my Math classes, I noticed that several rows of students were looking intently out the window, so I turned to them and said, "What?" When no one responded, I walked over to the window, expecting to see some sort of unusual or interesting event. After scanning the area to try to determine what could possibly be so attention grabbing, I came to the conclusion that the big attraction was a line of students coming out of the classroom across the courtyard (on their way to the library or computer center I assume). That's right. It was just a bunch of kids coming out of a classroom. Now, of course, I could have punished them for not paying attention. I could have lectured them on the need to focus on my lessons. But instead, I walked over and opened up the door and yelled, "I can't believe that kids walking out of a room are more engaging than my lesson. Am I that boring?" Then I turned to the teacher across the courtyard and yelled, "My kids were so bored with me that half my class was mesmerized by your kids exiting the room." I turned back to my laughing students and said, "Let's hope somebody doesn't walk by with a bagel in their hand. You'll go wild."

To liven things up in my Junior High classroom, about once a quarter, while my students were busy working on an assignment, I'd walk down to do an office errand and stop off at the central intercom, deciding as I was walking which student needed a little jolt that day. At that time our intercom system allowed the main office to buzz into a specific classroom and broadcast a message. So, I'd pick up the microphone, beep into my classroom and say, "Johnny Wilson, I told you to stop talking and get your assignment done." The students thought this was hysterical, often saying that the offending student had actually been caught "committing the crime" by this disembodied voice on the intercom. Talk about convincing students that teachers have eyes in the back of their heads.

What works for me may not work for you; each teacher must find a way to add frivolity into the classroom. Most of the good teachers I know have subject-specific jokes: math jokes, grammar jokes, or science jokes. I'm known for telling silly math jokes. In a recent lesson on imaginary numbers in my Math class, when an equation included "$9i$," I burst into "Nine eyes have seen the glory of the coming of the Lord." It needn't be a big deal; sometimes it's the little things that really serve to break the ice during otherwise serious moments. At the end of the week I often have "Disco Friday" for the last five minutes of class, during which I play old disco tunes and have students try to Name that Tune. At least once a year I use a card trick to convince students that I can actually read their minds. All of these simple methods help provide a needed counter-balance to the intensity and seriousness I want students to bring to their classroom work.

Closely linked to the need to provide equal amounts of seriousness and frivolity is the need for maintaining a balance between structure and spontaneity. As I've said throughout this book, children thrive in environments that are consistent and predictable. Structure helps children make sense of the world around them and gives them a sense of control. However, too much structure and predictability can make life pretty boring. The trick is to find ways to add spontaneity without disrupting the important routines that kids need to feel secure. This can be as simple as having breakfast foods for dinner one day (or dinner foods for breakfast). During Christmas my kids loved to spend one night sleeping in sleeping bags under the Christmas tree. When my sons were younger and my wife needed a break from the kids on the weekends, I'd often announce that we were going on an adventure. I wouldn't tell them where we were going or what we were going to do; the suspense was part of the fun. Often we took a couple of their buddies with us. We'd go to the local park and follow a stream through the woods; check out a new exhibit at the Science Center; play capture the flag at the neighborhood elementary school. The activities were almost always free or low cost and we had a great time.

With a little creativity, even challenging circumstances can become fodder for family fun. One winter our basement flooded and the entire family room needed to be dried out and re-carpeted. One morning as I was surveying the newly carpeted room, dreading the next step of moving all the furniture back in before my son's upcoming birthday party, I realized that this wide-open space was begging for some spontaneous fun. So, rather than replacing the furniture, we left the room empty and invented "balloon volleyball," outlining the court with masking tape and developing some simple rules of play. The birthday party guests had a great time.

During the summer, our backyard would often be filled with my sons and their friends engaged in one of their favorite activities— water fights. They would usually start out with water balloons or squirt guns, but when I joined the battle as their chief opponent, I often upped the stakes by filling a bucket with water and chasing them down. They usually retaliated by going directly for the hose.

One effortless activity that I used to introduce the idea of being away from home was putting up a tent in the backyard. It's a great interim step to going camping or preparing the kids for sleeping over night away from home. The boys and I would head for the tent as soon as it got dark. We'd tell scary stories, play cards, or wrestle on the sleeping bags. As they got older, they'd invite friends over to join them in this urban campground and I was usually kicked out of the tent at some point. However, I continued my role of adding a little fun and excitement to the event by scaring them in some way; throwing pinecones at the side of the tent, making scary noises outside, etc.

Praise versus Honest Feedback

Parents and educators who have the most influence over young people are those who tell children the truth; those who balance honest, earned praise with equally honest corrective feedback. I'm not sure when it happened, but somewhere along the line, giving young people honest feedback became a wicked thing to do, whether it's pointing out incorrect knowledge (two plus two does *not* equal seven) or identifying inappropriate or unacceptable behavior (stop hitting your brother). A friend of mine who coaches high school boys vented to me one afternoon about his team. He had a group of talented athletes but was having trouble getting them to perform to their potential. As he described the problems he was having with these young men, he finally blurted out, "Why do I have to spend so much time worrying about their feelings?" I chuckled and he continued, "I can't even give them an instruction, like 'stand over here during this play' without them pouting or getting huffy." I've watched this coach for years and understand his frustration. He's not yelling at the kids. He's not humiliating them. He's just providing honest feedback to help them learn to be better players. Yet many of these young men have spent their whole lives being told that everything they do is perfect. It should be no surprise that, after sixteen or seventeen years of this type of treatment, they wouldn't take too kindly to being told differently.

I've watched as teachers, bowing to the gods of self-esteem, fall all over themselves trying to avoid telling a student that the answer he gave is incorrect. They've been convinced that, to protect the child's fragile ego, they need to refrain from correcting him. So, they wait for the appropriate behavior to magically appear and then praise the child. How are kids supposed to learn if they only get feedback when they're doing something correctly?

When children's behavior and performance isn't judged honestly, when feedback isn't truthful, children stop listening. A child will only believe positive feedback if she has experienced the honesty of negative feedback. As difficult as it can be to tell kids the truth, it is critical that parents and teachers have the guts to do it. As unpleasant as it may be, this lays the groundwork for better communication and more powerful influence as a parent or teacher. Without exception, the best relationships I have had with students often began with some degree of confrontation. It is almost as if the student is challenging me, testing my integrity. Will I do the typical teacher thing and either spew a list of meaningless accolades or ignore inappropriate behavior? Or will I have the backbone to tell the truth with firmness and fairness?

If you want kids to trust you when you praise them, they have to trust you to go to the opposite end of the spectrum with them as well. Would you trust someone who only tells you the good stuff? Don't you appreciate having someone (spouse, parent, friend) who you know will tell you the truth no matter how uncomfortable it may be to hear? Isn't this the person you trust the most? Children need and deserve such adults in their lives. Unfortunately, most adults find it very difficult to give children negative, or honest, feedback. It may help to think of this approach as another way of teaching your child.

Honesty can go a long way with kids. There have been countless cases, both as a parent and as a teacher, where I have crossed over into this unnerving ground, and in every situation, honesty was the best move. However, there are some important ground rules to keep in mind when using this approach. Kids will only pay attention to honest feedback when they respect the person providing it and trust that person's wisdom. You must be clear on the outcome you hope to achieve. You must adjust to the child's age and maturity. The honest approach will vary in style if you are dealing with a six-year-old or a teenager. If you are speaking to your own child, you are doing it because you love her. If you are speaking to a student you are approaching him because you care about him. It is important for the child to perceive that your honesty is a form of caring, so a calm voice and relaxed demeanor are mandatory. This shouldn't be a lecture; it should contain only the one or two key messages you want to convey. You need to focus on the crucial point and verbalize it clearly and concisely. You shouldn't apologize or try to soften the feedback because that compromises the seriousness of your message. It is highly likely that the child will resist your feedback at first. That's normal. Don't fight it. Allow the resistance to occur and then gently focus on your message. Do not linger or extend the conversation because you think the message was not heard. If you have followed the guidelines above and it is an important subject, it will be heard. After you follow through with this strategy, you will likely feel bad. But it will diminish as you see that your approach pays off in changed and improved behavior.

Several years ago I had a high school student in class who had very special needs. I had taught this student in Junior High and knew he was an intelligent kid with an active interest in technology and science fiction. However, his hyperactive, out of control behavior and immaturity had made him well known among the faculty. When he entered my class as a junior, it was apparent that very little had changed with this student's behavior. Although as an older adolescent, he had probably physically outgrown his hyperactivity, by that time his inappropriate behavior had been so consistently tolerated, excused and inadvertently reinforced, that it had actually gotten much worse. In fact, he was in a class with younger students because he had not progressed as fast as others his age. This was a situation he thoroughly enjoyed because he could intimidate many of his younger peers.

Once I saw his typical behavior pattern emerging, I pulled out the standard discipline techniques. As I expected, detention and being sent to the office didn't work at all. He was intimately familiar with these strategies and they simply weren't sufficient to inspire change. So, I decided to take another tack. Time was running out for this young man. He was no longer a child whose behavior could be dismissed as immature. He would soon be out in the real world with people who were far less tolerant and forgiving than those he had encountered in the school system. I decided that the kindest thing I could do for this young man was to be painfully honest with him. So after one particularly outrageous episode, I took him outside and spoke to him in a very calm and straightforward voice. He was usually so effective at pushing teachers' buttons, that the response he typically got was anger and frustration. Because my calm, controlled response was so unexpected, I got his attention immediately. I proceeded to outline for him the reasons why kids disliked him, clearly describing the behaviors that provoked these negative responses. Several times he slipped into his usual childish avoidance behavior, but I was able to refocus his attention and complete my frank descriptions. I told him very honestly how other kids viewed him and I speculated on why I believed he chose to act the way he did. As the discussion progressed I could see he really was listening to my words. I told him that sometimes his behavior was perceived by the other kids as being goofy. By the end of our discussion, we had come to an understanding about the kinds of behaviors that were expected and acceptable in my class and he even requested my suggestions on what to do to get the kids to like him. For the remainder of the semester the two of us worked on his social skills and he did his best to follow the expectations I had for him. When he occasionally slipped up, I would signal him that he was doing one of those "goofy things." Once reminded, he usually got himself back in control. When he left my class he didn't wear the label of "goofball" as proudly as he had before. By the time he left high school, he was on the road to maturity.

The most drastic form of honest feedback is rejection. When other discipline techniques have failed to change a child's inappropriate behavior, rejection might be the best choice. This tactic should be used sparingly and with great caution. It also must be something you really believe will work. Although it flies in the face of most conventional expert wisdom, I have seen it work miracles with very difficult students. It's important to understand that this technique shouldn't be done in anger. Your demeanor should be calm and matter of fact. The child should understand that the use of this method is the result of her failure to respond to other approaches.

Experience is a great advantage in this area. Having the opportunity to try an unconventional strategy and see it work over and over again has given me the confidence to use it when necessary. I know specifically when this method should be used, with whom it should be used, how intensely it should be employed, and why it is successful. The method should be used in two types of venues. First, if you are dealing with a kid who is fully invested in making life miserable for you and everyone else with whom they come in contact, this strategy can be very effective. The second situation is when you and this child just seem to be like oil and water, and, despite your best efforts, the two of you drive each other nuts. Let's be honest, there are some kids (albeit few) that you just can't stand. In order to facilitate learning for all the students in your classroom, you and this student come to an agreement to avoid each other as much as possible. You get along by ignoring each other. Sometimes things can't be worked out and you just have to face that fact, which is okay. You are human and so is the student. But it isn't necessary for the entire classroom to bear the brunt of one student's interpersonal issues. Just stay away from each other. Although this may sound callous or difficult, I have used this method successfully many times and have found that, once you take away the potential for conflict (by removing yourself from contact with the student) the student's behavior begins to change. Occasionally students show no interest in reconciliation. That's okay, because even though my relationship with that student didn't turn out ideally, the chronic interruption and conflict he or she inflicted on the rest of the students was eliminated.

I want to emphasize that this method is a last resort. The majority of students will respond to less drastic approaches. However, when all else has failed, rejection can be a powerful lever for changing a student's behavior patterns. Without such drastic intervention, most of these students will continue to behave in ways that compromise their academic and social success. Although it takes guts for a teacher to follow through with this unorthodox approach, chicken teachers rarely make a difference in the lives of these students.

Scott was a very angry young man, an arrogant and defiant ninth grader in my Junior High Health class. He had been in trouble many times and was well known by the administrators. As the weeks passed, Scott challenged every aspect of my class and the school environment. Before too long, I reached a point where I truly disliked this kid. Finally after yet another defiant action in class, I knew it was time for the rejection technique. I took him outside of the room and calmly informed him that I did not like him and that I was sure that he did not like me. I informed him that we did not need to speak to each other or communicate in anyway. Scott was quite perplexed. He had never had anyone be so blunt with him, especially a teacher. Scott used his final wild card and told his parents what I had said. Of course the parents called and I explained that their son and I had conflicts that were too deep to fix in the short time left in the school year. Before the parents could make the request, I suggested that Scott be placed in another class . The fact that a teacher suggested rescheduling first neutralized the parents, depriving them of a valuable trump card. Scott stayed in my class. He and I didn't speak or communicate in any way for weeks. Then one day Scott made a very slight gesture of cooperation. I acknowledged it and that was the beginning of the rebuilding stage. By the end of the school year, Scott and I were not good buddies by any stretch of the imagination, but what we did have was an unwritten agreement to be civilized. The agreement wasn't something we sat down and talked about, but an agreement reached day by day through the interactions of two people just trying to get along. In the meantime the class ran smoothly and Scott was no longer a problem.

Why does rejection work for some kids when other methods fail? Kids most commonly act out for two reasons: they are seeking power or they want attention. If the student is involved in a power struggle with you, rejection immediately neutralizes that power. If you refuse to become engaged, the power struggle disappears. If the student's goal is to get attention, rejection effectively pulls the rug out from under him. When you withhold your attention, he doesn't get what he is seeking. This is the reason why, for most kids, the end result of this approach is a renewed desire to reestablish a relationship with you. But this time they know they have to use appropriate behavior to get your attention.

Parent versus Friend

Although I've titled this section "parent versus friend," I don't really believe that the two are mutually exclusive. It's many parents' interpretation of what it means to be their child's friend that causes problems. In my opinion, a true friend is someone who cares about your well-being, whose company you enjoy, who stands by you regardless of the circumstances, who tells you the truth, and who encourages you to become the best person you can be. A good parent does all of these things for her child. So, if that's your definition of friendship with your child, you're in good shape. But the relationship between a child and a parent isn't the same as a relationship between two adults. You probably don't have to spend a lot of time making your adult friends do things they don't want to do or stopping them from doing something they want to do but you don't want them to do. As a parent, a good deal of your time may be spent in this less than pleasant task. You probably don't spend a lot of time teaching your adult friends things they don't care to learn; yet your children need you to teach them about manners, hygiene, self-control, responsibility, decision-making, and the myriad other things parents teach their children. Your adult friends can look after themselves; your children can't.

As the adult, you have responsibilities, experience, and knowledge that your child doesn't have. That means your relationship with your child shouldn't be a democracy, with you and your child holding equal power. Sometimes you need to make unilateral decisions, often ones that your child won't like. The payoff to responsible parenting is that, once you get through the struggles of childhood and adolescents, your adult children can, indeed, be your friends in every sense of the word. However, parents who refuse to take on the tougher, less pleasant responsibilities of parenting run the risk of producing adults who are so immature, dysfunctional, self-centered, or just plain unlikable, that their parents can hardly wait for them to get out of the house.

I see many teachers also struggling with the balance between being their students' teacher and their friend. As with parents, the two are not mutually exclusive. Yet, just as the relationship between a parent and a child cannot be the same as the relationship between two adult friends, a teacher's relationship with a student must err on the side of fulfilling the responsibilities the teacher has to that child. Like parents, teachers often have to make students do things they don't want to do or stop them from doing things they want to do. Classrooms shouldn't be democracies. Teachers have wisdom, knowledge and experience that students don't have. This is not to say that teachers should not be caring and compassionate toward their students. It simply means that caring and compassion must be balanced with the limits, expectations, and guidance students need to grow up to be responsible, productive, educated adults.

In my years of teaching I have found many ways to show caring and compassion for my students, without compromising my role as a teacher. I pay close attention to clues to my students' outside interests so that I can connect with them through something they care about. I might see the name or picture of a favorite band on a T-shirt or notebook cover and I go home and ask my sons the name of a song by that band, so I can talk about it with the student. I find out which guys are into their cars and then talk to them about car stuff. When a student is involved in a school activity, whether sports, drama, music, art, or other activities, I ask them how it went the day after their performance. Students often ask me to attend these performances and I try to oblige as often as I can.

I've found that the smallest gestures often reap the greatest rewards. I had noticed that one of my students, who is normally attentive and awake, had begun showing signs of distress and was resting his head on his desk more than usual. One day at the end of class I approached his desk and put a single Rollo candy on his desk and quietly said, "It looks like you need this more than I do today." I walked away, the bell rang and he picked up his backpack and left class. The next day as students were working on their math problems, this young man approached my desk and asked "Why did you give me that candy yesterday?" I told him that he didn't look like his normal self and I thought he could use a little something. In the discussion that followed, he revealed information that lead to his being tested for learning disabilities.

Excellence versus Strengths and Weaknesses

This is one area where the balance seems to be precariously tipped one way or the other. In the "Not Like Mike" chapter, I discussed the dangers of the unrealistic perceptions that too many parents have of their child's capabilities. We've all heard stories about stage mothers in the entertainment world. Unfortunately, it seems that the stage mother phenomenon has expanded to much of the rest of the parent population, with every parent believing their child is the next star of whatever endeavor he attempts. Parents need to be realistic in assessing their child's strengths, as well as their weaknesses. That way they can help their child build on strengths and minimize their weaknesses. It's important to remember that no child can be good at everything and pushing a child to do so is counterproductive. When a child is expected to be equally outstanding at everything she does, the consequence is often that she is so busy trying to be exceptional at everything that she isn't able to give her time and energy to those things at which she truly does excel. Another potentially devastating effect of ignoring this important balance is that it often sets young people up for a painful fall when they are inevitably confronted with reality.

Being honest about a child's abilities also helps parents identify ways to build on strengths to help address weaknesses. For my oldest son, one of his key strengths became apparent within the first year of his life. This child lived to move. He crawled at five months, walked at eight months and was running, jumping and kicking a ball before his first birthday. His first word wasn't Mommy or Daddy, but "boogie," which was his term for ball. He didn't care what he played as long as he could be moving, and it usually involved some type of ball. When he was about eighteen months old, he would anxiously await my return from work each day, ready for a marathon game of whatever ball/movement-related activity was the current favorite. Usually exhausted from a full day of teaching and coaching I was forced to design an activity that would satisfy my son and not demand too much of my dwindling energy. After some trial and error, we finally settled on one that pleased both of us. I sat on the floor of my bedroom across from a large wall area and my son positioned himself between the wall and me. I would toss the ball against the wall and my son would try to intercept the ball before it bounced back to me. We often played this game for an hour or more before dinner. My son would dive for the ball, block it with his body, or jump up to knock it out of its pathway. We laughed at his interceptions and laughed louder at his acrobatic misses. He truly enjoyed the physicality of the game and was learning coordination and concentration at the same time. This went on for a couple of years.

It quickly became clear that one of this child's gifts was his athletic ability and we consciously created situations and environments that took advantage of that strength. His self-confidence has been a direct result of the success he has experienced in team sports and other physical competitions. He was fortunate to attend an elementary school that had a nationally recognized circus arts program, where he learned to juggle and unicycle and was able to successfully participate in all-city competitions. His kinesthetic abilities earned him recognition, admiration and respect from his classmates. However, as much as this kinesthetic talent was a gift in athletic endeavors, it proved to be a challenge when it came to academic achievement. Reading was extremely difficult because he had to be still and rely only on his eyes and his brain. Once when he was reading to my wife and had been dutifully trying to sit still as he struggled to make it through a difficult passage, he actually said, "Mommy, this hurts." I can remember listening to him read before bed every night, his eyes and head motionless concentrating on the book while the rest of his body moved constantly, twisting and contorting, hanging over the side of bed, or walking around. He just had to move. When the situation required that he actually sit still while reading, he would still find some way to move, often tapping his big toe inside his shoe or running his tongue around inside his mouth.

Although we knew it was important for him to eventually learn to sit still and focus (we realized that his teachers weren't going to let him walk around the room all day), at home we took advantage of his kinesthetic abilities as a way to help him learn. We designed activities that allowed him to learn while moving. When he was first learning to read, we would print the names of common objects (door, refrigerator, wall, light, etc.) on note cards and tape them on their corresponding objects. We'd then tell him to go find something that starts with a "D" and he'd race around looking for a word that started with "D." When he found it, he'd spell the word out loud, say the word, and then we'd call out another word to find. As he got older and was able to read simple sentences, we transformed reading practice into a treasure hunt. When he walked in the door after school, he would find a note card with instructions that included something like, "Walk backwards into the kitchen, hop twice on your right foot, then open the refrigerator and you will find your next clue." He would have to find each clue, read and follow the instructions, which ended with some small treat.

Realizing that paper and pencil practice for his weekly timed arithmetic fact tests wasn't going to work for this child, we devised a movement game to help him prepare. For example, when he was learning his addition facts, we put the answers for each addition problem on a piece of paper and spread the papers across the family room floor. Then we'd call out, "4 + 4" and he would run and stand on the piece of paper that said "8." He would then say, "4+4 = 8" and we'd move on to the next problem. We used this simple game for learning spelling words, matching countries with their capitols, or any other memorization type of activity. We found that this was a great way for him to learn new information in a way that really stuck. Over time, he learned to use this strength himself when learning new material. He often practiced facts he had to memorize as he was juggling or bouncing a basketball.

It's important to note that we never expected his teachers to make this level of accommodation for him in the classroom. With twenty five to thirty other students in the classroom, that would have been completely unrealistic. He knew that at school he was expected to follow the rules that all the other students followed, which he was able to do, knowing that at home he would have the opportunity to reinforce what he was learning in the classroom in ways that worked better for him. Rather than forcing the school to completely adapt to his individual needs or forcing him to completely adapt to the school's structure, this balance of individualized support at home versus learning to live within the structure of the school was sufficient to allow him to gradually develop his own ways of operating in environments that are less than a perfect fit for him.

This child had clear strengths that we promoted and helped him use to his advantage. In his physical endeavors, there was no need for us to push him to excel. His motivation always came from within. In school, he worked hard and was able to get through school with a respectable academic record. However, it would have been counterproductive to push him to take Advanced Placement classes and to get A's in all of those classes.

Small Stuff versus Big Stuff

This is probably one of the most important areas in which parents need to strive for balance. The key to maintaining this balance is keeping your eye on the prize—your Big Five. If a decision, conflict, or problem doesn't fit into your Big Five, then it probably isn't worth the time and effort you will expend trying to address it. Paying attention to that unimportant situation will divert your attention from the big stuff.

I realize that this can be difficult when you're enmeshed in the every day details of life with children. Particularly for new parents, every decision seems to take on monumental importance. But, if you let your Big Five guide your decisions, you can keep yourself focused on those things that are most important for your family.

One way to stay focused on the "big stuff" is to continually ask yourself, "Will this matter in ten years? What's the worst that could possibly happen?" The classic example of this is the parent who is completely stressed out over her toddler's difficulty with toilet training. It really is true that no child goes to kindergarten still wearing diapers. So, is freaking out about your child's accident really worth the energy? If your teenager wants to dye her hair purple, you need to ask yourself, "Is it likely that she will have purple hair when she's thirty-five?" Probably not. And what if she does adopt purple hair forever? What's the worst that could happen as a result of purple hair? Is it worth the battle with her right now?

Deciding early on to choose your battles, and choose them wisely, will make parenting infinitely easier and you will ultimately be more effective. If you approach every situation with your child as a battle, your relationship will soon become characterized by conflict. Also, when everything is a battle, it's difficult for your child to determine what is really important to you. On the other hand, some parents choose to avoid *all* battles, which is just as damaging. When you focus on the important battles, guided by your Big Five, you are able to bring to that issue the time, energy and sense of importance it deserves.

CHAPTER 11: THE ANSWERS

This book began by challenging you to take a good hard look in the mirror and ask yourself, "Am I a chicken parent or a chicken teacher?" Congratulations for having the courage to take that challenge. Parenting and teaching are tough jobs. However, if you use the Big Five/Five Steps to guide the children in your care toward positive adulthood, you will find the job more manageable and you will be more successful in this important endeavor.

The Big Five/Five Steps is about knowing where you want to go and having a plan to get there. It's about defining your goals and taking conscious steps to achieve those goals, rather than reacting to situations as they come up, with little forethought and direction. You have the potential to be a powerful influence on the future of a child. One of the things I hope you have realized from reading this book is that the experts don't have the answers you need to be an effective parent or teacher. *You* are the best expert for your family or classroom. *You* know your child or students better than some PhD sitting in an ivory tower thousands of miles away. Rather than jumping on whatever teaching or parenting "expert" bandwagon that comes along, what works in your situation is best guided by the long-term goals you have for the children in your care, your own experience with what works, and your ability to think logically and strategically about how to best move children step-by-step toward the Big Five characteristics you want them to embody as adults. Does that mean that you should ignore what the experts say? Does it mean you shouldn't try to learn new information and strategies to make you a better parent or teacher? No. What it means is that your Big Five and the plan you develop for getting children to those priorities comes from you. This foundation is the structure for everything you do. If new information or strategies seem appropriate or valuable within that structure, by all means incorporate those things into your approach. But, before you do so, subject it to the Big Five/Five Step test: 1) Does this contribute to my Big Five? 2) What will my child/ students learn from this? 3) Will this help me take charge and fulfill my responsibilities as a teacher or parent? 4) Does this contribute to a balanced approach? 5) Will it work?

The Big Five

Your Big Five are the foundation of your parenting or teaching. However, they aren't just lofty goals. They represent the priority areas on which you should focus your time, energy and attention. Your Big Five are only valuable if you use them to guide your daily decision-making with your children. If you haven't yet determined your own Big Five, take the time to ensure that this important foundation is carefully considered and reflects your best thinking. If you have, be sure your children or students understand your Big Five, know exactly what they mean to you and how they influence the behavior you want from them. Use your Big Five to shape your family or classroom expectations and consequences. For example, if one of your family's Big Five is to "be responsible for your own actions," then you may have an expectation that your nine-year-old has daily chores that must be accomplished before he watches television. If those chores aren't done, the logical consequence is no television. The consequence serves as a reminder to the child to be more responsible. If one of your Big Five is honesty, then you would expect your teenager to tell you the truth about how she is doing in school and would impose a consequence when she hid her progress report to keep you from finding out about her failing grade. If one of your classroom Big Five is that students "treat others with respect," then you would impose appropriate consequences if you hear one student calling another a derogatory name.

One of the best ways to help children understand your Big Five is to make sure you are a powerful and consistent role model of these characteristics. The old saying, "Do as I say, not as I do" doesn't work well with children. The more our behavior resembles the behavior we want from children, the easier it will be for them to internalize those characteristics. If you want your children to be responsible for their own actions, let them see you behaving in responsible ways. If you want children to make good decisions about their health, they need to see you making good choices about your own health. You can help young children understand how your behavior embodies a desired characteristic by labeling your actions for them. "I held the door open for that older woman because that's a respectful thing to do," or "I need to drop the cookies off at preschool even if we're not going to be there today because that's being responsible."

Does that mean you need to be a perfect role model? No. As I've said before, children are resilient and they know you're human. However, you do need to make sure that, on balance, your behavior is consistent with what you say to kids about your most important priorities.

Once you've established your Big Five, when you find yourself wondering what to do, you can ask yourself a simple question, "How does this situation impact my Big Five?" If your response is "not at all," then instead of expending your finite time and energy on sweating the small stuff, you can save it for the big stuff.

Although parenting or teaching can seem like a never-ending response to crises or difficult situations, being clear on your Big Five provides a laser-sharp focus to your daily life with children. Feeling as though you are always putting out fires (especially when the same fire never really goes out, but seems to reignite on a regular basis), is extremely stressful. Rather than waiting for situations to arise and then reacting in the heat of the moment, the up-front work you do to clarify your highest priorities allows you to respond more thoughtfully, deliberately and consistently to difficult situations. It also gives children a predictable framework for understanding how you will respond to their behavior, which is a valuable source of stability for young people. As they begin to internalize the Big Five, they become better and better at anticipating the consequences of their behavior: "If I lie to my parents about being at my girlfriend's house last night, that's dishonest, and since honesty is a big deal for them, I know they will give me a consequence that will make me sorry I made that choice." When life is predictable, kids make better choices.

Identify the Lesson

As a parent you are your child's first and best teacher. Everything you do teaches a lesson, whether you intend for it to or not; it's up to you to decide what your child will learn. The sum total of your child's experiences during these formative years will largely determine the kind of adult he becomes. As the person who loves and cares about your child the most, you need to step up to the plate and parent with that long-term goal in mind. Making the tough decisions, taking the hard stands, hanging in there even when things are unpleasant, that's your job as a responsible parent. Will your child always be happy? No. Will your child thank you for playing that unpopular role? Certainly not in the foreseeable future, perhaps later on when she's a parent herself. Will your child be a better adult as a result of it? Absolutely.

The question, "What will my child learn from this?" should be a constant refrain in your parenting approach. When you are tempted to give in to your child's whining, tantrums, or arguing, ask yourself, "What would my child learn if I gave in?" Remember that uncomfortable, frustrating, even painful situations can be powerful learning experiences. Don't be afraid to take advantage of these maximum opportunity moments to teach your child valuable lessons. I hope I have convinced you that, even if you *could* protect your child from ever feeling sad, frustrated, or angry, it would be an unloving, irresponsible thing to do. If you have a tendency to jump in and protect your child rather than letting her face the natural consequences of her behavior, restrain yourself by re-framing the situation to highlight the positive lessons she will learn through the experience.

If you haven't taken the time to reflect on the experiences, both good and bad, that made you the person you are today, do that important work. It's also helpful to think about the people who were instrumental in your success. For most of us, those people include individuals who pushed us to be the best we can be. Don't you want to be that person for your child? Don't cheat your child by denying him the valuable experiences he will need to survive and thrive in the adult world just because you want to protect him from feeling bad.

If you are a teacher, it's not a big leap to say that every interaction you have with a child is a lesson. I'm sure you spend plenty of time thinking about what academic lessons you want your students to learn from certain activities. But do you spend equal time considering the other lessons your students are learning in your class? Are they learning responsibility? Are they learning civility? Are they learning compassion? Are they learning self-reliance? Is your behavior as a role model consistent with your Big Five? Just as with parents, your students are constantly watching you. When they are allowed to get away with inappropriate behavior at school, the lesson they take away with them is that you condone their actions, regardless of your actual feelings about the behavior. When students are allowed to interrupt other students or the teacher, they are learning that it's okay to treat other people in an uncivilized manner. When students are allowed second, third, fourth chances to turn in assignments, take tests, etc., they are learning that they needn't be responsible for their own behavior. Conversely, when students see you handle conflict in a calm and mature way, they learn that problems can be resolved without losing control. When they see you living your life in a balanced and stable way, you are providing a role model for healthy adulthood.

Remember that self-esteem is not something you can *give* children. You can't improve children's self-esteem by telling them they're wonderful and special; by denying them the opportunity to learn from failure as well as success; by false, undeserved praise; or by coddling them and protecting them from the realities of the world around them. All of these things teach unintended lessons that actually undermine self-worth and self-confidence. You *can* help children build self-worth and self-confidence by providing plenty of opportunities for them to *be* worthwhile; to be active, contributing, valuable members of their families, schools and communities and recognizing those efforts. You can communicate high expectations for them and give them honest, useful feedback on their performance and behavior so that they can continue to improve. You can increase their resilience by allowing them to struggle through difficult situations, in turn communicating your confidence that they are strong and competent enough to survive these challenges. You can help a child feel special by helping that child identify his unique strengths and talents, then providing experiences that help him use those strengths and challenges to be successful.

Take Charge

So, you've identified your Big Five and are integrating these fundamental concepts into your everyday life with your child or your students. You have empowered an alter ego sitting on your shoulder to continually ask, "What will my child/student learn from this?" Once you've built this important foundation, you're ready to Take Charge. Taking charge means that you embrace your role as the responsible adult in children's lives. It means that you face and conquer the fears that prevent you from fulfilling that role. You realize that your job is to set and enforce guidelines that will help your child gradually learn to manage her own behavior. You understand that kids won't like those guidelines, will push against those guidelines, and may occasionally dig into an impressive bag of tricks to try to get you to back away from those guidelines, but you hold firm because you know the important lessons that will be learned. It means that you accept both the pleasant and the unpleasant parts of being the responsible adult, the hugs and kisses as well as the "You're the meanest Mom in the world; I hate you" epithets. It means that you are willing to sacrifice to ensure that your child learns the lessons she needs to become the kind of adult you want her to become. You realize that once you commit to being a parent, your children should be your highest priority and your behavior should clearly demonstrate that fact. You accept that your child needs your attention and time, quality as well as quantity, and her need for attention and time will be on her own schedule, not yours. You accept the fact that you probably can't have it all at the same time. You recognize that your child's childhood is hers, not a second chance at the childhood you always wanted.

Taking charge means you take the hard, usually unpopular stands that protect your child from too much: too much stuff; too much non-parent time; too much guilt; too much instant gratification; too much technology; too much information with too little learning; too much stress; too many choices; too much coddling; and too much media.

Balance the Approach

One of the greatest gifts adults can give children is stability. In today's uncertain, rapidly changing world, far too much in children's lives is unpredictable. In order to do the important work of growing up, children need to be able to focus their time, energy and attention on the developmental challenges they face at various points in their lives. When that energy is diverted by having to cope with chaos and uncertainty, healthy development becomes more difficult for kids. Conversely, stable, predictable home and school environments free children to develop to their fullest potential. It's important to remember that stability isn't an all or nothing condition. Aspects of children's lives will always be in flux. Families move; parents divorce or remarry; friends or loved ones die. A new baby, a child or parent's illness, changing classes or schools all can disrupt children's routines. Total stability and predictability is an unreasonable goal. However, even the smallest attempts to bring stability and routine to children's lives are productive. Even in the most chaotic home, a regular time and place to do homework or a predictable bedtime routine are powerful buffers. In a classroom, teaching students routines early in the school year sets up a classroom environment where everyone's attention can be focused on learning, not on managing behavior. As with so many other things, balance is the key. Don't stress yourself about those things over which you have no control. You may not be able to change the fact that your work hours (and thus your child's daycare hours) change each week. But you can start a routine that whenever you pick your child up from daycare, the first thing you do is to give him a hug and say, "Tell me something funny/interesting/ weird that happened today." If you are a teacher, you may not be able to control the fact that your class time is interrupted by assemblies, announcements and special events but you can establish a routine for how homework is handed in or corrected; or you can have a predictable schedule of learning activities that happen each class period.

When it comes to balancing your approach, remember that many of the myths we have about what makes a good parent or teacher are false. The best parent or teacher is the one who most fully prepares children for the realities of the world they will face as an adult. That means that effective parents and teachers have a plan for gradually building independence, self-reliance and competence. They recognize the valuable lessons taught by both pleasant and unpleasant experiences. They communicate their confidence in children by refraining from coddling or rescuing them. Effective parents and teachers understand that being loving and caring means showing affection for children, taking pleasure in being with them, and accepting children for the unique individuals they are. They also know that being a loving, caring parent or teacher means being willing to go to an uncomfortable place to ensure that children learn the lessons they need to grow up to be healthy adults. It means telling children the truth, even when the truth is painful. It means providing honest feedback on children's strengths and weaknesses so that children can reach for and achieve realistic goals. It means watching as children struggle through sadness, frustration, or pain, knowing that these experiences also teach valuable lessons. Effective parents and teachers realize that just concerning themselves with how children are *feeling* is only half the battle. Children can *feel* great while *behaving* abominably.

Finally, a balanced approach starts with a balanced adult. As a parent or teacher you are in a powerful position to model healthy adulthood for children. The more your own life exemplifies balance, the greater your ability to influence the development of a healthy balance in children's lives.

See if it's Working

Effective parenting or teaching isn't rocket science. It *does* require reflection, logic and planning. Part of the logical process is to constantly check to make sure what you're doing is working, which is dependent on reflection and planning. In order to know if something is working, you need to be clear about what you want to have happen. In addition, your response to a given situation often has both short-term and long-term consequences, both of which are important to evaluate. So, if your child refuses to put his toys away and you spank him as punishment, he may, in fact, pick up his toys, which means that spanking worked to achieve your short-term goal. However, it's unlikely that spanking him will achieve your long-term goal, making him responsible for his own behavior. A more effective solution for achieving both goals might be to tell him that, *after* he picks up his toys, *then* he can watch television (or have a snack, or go to the park, or whatever else might be an effective motivator). That way you get the toys picked up *and* your child learns that when he behaves responsibly, then he gets privileges. Remember that discipline is only truly effective if it moves your child closer to self-discipline and self-management. The goal of discipline is not to *control* children but to *teach* them how to control themselves.

To help ensure that the daily interactions with your children or students are moving them gradually toward your Big Five, take time regularly to reflect on the big picture of "is it working." For each of your Big Five characteristics, ask yourself the question, "Is my child (or are my students) closer to this characteristic than they were six months ago (or a month ago, or last year)? Is my child more responsible? Are my students more respectful? If you are not seeing the progress you would like, go back and examine the lessons that are being learned. Is your behavior teaching unintended lessons? Force yourself to be conscious of your daily interactions and focus on the lessons you do want children to learn in order to move them closer to that element of your Big Five.

According to child psychologist Penelope Leach, "Children are a part of many people's present and the whole of everybody's future."[37] As a parent or teacher, you have an incredible opportunity to positively influence the future of our nation's most precious resource. You have taken an important first step by reading this book. You may agree with some of the things I've presented, you may disagree with others. That's okay. The goal of this book is not to get you to do what I do as a parent or teacher. My goal is to get you to think carefully and logically about what *you* should do as a parent or teacher. If I have encouraged you to challenge your current thinking about our system for developing healthy adults, my goal has been met. If I have convinced you that you are the true expert for your children, you're on your way. Change begins with the awareness that change is required. You have both the capacity and the ability to make the changes needed to become a powerful adult in the lives of children.

Final Thoughts

A recent article in my local newspaper highlighted an interesting phenomenon occurring with today's parents. With over 28,000 books available to help guide them through every aspect of parenting, parents are eager consumers of this explosion of advice. The interesting twist is that, although parents are quick to *purchase* these guides, they often don't read them, or if they do, they seldom follow through on suggested changes. The article quotes Gary Krebs, director of publishing at Adams Media, "When people buy a book, they feel they are accomplishing something. They feel as though their problem's solved, even if they never read the book, but just take it home. ... This is particularly true about child-care books, because parents today are so busy they don't have time for major counseling or rethinking their entire lives, and they hope perhaps a book can solve their problems fast."[38]

In other words, parents are looking for a quick fix but are unwilling to put in the sustained time and effort required to effect genuine change. Purchasing, and even reading, parenting books gives them the *illusion* of striving to be a better parent, without having to take a hard look at their current parenting habits and change their behavior. Please don't do that with this book. You've taken the time to read it; don't be satisfied with the illusion of change.

Successful change comes more easily when tackled in small steps. Pick one small change to work on this month and concentrate on successfully reaching that goal. You may want to start with identifying your Big Five or practicing refraining from rescuing your child from consequences. Then build on that effort and identify another step for the next month. These step-by-step efforts will eventually pay off. You may notice a more cooperative home environment and a decrease in feelings of chaos or lack of control. You will start to sense the momentum changing in a more positive direction and the joy that you should be experiencing from parenting will begin to resurface. Don't wait. You only have a few more sentences to read so start right after you put this book down.

I don't need to tell you that parenting is the most important job you will ever have. You have a limited amount of time to be a powerful influence on your child. Take advantage of this window of opportunity and initiate those small changes. The time you invest will not be wasted. Indeed it will be the greatest investment you will ever make.

Remember, you are not raising a child. The work you do today will determine the kind of adult your child will become in the years ahead. I know you love your children. Your goal now is to ensure that you *like* them when they are sitting across the table from you at Thanksgiving next year and the year after that and the year after that...

End Notes

[1] National Center for Education Statistics

[2] See, for example, Darling-Hammond, L. (2000). Teacher quality and student achievement: A review of state policy evidence. *Education Policy Analysis Archives, (8)1.*

[3] Status of the American Public School Teacher, 1995-96. National Education Association.

[4] National Commission on Teaching and America's Future (2003). No Dream Denied: A pledge to America's Children. *National Commission on Teaching and America's Future:* Washington, DC.

[5] US Census Bureau

[6] Damon, William (1995). Greater Expectations: overcoming the culture of indulgence in America's homes and schools. Free Press; Maxwell Macmillan International.

[7] See, for example, Smelser, J. (1989). Self-Esteem and Social Problems in Mecca et al. (Eds.) *The Social Importance of Self-Esteem.* Berkeley: University of California Press, 15-17 or Schroeder, D. et al. (1993). Is There a Relationship Between Self-Esteem and Drug Use? *Journal of Drug Issues,* 23, 658-659.

[8] Maslow, A. & Lowery, R. (Ed.). (1998). *Toward a psychology of being* (3rd ed.). New York: Wiley & Sons.

[9] Catalano, RF, Hawkins, JD. (1996). The social development model: A theory of antisocial behavior. In JD Hawkins (Ed.). *Delinquency and crime: Current theories* (149-197). New York, NY: Cambridge University Press.

[10] Kohlberg, L. (1987). Child Psychology and Childhood Education: A cognitive-developmental view. New York: Longman.

[11] Josephson Institute (2002). *The ethics of American youth: Press release and data summary.* http://www.josephsoninstitute.org/Survey2002/survey2002-pressrelease.htm

[12] Howell, J. (Ed.) (1995). *Guide for Implementing the Comprehensive Strategy for Serious, Violent and Chronic Juvenile Offenders.* Washington, D.C.: U.S. Department of Justice, Office of Juvenile Justice and Delinquency Prevention.

[13] Hawkins JD, Catalano RF, Miller JY (1992). Risk and protective factors for alcohol and other drug problems in adolescence and early adulthood: Implications for substance abuse prevention. *Psychological Bulletin,* 112(1), 64-105.

[14] Vedantam, S. (2003, January 14). Study: More kids given drugs for mental illness. *Washington Post.*

[15] Reynolds, P., Elkin, E, Layefsky, M., Lee, G. (1999). Cancer in California school employees, 1887-1992. *American Journal of Ind. Medicine.* Aug: 36(2): 271-8.

[16] National Center for Education Statistics (2001).

[17] Males, Mike A. (1996). *The scapegoat generation: America's war on Adolescents.* Common Courage Press, ME, Monroe.

[18] Chall, J. (2000). The Academic Achievement Challenge: What really works in the classroom. New York, NY: Guilford Publications.

[19] Minear, R., Proctor, W. (1989). *Kids Who Have Too Much.* Nashville, TN: Thomas Nelson Publishers.

[20] See, for example, Casper, L. (1996). *Who's minding our preschoolers?* U.S. Bureau of the Census, Current Population Reports, 70, 53: Washington, DC. or Hayghe, H. (1997). Developments in women's labor force participation. *Monthly Labor Review,* 122(12): 22-30.

[21] Cohen, D., Farley, T., Taylor, S., Martin, D., and Schuster, M. (2002). When and where do youths have sex? The potential role of adult supervision. *Pediatrics, 110(6)*.

[22] Brazelton, T., Greenspan, S. (2000). The Irreducible Needs of Children: What Every Child Must Have to Grow, Learn, and Flourish. New York, NY: Perseus Publishing.

[23] Washington Post, November 18, 1999.

[24] See, for example, Henderson, A., Mapp, K. (2002). A New Wave of Evidence: The impact of school, family, and community connections on student achievement. Annual Synthesis 2002. Austin, TX: National Center for Family and Community Connections with Schools, Southwest Educational Development Laboratory or Hoover Institution (2000). Teacher Quality is Most Important Factor. Hoover Institution Newsletter 2000. http://www.stanford.edu/PubAffairs/Newsletter/ 00summer/teacher.html.

[25] Depression and Suicide in Children and Adolescents in *Mental Health: A Report of the Surgeon General* (1999). Retrieved June 23, 2004, from http:// www.surgeongeneral.gov/library/mentalhealth/chapter3/sec5.html.

[26] Luther, S. & D'Avanzo, K. (1999). Contextual Factors in Substance Abuse: A Study of Suburban and Inner-city Adolescents. *Development and Psychopathology*.

[27] Goleman, D. (1995). *Emotional Intelligence*. New York: Bantam Books.

[28] Morris, K. (1999, October 15). Lobbying, angling, intelligence-gathering: Parents push to get the 'right' teachers. *Seattle Times*.

[29] Los Angeles Times and The Washington Post (1999, November 18). Study: Kids' use of media a full-time job. *Seattle Times*.

[30] Reid, T. (1999). *Confucius Lives Next Door*. New York, NY: Random House.

[31] See, for example, Darling-Hammond, L. (2000). Teacher quality and student achievement: A review of state policy evidence. *Education Policy Analysis Archives, (8)1*.

[32] WASL Facts. Retrieved June 23, 2004 from http://www.curewashington.org/ WASL_Facts.htm.

[33] Superintendent of Public Instruction (2003). *SPI Education Profile: District WASL Scores for 2001-2000. Retrieved May 23, 2003 from* http://www.k12.wa.us.edprofile/ districtreport.asp?sReport=districtWASL2001-2002

[34] Vinh, T. Testing changes proposed by state schools' official. (2002, November 16). *Seattle Times*.

[35] Brazelton, T., Greenspan, S. (2000). *The Irreducible Needs of Children: What Every Child Must Have to Grow, Learn, and Flourish*. New York, NY: Perseus Publishing.

[36] Goleman, D. (1995). *Emotional Intelligence*. New York: Bantam Books.

[37] Leach, Penelope (1994). *Children First*. Random House, New York: New York, pg. 26.

[38] Dunnewind, S. (2003, January 25). Parenting books: Finding a good guide can be a gamble. *Seattle Times*.